The Blind African Slave

Wisconsin Studies in Autobiography Series

The Blind African Slave,

Or Memoirs of
Boyrereau Brinch,
Nicknamed Jeffrey Brace

Edited and with an introduction by

Kari J. Winter

THE UNIVERSITY OF WISCONSIN PRESS

The University of Wisconsin Press
1930 Monroe Street
Madison, Wisconsin 53711

www.wisc.edu/wisconsinpress/

3 Henrietta Street
London WC2E 8LU, England

Library of Congress Cataloging-in-Publication Data
The blind African slave, or, Memoirs of Boyrereau Brinch, nicknamed Jeffrey Brace /
edited and with an introduction by Kari J. Winter.
p. cm. —(Wisconsin studies in autobiography)
Narrative originally transcribed, with commentary, by Benjamin F. Prentiss.
Originally published: St. Alban's, Vt.: Printed by Harry Whitney, 1810.
Includes bibliographical references.
ISBN 0-299-20140-6 (hardcover: alk. paper)—
ISBN 0-299-20144-9 (pbk.: alk. paper)
1. Brinch, Boyrereau. 2. African Americans—Social conditions—18th century. 3. Slaves—
New England—Biography. 4. Slaves—New England—Social conditions—18th century.
5. Slavery—New England—History—18th century. 6. Slave trade—Africa—History—
18th century. 7. Slaves' writings, American. 8. Africa—Description and travel.
I. Title: Blind African slave. II. Title: Memoirs of Boyrereau Brinch, nicknamed Jeffery Brace.
III. Winter, Kari J. IV. Prentiss, Benjamin F. (Benjamin Franklin), 1774 or 5–1817.
E444.B86B58 2004
306.3'62'092—dc22
2004007741

to the memory of
Boyrereau Brinch / Jeffrey Brace
circa 1742–1827 and
John H. ("Jack") Winter
1931–2002

Contents

Illustrations

Tables

Preface

Searching for Jeffrey Brace

When I first read a fragile copy of *The Blind African Slave* in the Special Collections of the Bailey-Howe Library at the University of Vermont, I was persuaded and moved by the narrator's voice and the stories he told about his capture, the perfidy of English slave traders, the horror of the Middle Passage, the brutality of slavery in New England, and the difficulties of "free" life in Vermont. At the same time, I was perplexed by the text's disappearance from history. Memoirs of former slaves who remembered Africa are exceedingly rare, as are first-person accounts of black soldiers who served in the American Revolution.[1] Of the autobiographical narratives by slaves or former-slaves published before 1810, only one—that of Olaudah Equiano—is longer than that of Boyrereau Brinch/Jeffrey Brace. How then can we account for the disappearance of *The Blind African Slave* from scholarship and history?

The answer appears to be simple: no one until now has undertaken and published in a widely accessible form the historical research necessary to "authenticate" Brace's story and indeed his existence.[2] In fall of 2001 the University of North Carolina at Chapel Hill Library made the book widely available for the first time by publishing it online, but as of March 2003 it was still absent from the world's largest library, the Library of Congress. The rare interested scholar would have expected Brace to be hard to trace. I certainly did. Nonetheless, at the urging of William L. Andrews, I decided to search for traces of Jeffrey Brace. What I found astonished me. I learned that despite Vermont's reputation for being the whitest state in the union, for over two hundred years Brace's descendants have lived and continue to live in St. Albans and the surrounding regions of northern Vermont.[3] I found a packet of legal documents in the National Archives in Washington D.C., and original letters written by a St. Albans judge in the University of Vermont's Special Collections that substantiate the major facts of Brace's life: birth in Africa, enslavement in Connecticut, service in the Revolutionary War, and settlement in Vermont (Appendix B). That was just the beginning. My further research in New England; Washington, D.C.; Barbados; and London revealed that Brace recalled names of people and details of place with remarkable accuracy. His contemporaries testified to his honesty and extraordinary memory. When he applied for a military pension, the judge of Franklin County Court endorsed his application by certifying that "the said Jeffrey Brace['s] reputation for truth & veracity stands unimpeached & will gain Credit where ever he is known" (Frederic Bliss, 20 June 1818, Appendix B). The author of Brace's obituary recalled his powerful memory: "He had for many years been totally blind, yet his mental powers appeared to be hardly impaired. The powers of his memory were frequently tested by repeating whole chapters of the scriptures nearly verbatim" (*Northern Spectator*, May 9, 1827).

Like most enslaved people, Brace had difficulty recalling dates with precision. Frederick Douglass describes this difficulty as a "destitution" in his 1855 autobiography, *My Bondage and My Freedom*, in which he explains that because slavery severed children from their parents and deprived slaves of means to measure the passage of time, "I never met with a slave who could tell me how old he was" (28). By the time Brace died, some of his friends believed that he was nearly 100, but the dates in his memoir suggest that he was closer to 85. With the help of Vermont historian Raymond Zirbliz, I have prepared an approximate chronology of Brace's life compiled from information he provides in the memoir as well as from supplementary documents (Appendix C).

In a legal deposition related to his military pension application, Brace states that after he was manumitted he took the name "Brace" because it was the name of his father. Although he never comments on how "Brinch" became "Brace," I believe the phonetic change attests to his simultaneous desire to connect himself to his paternal legacy and to acknowledge that his identity has been altered or hybridized. He explains in the memoir that he accepted the name "Jeffrey" in place of "Boyrereau" because it was bestowed on him by his first master, Captain Isaac Mills, after a battle with a Spanish vessel in which Brace fired the first shot and received five wounds.

"In consequence . . . the captain gave me the honorable nick-name of *Jeffrey*. I say honorable, as I was named after Sir Jeffrey Amherst, General and commander in chief of the expedition for the reduction of Canada, the year before" (chapter 7). There is no sign in the text that Mills was following the slaveholding tradition of bestowing an aristocratic name on a slave as a form of mockery. While readers familiar with Jeffrey Amherst's wretched treatment of Indians might find this nomenclature regrettable, Brace accepted the name as a badge of honor. Since "Jeffrey Brace" is the name he claimed for himself as a free man in the last decades of his life, it is the name by which I refer to him.

This book was inspired by William L. Andrews, whose value as a reader, critic, and friend is immeasurable. I am indebted to many wonderful colleagues at the University of Vermont. Those particularly helpful on this project include Philip Baruth, Emily Bernard, Anthony Bradley, Mary Jane Dickerson, Kathryn Dungy, Tina Escaja, John Gennari, Huck Gutman, Major Jackson, Mary Lou Kete, Lokangaka Losambe, Helga Schreckenberger, Helen Scott, Stephanie Seguino, Lee Thompson, Nancy Welch, Joseph Won, and Robyn Warhol. I am also indebted to the University of Vermont's marvelous cohort of librarians, especially Connie Gallagher, Jeffrey Marshall, Chris Burns, Ingrid Bower, Trina Magi, Patricia Mardeusz, Nancy Rosedale, Mara Saule, and Peter Spitzform. A grant from the Dean's Fund of the College of Arts and Sciences enabled me to conduct research in Barbados. The English department supported my research in London, thanks to funds negotiated through our new faculty union. My research assistants, Sara Rubin and Tracey Provost, provided invaluable assistance. Peter Frechette and Rebecca Cutkomp also provided important support. Many thanks to my students in "Slavery and American Literature" and "African American Writers in New England: Jeffrey Brace through John Edgar Wideman," especially Gregory Askew, Sophia Emerson Blount, Elizabeth Laucks, Bjorn Pink, and Ashley Shuford.

About a year into my research, I was contacted by Raymond Zirblis, a Vermont historian who had been researching Brace for several years and who generously shared his sources with me. I am especially grateful for his discovery of Brace's obituary in a Poultney newspaper. I appreciate his collaboration and friendship. John Buechler, former head of the University of Vermont's Special Collections, shared his ground-breaking research on Brace with me after a talk I gave to Friends of the Library in the spring of

2002. I had several informative telephone conversations with James Brace Sr., a descendant of Jeffrey Brace, who lives with his family in St. Albans. Aided by clues provided by Win Heald of the Heald Funeral Home in St. Albans, my mother, Dorothy Winter, discovered the grave of Jeffrey S. Brace (the original's great-grandson), and my father, Jack Winter, scraped it off with a credit card so that we could read the inscription. Together we also found the grave of another great-grandson, Peter Brace. Richard and Anne Dennis showed me around Poultney, Vermont, and helped me locate the probable site of Jeffrey and Susannah Brace's farm. I am grateful for their warm hospitality and enthusiasm. Thanks also to Ethan and Judi Ward for inviting me into their eighteenth-century home built by Judge William Ward, which was just around the corner from Brace's farm in East Poultney. I am indebted to Elise Guyette for her careful comments on the manuscript. Thanks to other people throughout Vermont, including Don Miner, curator of the St. Albans Historical Museum; John Denison and other volunteers at the St. Albans Historical Society; Carl Johnson, a St. Albans town historian; Peter Mallett, a Georgia town historian; and Jane Williamson, curator of the Rokeby Museum in Ferrisburg.

Natalia Smith, who worked with Bill Andrews to compile the University of North Carolina's massive database, "North American Slave Narratives, Beginnings to 1920" (http://docsouth.unc.edu/neh) helped me obtain a hard copy of the original memoir, which greatly facilitated my work. I was aided by many scholars, librarians, and archivists in Barbados, including David Williams, Cherri-Ann Beckles, and Carlton Cole at the Barbados Department of Archives, and the staff at the Barbados Museum and Historical Society. I am deeply indebted to Pedro Welch at the University of the West Indies—Cave Hill Campus, both for his own research and for his insightful comments on mine. Thanks to staff at the National Maritime Museum in Greenwich, England; the Public Records Office in London; the National Archives (especially Clifford MacWha) and the Library of Congress in Washington D.C.; and the New England Genealogical Society in Boston.

A smart audience of graduate students and scholars at the University at Buffalo raised thought-provoking questions; special thanks to Yvonne Dion-Buffalo, John Mohawk, and Oren Lyons. I am grateful to Dean Charles Stinger at the University at Buffalo for granting me a release from teaching in Spring 2004 that enabled me to complete revisions of the manuscript.

Conversations with John Edgar Wideman enhanced my work. Margot

Minardi shared her research on Belinda and Chloe Spear with me and provided useful suggestions on an early draft of this book. Terry Rowden, Wilfred Samuels, and Mark Schoenfield made insightful suggestions on the work-in-progress. Betty Moss's encouragement helped me keep working. My undergraduate advisor of a quarter century back, Robert Ferrell of Indiana University, offered enthusiastic support. Thanks to the scholars who responded to my queries on the H-West-Africa discussion list, especially Wendy Wilson Fall, Paul Lovejoy, and Jerome Handler, with whom I had several cyberspace conversations. The genealogical database assembled by the Church of Jesus Christ of the Latter Day Saints (familysearch.org) proved invaluable in providing alternate spellings of names and in helping me locate many of the people Brace mentions. I benefited from the comments and suggestions of the anonymous reviewers from the University of Wisconsin Press, as well as from those of the editor, Raphael Kadushin. All remaining errors in the text are of course my own.

Finally, thanks to my family—Dorothy Winter; Kris, Allan, Alexander, and Jonathan Rinkus; John, Amelia, Selma, and Hugo Winter; Joan and Emil Magnuson; and Bernice Woodrum Grinde—for their support and love. My father, Jack Winter, took an unprecedented interest in Brace's life, and I regret that he did not live to see the book's publication. My husband, Donald A. Grinde Jr., commented helpfully on multiple drafts of this book and also helped to manage life so that I had time to work. Our son, Zane Winter Grinde, sustained me with his infectious joy.

Notes

1. Other accounts of African American Revolutionary soldiers include the following. Boston King, a South Carolina slave who fought for the British during the revolution and eventually fled with his wife to Sierra Leone, published memoirs in 1798. James Forten, a free black Philadelphian who served as a powder-boy for the rebels during the Revolution, published a book, *Letters from a Man of Colour,* in 1813. A well-known abolitionist and prosperous sailmaker, Forten was the progenitor of a prominent family that included the poet Sarah Forten and the poet-activist-diarist Charlotte Forten Grimke (1838–1914). James Roberts, a Maryland slave who served in both the Revolution and the War of 1812 only to find himself re-enslaved, published a short memoir in 1858 in which he warned his readers to

> take counsel from me, one who has fought in the revolutionary war, and thereby caused the chains of slavery to be bound tighter around the necks of my people than they were before. . . . Therefore, my earnest and departing request is, that should this country ever again engage in war with any nation, have nothing to do with the war, although the fairest promises should be made to you. . . . But for our faithfulness and manly courage,

we should all be free men and women this day. Avoid being duped by the white man—
he wants nothing to do with our race further than to subserve his own interest, in any
thing under the sun. (31–32)

James Mars, an enslaved son of a Revolutionary War veteran (Jupiter Mars),
published a memoir in 1864.

2. In 1978 John Buechler, the head of Special Collections at the University of
Vermont, published a brief article on Brace and the history of early publications
in St. Albans, Vermont. He speculates that Brace's memoir, the first book published in St. Albans and the first published by Harry Whitney, "probably met with
a modicum of success, enough at least to suggest another printing venture" to
Whitney (36). Buechler then substantiates the book's peculiar disappearance:

> The Blind African Slave has been overlooked by nearly all the bibliographers and does
> not appear in such standard bibliographies as Sabin's Dictionary of Books Relating
> to America and the catalogue of the Library of the British Museum; not even the great
> Vermont bibliographer, Henry Stevens, Jr., could locate a copy . . . even though
> Stevens was the greatest discoverer of rare American books of his century, and his
> British Museum catalogue of Christmas 1856 was compiled within fifty years of the
> publication of The Blind African Slave in his own native state within a few miles of his
> birthplace! Lucius E. Chittenden, an avid collector of Vermont imprints, could not
> procure a copy for his collection; nor was the little book known to M. D. Gilman, com-
> piler of the Bibliography of Vermont (Burlington, 1897), nor is it listed in Matt B.
> Jones' additions to Gilman. . . . No copy exists in the Black Collections at Oberlin Col-
> lege, Atlanta University, or Howard University, and not even the fine Schomburg
> Collection of the New York Public Library owns a copy. (36–37)

In 1985 Charles T. Davis and Henry Louis Gates did include The Blind
African Slave in the bibliography of their edited collection, The Slave's Narrative,
and one of the contributors, Susan Willis, gave it serious, though brief, attention,
asserting that "the Boyrereau Brinch text is atypical. . . . The narrator, not fully
aware of an audience and the purpose to which his narrative might be put, is not
constrained to supply meaning. Brinch, in the process of relating the past, re-
experiences the lack of perspective which conditioned his life as a slave and narrates the raw unevaluated material of experience as an assemblage of undigested
bits and pieces" (202).

3. Although the current Braces could trace their ancestry to nineteenth-
century African Americans buried in the St. Albans cemetery, they had no knowledge of Jeffrey Brace or of his memoir before I contacted them. In telephone in-
terviews in July and August 2001 James Brace, Sr. of St. Albans indicated that he
had not been aware that one of his ancestors fought in the Civil War, much less
that the progenitor of Vermont's African American Braces fought in the Revolutionary War.

The Blind African Slave

Introduction

In 1810 in St. Albans, Vermont, a small town near the Canadian border, an anomalous narrative of slavery was published by an obscure printer. Entitled *The Blind African Slave; Or, Memoirs of Boyrereau Brinch, Nicknamed Jeffrey Brace*, it was greeted with no fanfare, and it has remained for nearly two hundred years a faint specter in our cultural memory. Published two years after the United States Congress officially abolished the trans-Atlantic slave trade and two years before the outbreak of the War of 1812, *The Blind African Slave* lacked significant political appeal at the moment. For the antebellum abolitionists, it held little propaganda value since it described slavery in New England, not in the South. In the nineteenth and twentieth centuries, few readers expressed interest in the experiences of African Americans in "free" states like Vermont. Perhaps twenty-first century readers will recognize the historical significance of a memoir that offers us an opportunity to view the slave trade, West Indian culture, the Seven Years War, New England slavery, the Revolutionary War, and early Vermont culture from the perspective of an extraordinarily perceptive African victim and participant. Brace's tragic experiences followed the patterns of bondage forced upon millions of people, most of whose voices were silenced. Through his narration, Brace forges meaning and an identity from his violent, fragmented, courageous life.

Childhood in Africa

Because it is an "as-told-to" autobiography, *The Blind African Slave* is a composite text shaped by the interests, politics, research, and desires of its abolitionist editor, Benjamin Prentiss, as well as by the voice, memory, politics, and desires of its narrator-subject, Jeffrey Brace. In the opening quarter of the book, Prentiss constructs a third-person voice that blends his voice as "author" with the voice of Brace as "narrator." Because Brace at the time of his capture was a teenager who knew no English, his ability to translate his childhood memories into places and concepts comprehensible to English readers was circumscribed. Prentiss supplemented Brace's narration with his own research into African history and geography. A well-intentioned but inexperienced researcher and writer, Prentiss cited, with varying degrees of accuracy, a range of popular autobiographical, encyclopedic, and literary texts written by Europeans about Africa and slavery.[1] The Africa section of the memoir echoes conventions of eighteenth-century travel literature in that it describes family structures, laws, customs, religious beliefs, royalty, government, trade, architecture, geography, and agriculture. Prentiss and Brace include an extensive list of the names of flora and fauna in "the Bow-woo language," a West African language that Brace believes derives from Hebrew. Trying, literally, to place Brace on the map, Prentiss was both aided and impeded by sources that were hazy, Eurocentric, and sometimes fantastical. He concludes that Brace's homeland, the Kingdom of Bow-woo, is "situated between the 10th and 20th degrees of north latitude, and between the 6th and 10th of west longitude," and that the Niger River runs through it. Contemporary maps, such as that in Jedidiah Morse's 1802 *New Gazetteer*, thus place Bow-woo in the middle of West Africa, north of Guinea, west of Nigritia, and south of the Sahara or the Great Desert of Barbary in an area known as Benown, to use Morse's descriptors. If Prentiss was correct, Brace came from the middle Niger valley, or the country that is now called Mali. This is a plausible scenario given the fact that from 1701 to 1810 nearly three-fifths of all African slaves were taken from West Africa (Rawley 430).

As heard and spelled by Prentiss, Brace's names for the people and places of his childhood are hard to trace in external documents. Historian Richard L. Roberts noted in 1987: "Since most Malian languages were until recently oral, the spelling has usually been filtered through French. For historians, this poses particular problems in the spelling of surnames and place names" (xi). However, several pieces of textual evidence confirm the likelihood that Brace came from Mali.[2] Brace's "kingdom of Bow-woo" bears phonetic resemblance to the "Bobo" ethnic group which, like Brace's people, occupied lands near tributaries of the Niger River. The Dogon people, who have lived in this region since the Iron Age, practiced (and continue to practice) a religion similar to that described by Brace, which includes a belief that Africans are "creatures of light emanating from the fullness of the sun" (Griaule 17). In chapter 2, Brace describes "peace, humanity and courtesy to strangers" as the salient characteristics of Bow-woo society, another correspondence to the Dogon, who "have a strong orientation toward harmony and communion among members of clan and village. Conflicts are largely avoided and differences of opinion are seldom raised. . . . Hospitality and openness are essential values: each Dogon, it is felt, should be accessible at all times for anyone. In the Dogon language there are many ways of welcoming a stranger. Whereas for numerous other African groups strangers are enemies without any right to respect, the Dogon consider strangers as guests" (Van Beek 14). Many other tribal peoples in the central Niger valley, such as the Bambara, the Bozo, and the Kouroumba, developed world views "based on an equally systematic and equally rich metaphysic, the fundamental principles of which are comparable to those of the Dogon" (Griaule 3). Dogon mud-brick architecture resembles Brace's description of his home town, where the houses are "placed in rows, & are joined"; the rows of houses are "long and low, none more than one story high, except the King's Palace. They are generally built of a kind of clay, made into a cement, which is strengthened by being bound together by small sticks of timber in the body of the walls" (chapter 1). Although not a Muslim society, the Kingdom of Bow-woo was influenced by Islam, and Brace believed the kingdom to be "a province or colony of the Empire of Morocco," an Islamic empire that had controlled trade routes through the Saharan desert into Mali for centuries (Shillington 181–83).

Acts of remembering or (re)creating the sites of childhood must have been both pleasurable and empowering to Brace. He rejects Euro-American representations of Africa as a wilderness inhabited by savages incapable of genuine affection, memory, discipline and rationality. One of Brace's most important rituals of memory in the book's first chapter is to invoke the name of each of his paternal and maternal ancestors as well as of his siblings. He begins: "the grand father of Boyrereau, on the father's side, was honored with the title of councillor and governor of the country of Hugh Lough. His name was Yarram Brinch." He continues: "the father of the present narrator succeeded to the title of governor of said county, whose name was Whryn Brinch; he was also Captain of the king's Life Guards. . . . His mother's name was Whryn Douden." Brace recites the names of his three brothers and four sisters, observing that "the mention

of [their] names, calls from a heart almost subdued by grief, one sad tear
of fraternal remembrance consecrated to religious resignation. The eldest
brother's name was Cressee, 2d Deeyee, 3d Yarram; the eldest sister's
name Desang, 2d Bang, 3d Nabough, 4th Dolacella." He identifies his maternal grandfather as "Crassee Youghgon . . . who was a distinguished officer in a former war, and after a glorious campaign, he returned with the
trophies of victory, covered with wounds to the capital, amid the acclamations of a grateful people, was created first Judge of petty offences and civil
differences in the country of Voah Goah." It would become a convention
"in fictional and factual narratives recounted by or about former slaves"
for enslaved people to claim "high-born African descent" (Carretta, "Defining" 390).[3] However, I would argue that when Brace situates himself as
"the third son, and seventh child of an ancient and honorable family" (21),
he is not claiming class distinction so much as rejecting the constituent element of slavery that Orlando Patterson calls "natal alienation." Patterson
explains that part of the process of transforming people into slaves involved severing them from their ancestors and descendants, thereby ren-
dering them "genealogical isolates" with no sense of kinship. Patterson argues: "It was this alienation of the slave from all formal, legally enforceable
ties of 'blood,' and from any attachment to groups or localities other than
those chosen for him by the master, that gave the relation of slavery its
peculiar value to the master" (7). Enslavement physically severed Brace
from his people, his culture, his land, and his language, but his determination to remember and to continue locating himself within a network of
familial relationships helped him to survive unbroken in mind and spirit.

Blending Brace's stories with Prentiss's research, *The Blind African
Slave* represents Brace's native culture as an absolute monarchy in which
"the first grade of nobility" performed "the office of councilors of state," at
the king's discretion. The king was commander-in-chief of the military,
and the culture prized bravery highly while cowardice in battle was seen
as a capital offense. As in Europe and its colonies at the time, corporal
punishment was commonplace. Adultery, "if clearly proved by at least two
witnesses" (a high standard of "proof"), was punished by a grisly execution
of both offending parties (the woman and the man), a detail that Brace
and Prentiss probably include to emphasize the ideal of chastity in Bow-
woo culture, and to highlight the outrage of the rapes committed by the
slave traders on African women (chapter 1). Equiano, influenced by Anthony Benezet's *Some Historical Accounts of Guinea* (1788), similarly as-

serts that adultery "was sometimes punished with slavery or death; a punishment which I believe is inflicted on it throughout most of the nations of Africa; so sacred among them is the honour of the marriage bed, and so jealous are they of the fidelity of their wives" (33). Brace departs from Equiano and Benezet by asserting that in the Kingdom of Bow-woo, adulterous men are punished as severely as their female partners.

Brace relates that Bow-woo's king traveled to Morocco every year, apparently to pay tribute to the Emperor and to conduct trade. He mentions that this travel always took place during the rainy season because "in any other season of the year, it is dangerous to pass the great deserts of sand [the Sahara] which lie between" his home and Morocco. He identifies the rainy season as lasting from May through September, which is indeed the typical rainy season in northern West Africa (Udo 12). After accompanying the king on a trip to Morocco, Brace's father returned to his family bearing products that he had procured from white people there, including silk and pistols, two of the most common products that Europeans imported to Africa to exchange for slaves. Hearing about white people for the first time, Brace asked his father: "White people! What kind of beings are they?" (chapter 3). His father responded: "Why . . . they have every appearance of men, like our people, only they are pale as the moon and are covered with clothes from head to foot" (chapter 3). Brace recalls being mildly interested in the pale strangers, but because he was well-accustomed to diverse peoples his attention soon shifted to the pistols.[4]

In chapter 2, Prentiss and Brace represent Brace's homeland in complex terms, attending to language, landscape, agriculture, animals, food, and social history as well as to Brace's personal experiences. They scrutinize West Africa's natural landscape with the eyes of botanists and farmers, describing and classifying the vegetation and animals of the region in both English and in Brace's native tongue. Like most travel narratives of this era, the opening chapters of *The Blind African Slave* blur the lines between memory, exotica, and scholarship.[5] Brace was an elderly survivor of profound trauma who was recalling his childhood in an intensely politicized context. Although he was trying to help, Prentiss nonetheless was immersed in a Eurocentric culture that offered few possibilities for genuine understanding of the African landscape, much less African cultures. He weakens the text's credibility by romantic assertions such as "The Unicorn is a noble animal, and a native of that part of the world." While readers should note that this apparently fanciful assertion may reflect

Brace's efforts to describe the northern white rhinoceros, an enormous animal with a long front horn that is native to West Africa, we should also remain aware that autobiography is never merely factual. Brace and Prentiss were collaborating in the production of meaning and myth, not simply facts.

While reconstructing his African roots, Brace was also searching for his ontological place in the universe. Like people in all cultures, Brace wanted a story—a myth of origins—to illuminate his existence. He eventually embraced Christianity, but he rejected the racism that infused Western Christianity. Christians often justified slavery as a "beautiful patriarchal institution" modeled after the households of biblical patriarchs. They asserted that Africans were descendants of Ham, condemned by God to perpetual servitude, based on their reading of Genesis 9.25, in which Noah responds to his son Ham's witnessing of him lying naked in a drunken stupor by cursing Ham's son, Canaan, saying, "Cursed be Canaan; a servant of servants shall he be unto his brethren." Brace based his search for meaning—psychologically, politically, and ontologically— on reading and rereading the Bible. To refute the notion that Africans descended from Ham, Brace highlights similarities that he perceives between the customs, languages, and religions of the peoples of Bow-woo and those of ancient Israel.[6] He suggests that if he had been inducted into the adult religious society of Bow-woo, he would have learned "the origin of all nations; the veil of superstition would be rent in twain. Man in his native elements would be held to view; their origin and descent would be portrayed; each kingdom and nation would be clearly seen and known, if real distinctions are; the proofs would be strong and convincing; if all mankind were naturally equal, we, however sable, if wise and virtuous, should be on a level with all mankind" (chapter 3). In a particularly bold rhetorical move, Brace suggests that the Bible "is verified by the ancient customs of my forefathers," rather than claiming more modestly that the Bible verifies his people's traditions (chapter 3). Brace concludes that the religious traditions of Bow-woo were "anciently introduced" by Jethro, the priest of Midian who was Moses's father-in-law. In Exodus 18, which Brace cites, Jethro tells Moses to establish ordinances and laws for his people, and Moses obeys him. Thus Brace suggests that the traditions of Bow-woo, like the traditions of Judaism, Christianity, and Islam, originate with Jethro, a high priest from a foreign land.

Captivity and Middle Passage

The transatlantic slave trade was launched in the fifteenth century by Christopher Columbus, who promised Isabel and Ferdinand of Spain "slaves, as many as they shall order" (Rawley 3). On his second voyage from the Americas, Columbus transported five hundred enslaved Indians back to Spain. About two hundred died during the voyage, and their bodies were thrown into the sea. For the next four centuries Spanish, Portuguese, Dutch, French, and British monarchs, mariners, and adventurers vied for African and Indian slaves. James A. Rawley incisively summarizes the impact of the slave trade on the emerging global economy: "The opening of the Atlantic soon led to the development of the commercial empire of the Atlantic. The wealth of the New World—especially sugar, tobacco, precious metals, coffee, indigo, and cotton—was extracted by black labor imported from Africa through the capitalistic enterprise of western Europe. Negro slavery was essential to the carrying on of this commerce, which in turn was fundamental to the making of the modern world" (4). Before the trade was abolished, at least eleven million Africans were transported against their will to the Americas. England dominated the trade in the eighteenth century, and, according to David Richardson's estimates, "ships of the British Empire carried just over 3.4 million slaves from Africa in 1662–1807" (441).

Boyrereau Brinch/Jeffrey Brace was captured around 1758, during a peak period of the English slave trade.[7] To describe this event, Prentiss allows Brace to speak for himself—or, as Prentiss describes it, "here the writer takes the language of the narrator" (chapter 3). Brace describes a festive afternoon when he and thirteen of his friends went swimming in a river. When they got out of the water, they were surrounded by white men with dogs who succeeded in capturing eleven of them.[8] One moment he and his friends were engaged in a "delightful sport"; moments later they were bound, gagged, and "fastened down in the boat," surrounded by "a horrid stench" (chapter 3). A similar description of capture by the English is found in an autobiographical account of another African New Englander of the same era, an elderly woman named Belinda, who stated in a petition in 1782 to the Massachusetts Legislature that one day around the age of twelve she was "in a sacred grove, with each hand in that of a tender parent, [and] was paying her devotion to the great Orisa, who made

all things, [when] an armed band of white men, driving many of her countrymen in chains, rushed into the hallowed shades!" (142). She says that
she was ripped from the arms of her parents, whose "advanced age . . .
render[ed] them unfit for servitude," and thrown into slavery along with
"three hundred Africans in chains, suffering the most excruciating torment" (Belinda 142–43). Like Equiano, who writes "at the very moment I
dreamed of the greatest happiness, I found myself most miserable" (53),
Belinda and Brace juxtapose an idyll of carefree childhood with the unspeakable pain of captivity.

Noting that eighteenth-century slaves in Anglo-America often told
stories about being kidnapped by English sailors, Dickson Bruce argues
that these stories served an important psychological function, but that
they were rarely based on actual experience. He explains: "Kidnapping,
especially by whites, was a relatively rare event in the actual procuring of
slavery's victims from Africa. In this sense the stories may have been most
important for the way they dramatized a view among slaves themselves of
their enslavement as a matter of theft, an illegitimate taking of any of the
institution's victims from their lives and relations" (20). The era of the
slave trade predated the European colonization of Africa; thus, few Europeans lived in Africa in the eighteenth century. "Confined to the coast,
Europeans did business in places which were under the authority of
African rulers" (Rawley 12). It is a "virtually unanimous view among pro-
fessional scholars of transatlantic slavery and African history" that most
Africans who were transported to the Americas were first captured and/or
enslaved by other Africans (Handler "Survivors" 12). John Thornton summarizes the prevalent view: "Most were enslaved as a result of wars between African armies, or by raiders and bandits that arose from these
wars, or from the breakdown of social order that often accompanies war,
especially civil war" (84). For the most part, African dealers in slaves
forced Europeans to deal with them as equals in the slave trade (Behrendt
474–75). Nonetheless, the financial advantages of "stealing" Africans en-
ticed some Europeans to attempt to eliminate the African middlemen.
Europeans "could not steal [slaves] in significant numbers," but they did
sometimes try because the cost "of slaves on the African coast averaged 25
per cent of slave prices in the Americas between 1681 and 1697, 35 per
cent of American prices in 1698–1710, and 50 per cent at the end of the
eighteenth century" (Behrendt 474). Since greed was the engine of the
slave trade, slave trading attracted "freebooters" and "adventurers of all

varieties" (Barry 62). While "the Royal African Company and its succes-
sor, the Company of Merchants Trading to Africa (founded in 1750), continued to maintain forts and factories in the Gambia and along the Gold
Coast and Slave Coast[,] . . . responsibility for maintaining Britain's interest in the African trade . . . lay primarily in the hands of private merchants or 'separate traders' from 1712 onwards" (Richardson 445). Thus,
Brace's stories about himself and other Africans being captured directly
by English slave traders are not implausible. He and/or Prentiss may have
simplified Brace's story by eliminating mention of African intermediaries
in the slave trade, or they may have been accurately describing the particularities of Brace's experience.

Brace's own humanity, compassion, and judiciousness accentuate the
viciousness of the slave trade. He witnessed men who showed no vestige
of kindness, compassion, or honor—men who tortured, starved, raped,
and murdered children as well as adults. Some of his descriptions of the
methods used by the English to capture human beings and to traumatize
them into submission are unparalleled, but the basic structure of the
events that he narrates follows a typical pattern of the trans-Atlantic slave
trade.

Brace notes: "We were fastened in rows [with bolts and bars] . . . so
that we could set upon our rumps or lie upon our backs, as was most
convenient, and as our exercises were not much, we, it was concluded,
could do with little food; our allowance was put at two scanty meals
per day, which consisted of about six ounces of boiled rice and Indian
corn each meal, with the addition of about one gill of fresh water" (chapter 4). His descriptions are confirmed in precise detail by the historical
literature.

Edward Reynolds summarizes the conditions on slave ships as
"slovenly and foul. The height of the decks averaged between four and five
feet. In addition to the slave holds, some slavers built half-decks along the
sides of the ships, extending no farther than the sides of the scuttles,
where slaves, lying in two rows, one above the other, were crowded together and were fastened by leg-irons. . . . Slaves were brought upon deck
at mid-morning and those who had died during the night were thrown into
the ocean" (32). James Rawley observes: "The feeding of slaves early in the
trade became routinized. It was customary to give two meals a day. . . .
North American slavers commonly fed their slaves rice and corn. . . . Water was the usual beverage" (297–98). Brace underscores that "we were

Thomas Clarkson's 1791 diagram of a slave ship.

almost famished for want of water. We often begged salt water of the invalid who attended us. I would get it in my cap and cautiously drink it, which would run through us like salts" (chapter 4).

What the historical literature cannot provide is an understanding of the psychological toll exacted by enslavement. To illuminate Brace's accomplishment *in surviving to tell the tale*, we need the imagination of a novelist like John Edgar Wideman, who writes

> You are naked and chained to others who look like you, under the merciless control of brutal strangers who look and act nothing like you and, much worse, do not speak your language. To you their language is gibberish, the ba-ba-baaing of barbarism. They communicate their orders with blows, screams, shoves, crude pantomime. You are compelled at the peril of life and limb to make sense of verbal assault, physical abuse. You realize you're learning a new language even as you swallow the bitterness, the humiliation of learning the uselessness of your own. Much of this learning and unlearning occurs in silence inside your skull, in the sanctuary where you're simultaneously struggling to retain traces of who you are, what you were before this terrible, scouring ordeal began. In order to save your life, when you attempt to utter the first word of a new tongue, are you also violating your identity and dignity? When you break your silence, are you surrendering, acknowledging the strangers' power to own you, rule you? Are you forfeiting your chance to tell your story in your own words some day? ("In Praise of Silence" 548)

From the precision of his recollections half a century later, we know that Brace watched carefully. He managed to acquire dexterity in a new language and its value system without losing his old language and morality.

Brace observes that after loading the ship with human cargo, "the captain and many of the officers made choice of such of the young women as they chose to sleep with them in their hammocks, whom they liberated from chains and introduced into their several apartments" (chapter 4). He continues: "to add to the horror of the scene, the sailors who were not provided with mistresses, would force the women before the eyes of their husbands" (chapter 4). Rawley, like many historians, confirms that "[o]n the Middle Passage there was little check to sadism and lust" (298). Sexual violence was so thoroughly embedded in the system of slavery that it must be viewed not as incidental but as a constituent element of the trade—a practice that white men saw as a major benefit to their participation in slavery and that they used to subjugate and terrorize the slaves. As Hillary Beckles observes, "rape and other forms of physical and emotional violence at the hands of the white crew shaped the consciousness of African women in the passage, and established psychological structures that dictated subsequent attitudes to life on the estates. Many women arrived in the Caribbean already impregnated by [the] ship's crew" (*Natural Rebels* 27).

At the time of Brace's enslavement, the British were transporting approximately 42,000 African slaves each year. Brace states that his particular voyage from Africa took about five months, which would have been unusually long. In good conditions the voyage could be made in less than 40 days; in less optimal conditions it could take months. The pain of the passage may have made it seem interminable, and/or Brace may have been including the time between his original capture and his arrival in Barbados. Slave traders often sailed up or down the coast gradually collecting their enslaved cargo, which meant that the slaves collected first could spend many extra weeks aboard ship. Long voyages significantly increased the mortality rate; "the longer the time the higher the loss" (Rawley 301). Brace tells us that during the passage many slaves died from "disease, mourned themselves to death or starved; many of the children actually died with hunger" (chapter 4). He estimates that about three hundred slaves survived the voyage. The official logs of the port of Bridgetown, Barbados indicate that slave traders imported as few as two and as many as 630 slaves per voyage between 1757 and 1760. In the tables below I have highlighted the eleven ships that arrived from Africa between 1757 and 1760 carrying cargoes of slaves that fit the contours of Brace's description.

While the figures for mortality on slave ships have been widely debated, it is clear that the middle passage took the lives of many slaves as well as crew members. In 1788, the British abolitionist Thomas Clarkson uncovered "shocking facts about slave-crew mortality," and the British Parliament responded to the uproar by establishing "minimal requirements for sleeping and victualing sailors in the slave trade" (Rawley 286). Although the governments, companies, and individuals who controlled the slave trade wanted to maximize profits, they paradoxically undervalued the survival of their crew and their "cargo." They shared fully the ruling class's general disregard for human life. Disease and starvation ranked high as causes of death aboard ship. Brace is also correct in including "mourning" or depression as a leading contributor to slave mortality. Isaac Wilson, a surgeon aboard an eighteenth-century slave ship that lost 155 of 602 slaves in passage, "was persuaded that two-thirds of the deaths resulted from melancholy" (Rawley 291).[9] Beckles notes that "it is very dif-

Barbados/ An Account of What Numbers of New Negroes are Imported into this Island from the Ninth day of May 1757 to the Ninth of May One thousand Seven hundred and Fifty Eight following—

	Vessel's Name	Commander's Name	Number of Slaves
1757			
May 28	Snow Antigua Merchants	John Davis	17
June 8	Sloop Sea Horse	John Banks	78
June 13	Sloop Dolphin	Joseph Arnold	59
June 13	Snow Perfect	William Astley	127
Sept. 13	Schooner Peggy	Barnabers Bonney	105
Sept. 22	Brigg Iano	John See	98
Dec. 1	Ship Symo	John Farrar	438
Dec. 1	Ship Duke of Cumberland	John Nimos	364
Dec. 13	Ship Othello	Francis Malbourne	244
1758			
Jan. 3	Maj. Ship Litchfield	Mathew Barton, Esq.	22
Jan. 15	Brig Barb Packett	William Whitfield	56
March 7	Sloop Gambia	Henry Knowles	123
March 9	Snow Two Brothers	Edward Wanton	138
April 3	Snow Spattler (?)	Daniel Cook	336
April 3	Ship Chesterfield	Joseph Hesketh	396
		Total	2601

Note: Adapted from PRO CO 28/31

ficult for scholars to express in the language of the social sciences the results of the sexual exploitation, infection, nutritional deficiency, daily observation of death and sickness, and the physical torture, that characterized the middle passage" (*Natural Rebels* 28). To survive, Brace needed to listen to the stories of his fellows and to articulate his own suffering in narrative, elegy, song, protest, and jeremiad.

Barbados

The Blind African Slave offers a rare glimpse into 18th century Barbadian society from the viewpoint of an enslaved person. Brace's responses to Barbados contrast strikingly with the recorded responses of English adventurers. Richard Ligon, an upper class Englishman seeking his fortune

Barbados/ An Account of What Numbers of New Negroes are Imported into this Island from the Ninth day of May 1758 to the Ninth of May One thousand Seven hundred and Fifty Ninth following —

Dates	Vessel's Name	Commander's Name	Number of Slaves
1758			
May 13	Ship Nancy	James Waddington	312
July 26	Brigg Prince George	David Lindsay	133
Oct. 12	Sloop Bear	Andrew Key	25
Dec. 24	Snow William	Blackburn & Wilcox	141
1759			
Feb. 7	Ship Neston	John Jones	288
Feb. 28	Snow Prince of Brunswich	William Wise	10
March 8	Sloop Dolphin	Isaac Howland	128
April 10	Snow Two Brothers	Zebulon Wanton	140
		Total	1177

Note: Adapted from PRO CO 28/31

in Barbados in the mid-seventeenth century, recalled his first view of the island in rosy terms: "my first observation was, the form of the Island in general, which is highest in the middle; by which commodity of situation, the Inhabitants within, have these advantages; a free prospect to Sea, and a reception of pure refreshing air, and breezes that come from thence: the plantations overlooking one another so, as the most inland parts, are not bar'd nor restrained the liberties of their view to sea, by those that dwell between them and it. For as we past along near the shoar, the Plantations appear'd to us one above another: like several stories in stately buildings, which afforded us a large proportion of delight" (30). Seen by the English as "the brightest jewel in our crown of trade," Barbados was settled by the English in 1627 and it "was the first island to attract English settlers in considerable numbers" (Sheridan 124). Because it is the West Indian island closest to Africa (it is one thousand miles closer to Africa than Jamaica), it became "the first landfall in the New World for an English ship carrying slaves from Africa" (Rawley 157), and it emerged as "the mother colony, the centre to which newly-formed colonies looked for labour, experienced planters, capital, and leadership in matters of imperial politics and trade" (Sheridan 124). Despite the beautiful prospect of the island and the excitement of a busy international port in the mid-seventeenth

Barbados/ An Account of What Numbers of New Negroes are Imported into this Island from the Ninth day of May 1759 to the Ninth of May 1760—

Dates	Vessel's Name	Commander's Name	Number of Slaves
1759			
June 10	Ship Duke of Cumberland	John Ellsworthy	348
June 28	Ship Africa	Gurdon Saltonstall	139
Aug. 15	Snow Cesar	Peter Gwin	125
Aug. 18	Ship Pampadur	Thomas Shrelfall	630
Oct. 23	Brigg Prospet	Henry Howell	91
Nov. 6	Ship Blundell	Thomas Barcklay	354
1760			
Jan. 5	Brigg Jane	Daniel Hayes	41
Jan. 9	Snow Isaac	David Chatworthy	198 & 9°
Feb. 26	Ship Glory	William Spears	500
March 3	Brigg Nancy	James McDougall	91
April 9	Ship Prince Fury (?)	Thomas Chaffers	375
April 22	Sloop Betsey	Jeffrey Powers	2
April 22	Maj. Ship Chanfield	John Leacifo (?)	3 & 32°
April 24	Ship Ovoonok	Shitch Cowley	350
May 1	Ship Lenus MarrJoseph	Samuel Cox	100
		Total	3388

Note: Adapted from PRO CO 28/32

°Numbers of slaves are listed separately because they were consigned to different people.

century (Ligon observed twenty-two good ships and many small boats "plying to and fro, with Sails and Oars, which carried commodities from place to place: so quick stirring, and numerous, as I have seen it below the bridge at London" [31]), Ligon soon discovered that Barbados was filled with disease and famine, as well as with economic opportunity.

A century later, Bridgetown was still a busy international port whose raison d'être was the slave trade and whose internal reality was characterized by death and destruction. When the traumatized young Boyrereau Brinch arrived in port, he and his fellow slaves were removed from the slave ship and imprisoned in what he calls "a large prison, or rather house of subjection" (47). William Pierson observes: "So terrible was the experience of the middle passage that most black newcomers were in a state of psychological shock. It was at that moment, when the new slaves were most thoroughly shaken by the horrors of the Atlantic crossing, that they arrived in the Americas. The result was that once they learned they would not be eaten but, instead, put to work, the new slaves saw their release from the cramped and stinking holds of the slave ships as an escape" (145). Brace understood that the enslavers were attempting to use shock and trauma to achieve the psychological subjugation of the enslaved, but he does not represent removal from the ship as a form of "escape." He recalls that one of the slaves, a former judge in his African home of Yellow-Bonga, made a speech to the captain through an interpreter in which he stated: "Sir, we will sooner suffer death than submit to such abominable degradation" (chapter 4). The captain responded by subjecting the fresh lot of slaves to a regimen of whipping and starvation, until, Brace says, "[a]ll began to be subdued and to work according to their strength and abilities" (chapter 4). Far from conveying a sense of relative liberation, Brace represents Barbados as a site of relentless atrocities committed by men who were "dedicated to the subjugation of our spirits" (chapter 5). He describes, for example, a slave driver who responded to a young girl's attempts to protect her six-year-old brother by whipping the girl to death in front of her brother's eyes. After she died, the driver turned on Brace and "with a large tarred rope gave me about fifty stripes, which cut wails in every part of my body" (chapter 5).

Brace not only narrates what he experienced and observed, he also analytically illuminates the inner workings of the system of slavery. He points out that he was

starved, whipped and tortured in the most shameful manner, obliged to work unceasingly, in order I suppose that the clement, benevolent and charitable whiteman should be satisfied that the heathen spirit of an African boy of noble birth should be sufficiently subdued, rendered tame docile and submissive; and all for my good that I should thereby become a tame, profitable and honest slave. The natural man must be obliterated and degraded, that even the thought of liberty must never be suffered to contaminate itself in a negro's mind; and the odious thing, equality, should be taught by European discipline never to raise its head (chapter 5).

Brace's efforts to analyze his traumatizing environment may have enabled him to attain the emotional dissociation he needed to survive.

Brace mentions the names of three white men in Barbados: a hotelier/ slave breaker named Welch, an English ship captain turned small planter named Lecois, and a mariner named William Burke. Tracing these three names in conjunction with Brace's narrative illuminates the world of eighteenth-century West Indian society in compelling ways. (Unfortunately, the African names Brace mentions—Syneyo, Gow, Mahoo, Bangoo, Vrocea—are untraceable in colonial records.) The first white Barbadian whom Brace names is Welch. After spending about three months in the slave breaking prison or "house of subjection," Brace was sold to a New England ship captain named Isaac Mills who had been engaged in the West India trade since at least 1755.[10] While preparing to leave port, Mills placed Brace in the house of a sadistic man named Welch, who, according to Brace, "had a black wife and a white maid" (chapter 5). These surprising assertions raise useful historical questions. Was it possible for white men to marry black women in eighteenth-century Barbados? How would society have regarded their relationship? Did white women sometimes serve as maids for black women in the West Indian slave economy? Examining the history of families named Welch in Bridgetown provides some answers to these multifaceted questions.

Because Brace does not provide Welch's first name, I cannot pinpoint the specific man he encountered. However, records in the Barbados Department of Archives show that Welches were among the earliest seventeenth-century English settlers in Barbados, and they likely worked on the island either as indentured servants or as small farmers.[11] By the eighteenth century dozens of Welches lived on the island, concentrated largely in St. Michael Parish, the parish in which Barbados's largest city, Bridgetown, is located. The Welches of St. Michael Parish intermingled with the lowest classes of whites, freed people, and slaves. Such intermingling was not uncommon because the maritime activity in Bridgetown created such a high demand for laborers to staff taverns, hotels, and brothels that "freedwomen, slaves, and whites could, at times, interact in conditions of 'near equality'" (Welch and Goodridge 56).

As early as March 26, 1733 (about 30 years before Brace's arrival in Barbados), a three-year-old "free mulatto child" named David Welch was baptized in St. Michael Parish (Sanders, *Baptisms* 100). This David Welch could have been the offspring of the couple that Brace encountered; in any case, his baptism demonstrates that white Welches and black women were producing children together and that freed "mulatto" Welches existed in Bridgetown by the early eighteenth century. The numbers of freedmen and freedwomen gradually increased in Barbados during the seventeenth and eighteenth centuries, although their numbers remained small.[12] Archival documents indicate a long history of sexual and business partnerships among white Welches and freed blacks, as well as a steady growth in the number of free "colored" Welches in St. Michael Parish.[13]

Interracial marriage was not illegal in Barbados—there are recorded instances of it dating back to the seventeenth century[14]—but it was rare. While other West Indian countries legislated against "miscegenation," white Barbadians "hoped that the bio-social aspects of their white supremacy ideology, enshrined in the slave laws, would function as an adequate deterrent" (Beckles, *Centering Woman* 24). Thus it is unlikely that Brace's Welch was legally married to the black woman with whom he cohabited. Mixed race cohabitation was commonplace at the time. The best publicized instance of such cohabitation occurred in 1797, when George Points Ricketts was appointed governor of Barbados. One of his contemporaries, John Poyer, complained in his 1808 *History of Barbados:* "Unfortunately for the governor, unfortunately for Barbadoes, his excellency had brought with him from Tobago, a mulatto woman, who resided at Pilgrim [the Governor's house], and enjoyed all the privileges of a wife, except the honour of publicly presiding at his table. His excellency's extraordinary attachment to this sly insidious female was the greatest blemish in his character, and cast a baleful shade over the lustre of his administration. The influence which she was known to possess, produced a visible change in the manners of the free coloured people, who assumed a rank in the graduated scale of colonial society, to which they had hitherto been strangers" (639). Governor Ricketts was reprimanded by the Crown after this mistress, whose name was Betsey Goodwin, persuaded him to free a black prisoner. However, the slavocracy could not indict Ricketts's relationship with Goodwin without calling their own behavior into question. As Hilary Beckles observes, "Slave owners, and other males with capital, would commonly 'keep' black or 'coloured' mistresses primarily for sexual purposes. The evidence suggests that this was more popular in Bridgetown than on the plantations, though estate owners or managers probably had greater sexual access to a larger number of black women. In the towns, organized prostitution and resident mistresses were the general pattern" (Beckles, *Natural Rebels* 141). Pedro Welch and Richard Goodridge point to the variety of forms that these sexual liaisons took: "While concubinage involving white males and free colored women was sufficiently widespread to attract attention by most observers of the urban scene, there were also occasional glimpses of stable white-black house-holds. These might not have been 'sanctified' by marriages in the Church of England but they carried all of the other trappings of a marriage" (38). Brace likely observed in the Welch household just such a partnership.

Welch and his black "wife" appear to have shared more than a sexual relationship. Brace speculates that Welch ran a "boarding house," and he notes that Welch and the captain who brought Brace to the house went into a room where they regaled themselves with alcohol while Brace remained seated outside on the stoop. This description coincides with a distinctive pattern of interracial business relationships in maritime Bridge-town. Some free colored women found an avenue to economic survival and even prosperity by "operating 'hotels' (or brothels), taverns and haber-dasheries. We observe them acting as 'middlemen' in the local trading and market sector. Moreover, we see them developing a network of business relationships with white merchants and mariners which facilitated their own pro-emancipationist activities" (Welch and Goodridge 118). In the early nineteenth century John Waller observed: "There are a number of taverns in the town [Bridgetown], all of which are kept by mulatto women, who are possessed of considerable property, both in houses and slaves" (5). He added that these taverns were also "houses of debauchery, a num-ber of young women of colour being always procurable in them for the purposes of prostitution" (5). Brace describes Welch's black "wife" as a "brutish," "ostentatious," "large fat greasy Guinea woman; flat nose, thick lips, with teeth white as snow" (chapter 5). This description bears striking resemblance to Thomas Rowlandson's 1796 portrait of Rachel Pringle, a highly successful free black businesswoman who opened a tavern-hostelry-brothel in Bridgetown in 1780. It also resembles other "promi-nent freedwomen in the business, such as Sabina Brade who was de-scribed in 1807 as 'an old, fat black woman'; Betsy Lemon, a well-known mulatto figure in Bridgetown; Betsy Austin, whose hotel was said to offer the best in 'mental and corporeal' entertainment, though at exorbitant rates" (Beckles, *Centering Woman* 30). When Brace was in Bridgetown, the Welches may well have been running a prototype of this sort of estab-lishment. While the freedwomen who ran these "hotels" were frequently "brutish"—that is to say, pro-slavery, racist, and eager to profit from the exploitation of other women—at the same time they were working against enormous forces of race, gender, and class oppression to claim for them-selves a form of agency, empowerment, and even moderate prosperity.

Prostitution of both freed and enslaved women was pervasively practiced in Bridgetown; indeed, it was probably "more common at Bridgetown than in any other city in the British West Indies" (Levy 30). This form of sexual exploitation happened in a context where black women's bodies were routinely subjected to every form of violence and abuse imaginable. As Hilary Beckles has shown, white men grew attached to slavery not only because it was financially lucrative, but also because of the enormous interpersonal power they gained from it. Slavery in the Americas depended as much on the reproduction and elaboration of patriarchy as it did on the construction of race. Slave traders and slaveholders viewed

unrestricted sexual access to the slave women as a 'right' of mastery, and the refusal to exercise it on their part was considered strange if not irresponsible. . . . Ideologically, slaveowners understood well that they were entitled to commodify fully all the capabilities of slaves, as part of the search for maximum economic and social returns on their investment. Properly understood, this meant, among other things, the slaveowners' right to extract a wide range of non-pecuniary socio-sexual benefits from slaves as a legitimate stream of returns on capital, and an important part of the meaning of colonial mastery. (Beckles, *Centering Woman* xx, 22)

Brace testifies that sailors continued to rape slaves in Bridgetown, as they had done aboard ship, in a manner that terrorized the enslaved witnesses as well as the violated women. After the slaves disembarked, they were confined in a Bridgetown "prison," where, Brace observes, "the common sailors were allowed to come into the house and ravish the women in presence of all the assembly. Fathers and mothers were eye witnesses to their daughters being despoiled. Husbands beheld their wives in the hands of the beastly destroyers. Children bore testimony of the brutality practised upon their mothers" (chapter 51). During the 1760s Equiano observed the same systemic practice of rape in the West Indies. He recalls:

I used frequently to have different cargoes of new slaves in my care for sale; and it was almost a constant practice with our clerks, and other whites, to commit violent depredations on the chastity of the female slaves; and these I was, though with reluctance, obliged to submit to at all times, being unable to help them. When we have had some of these slaves on board my master's vessels to carry them to other islands, or to America, I have known our mates to commit these acts most shamefully, to the disgrace, not of Christians only, but of men. I have even known them gratify their brutal passion with females not ten years old. (104)

The dealers in slaves often profited financially from permitting sailors, clerks, and other white men to commit rape. Both male and female slave-holders encouraged the prostitution of their slaves. Beckles observes:

White males would often lease out their black mistresses and other slave women as prostitutes as a convenient way of obtaining cash. Dickson found this common practice in the 1770s, especially among men who were heavily in debt. Women were leased out to visiting "gentlemen", ships' captains and other clients for a spec-ified period. Monies obtained by these "whoremasters and mistresses" frequently exceeded the market value of the women. As such, slave owners considered the prostitution of women more lucrative than "breeding." (*Natural Rebels* 142)

Although many freedmen and freedwomen in Bridgetown, including some "colored" Welches, aligned themselves with ruling class values by adopting proslavery opinions and owning slaves, their lives remained pre-carious. John Waller noted in 1820, sixty years after Brace was in Barba-dos, that "a great diversity prevails among [the free people of color], but in Barbadoes, the great bulk of them are far indeed from being in a com-fortable condition. Many of these, however, having learned some useful trade, and being brought up in the habits of industry, accumulate a com-fortable independence. No property, however considerable, can ever raise a man or woman of colour, not even when combined with education, to the proper rank of a human being, in the estimation of an English or Dutch Creole" (95). Free people of color struggled to survive economically as well as to increase their civil rights. They played active roles in manumit-ting selected slaves, usually their relatives, sexual partners, and others whom they came to regard as friends. By 1739 the slavocracy felt so threat-ened by manumission that it imposed a manumission fee of £50. "In 1801, the manumission fees were significantly increased to £300 for the manu-mission of a female while the fee required for manumission of males was set at £200" (Welch and Goodridge 86). Because this fee was often pro-hibitive, those who were determined to manumit a slave searched for ways to circumvent it. "The one loophole which slaves and slaveowners could exploit was the fact that manumissions consummated in England were legal in the colonies. There the manumission rates were only 15s" (Welch and Goodridge 86). These realities produced an extraordinary collabora-tion between freed people (mostly freedwomen) and white mariners in Bridgetown. The free colored people who wanted to manumit one or more slaves would, for a token sum such as 10 shillings, "sell" the slave(s) to a mariner who would then draw up manumission papers on his next stop in London. Welch and Goodridge have identified "47 mariners who were involved in the manumission of some 400 slaves in the period 1795–1830" (90). The mariners were likely rewarded for their efforts with monies paid under the table or other forms of recompense. William Welch, a native of Bridgetown who became a London-based master mariner and commander of the ship *Berwick*, was involved in at least four such manumission projects wherein he collaborated with four free colored slaveholders (Sarah Hartle, Florella Clark, Christman Small, and Sussanah Ostrehan) to manumit six slaves (Michael, John Clarke, James George Clarke, Henrietta, Molly Sue, and Precilla Ostrehan) between 1806 and 1810. (See appendix for copies of three of Welch's Deeds of Manumission.) These Deeds of Manumission offer further evidence of intimate collaboration between white Welches and free colored people in Bridgetown.

Sexual and financial partnerships between black women and white men occurred despite the fact that "eligible white females were outnumbering white males almost by two to one by the 1760s," the time of Brace's sojourn in Barbados (Welch and Goodridge 40). Unlike the situation in any other West Indian colony, female slaves also outnumbered male slaves in Barbados, and life in Bridgetown "had a definite and distinct feminine stamp" (Welch and Goodridge 84). This predominance of women is reflected in Brace's account of the Welch "boarding house," which Welch passed through occasionally like a hurricane, while the women managed the daily life of the household and circumvented his wishes in his absence. This dynamic is evidenced upon Brace's arrival in the household, when Welch left the starving, thirsty boy sitting on a stoop by the door while he went off drinking with his associate. The "white maid" invited Brace into the house and fed him pork, onions, and a small biscuit. At first glance, this appears (both to Brace and to the reader) to be welcome nourishment. White people had long found pork plentiful and tasty in Barbados (Ligon 50), but it was rarely allocated to slaves, who subsisted mainly on "Guinea corn, which was also given to cattle" (Handler and Lange 86). Slaves in town had access to a more varied diet than plantation slaves, but the meat allocated to slaves was usually fish, which often was putrid (Handler and Lange 87). Many slaves in Barbados died from starvation and disease due to substandard and poisonous food. The pork and onions given to Brace turned out to be toxic, and he soon found himself "extremely sick." His sickness may account for why the pork was available to him in the first place. On August 20, 1760 James Douglas, the British commander-in-chief in the Leeward Islands, described to Mr. Coverdale, agent of the Naval Hospital in Barbados, an outbreak of food poisoning from pork. Douglas instructed Coverdale to stop feeding pork to his men, because it "often occasions a flux (much oftener than any other meat)" (Rodger 254). "Flux" was a contemporary word for dysentery, a disease characterized by severe diarrhea, and for similar illnesses characterized by excessive and abnormal discharges of bodily fluids, such as the vomiting that Brace describes.

Welch responded to Brace's vomiting by beating him to a pulp. The white woman attempted to stop the beating, whereupon Welch threatened her with violence. With the beating exacerbating the food poisoning, Brace remained violently ill for three weeks. During this time, he says, "the white woman paid every attention in her power, when Welch was gone; and my country woman paid every attention in her power,—but Welch's wife never entered the room during my sickness" (chapter 6). The white woman who befriended Brace may have been a fair-skinned slave or servant, an impoverished white servant, or even Welch's legal wife who may have been forced to cohabit with his mistress. Such triangular households were common, although white wives usually had more social power than the white woman in Brace's recollection. White maids were unusual in 1760, but the majority of white Barbadians were poor and in need of work. "In 1760, there were just over 5,000 slave holders in Barbados," out of a total population of 17,800 whites and 86,600 blacks (Beckles, *Natural Rebels* 58; *A History* 42). White laborers were regarded by the ruling class as ignorant, vicious, drunk, and lazy, "social failures and degenerates" who were a blight on Barbadian society. Most white laborers were "unable to find steady, well-paid employment; many resorted to the socially degrading poor-relief facilities, and some attempted the isolating backcountry, earth-scratching subsistence farming" (Beckles, *A History* 48, 47). Many of the poor whites were descendants of indentured servants imported from England by the original planters in the seventeenth century. In "the early narratives, histories, travel accounts and biographies . . . labouring white women are described variously as 'loose wenches,' 'whores,' 'sluts,' and 'white slaves'" (Beckles, *Centering Woman* xix).

One morning when the tortured young Brace was sitting on Welch's stoop weeping, an African woman walked by and began talking to him in

his native language. Astonished and afraid that it "was a delusion," Brace
hardly dared reply, but his countrywoman plied him with questions and it
soon emerged that she knew his city, his parents, and his extended family.
For the duration of Brace's time in Barbados, she befriended him sur-
reptitiously. On his request, she told him the story of her own capture
by French slave traders and her enslavement in Martinique, a French-
controlled island with an enslaved population of approximately 65,900
people in the mid-eighteenth century (Curtin, *The Atlantic Slave Trade*
78). Sold to a French merchant and put to work in his kitchen, she developed a relationship with an English captain named Lecois who dined frequently at the merchant's house. Captain Lecois helped her escape with
her African lover, whose name was Vrocea. Such escapes aboard ship were
not as uncommon as one might expect; in fact, runaway slaves were often
found on other islands, having made their escape on any one of the myriad
of small vessels that conducted an often illicit trade in the West Indies. In
a 1761 letter to Benjamin Southwell, the Agent at Barbados, Commodore
Douglas described British efforts to "discourage the French from send-
ing their free negroes and mulattos into their privateers," and he noted
that "at Barbadoes where they have such a short run both to St. Lucia and
Martinique . . . several of those negroes and mulattos have carried some
of the wherries off and made their escape" (Rodger 264). Wherries were
light boats that could race around harbors and rivers, easily evading the
large vessels or "men-of-war" of the colonial navies. These runaways contributed to the overall problem that colonial powers had in controlling the
West Indies, where British, French, Spanish, and American merchants
engaged in a lively and lucrative illicit trade amongst themselves. Brace's
portrait of Lecois accords well with the general profile of West Indian
merchants and mariners who were simultaneously profiteers from and
rebels against the official colonial structures of their societies.

In Brace's reconstruction of his conversations with his unnamed countrywoman, she states that after Vrocea died in a battle with a Spanish
vessel, she lived with Lecois, who "dressed me elegantly, treated me tenderly, seated me at the head of his table at all times; and . . . offered me his
hand. We were married about seven years ago, and have two little girls and
a boy" (Chap. 6). She describes Lecois as "considerably dissipated" and "a
natural tyrant," but claims that he treated her well, except sometimes
when he was drunk (chapter 6). I have been unable to trace the name
"Lecois" in Barbados; since there would have been no way for the young

Brace to understand its correct spelling, he may have been recalling "Lucas" or "LaCroix" (names well-established in eighteenth-century Barbados). In any case, Brace's countrywoman's "marriage" to Lecois fits the patterns of interracial relationships described above.

After enduring two or three months in Welch's "house of subjection," Brace tells us that he was collected by Captain Isaac Mills, who had "purchased me for his cabin boy, or private waiter" (chapter 6). A New England merchant active in the West Indies trade, Mills most likely was engaged in the Seven Years War as the captain of one of hundreds of vessels that were not owned by the king but were "the private property of the captains. . . . These little vessels were able to take on enemy privateers on their own terms with considerable success" (Rodger 245).[15] Battleships at the time were armed with guns numbering from eight to ninety, and Brace recalls that Captain Mills's frigate carried forty-four guns. Because Brace was unable to understand English, Mills put him "among the mariners," where he was "taught the military discipline by one William Burks, who taught me altogether by signs" (chapter 6). William Burke (1697–1788), a Bridgetown mariner, was a member of the standing English military forces in Barbados.[16] It is a testament to the power of Brace's memory that despite the trauma of kidnapping, the horror of the Middle Passage, and the confusion of acquiring painful knowledge in a foreign language, Brace was able to recall William Burke by name fifty years later.

An Enslaved Soldier in the Seven Years War

Perhaps Burke's military training remained impressed on Brace's memory because it contributed to his ability to survive the next two violent decades of his life, during which he served as an enslaved soldier in both the Seven Years War and the American Revolution. Purchased by Captain Mills around 1760, Brace found himself aboard a vessel that engaged in numerous skirmishes with Spanish and French vessels over the next two years. The British navy in the West Indies had relied heavily on black labor since at least 1729, when Admiral Charles Stewart wrote from Jamaica to the Navy Board in London proposing that "seasoned Negroes, boys and men" should be trained as "apprentices to the Master Caulker, carpenters or Builder, or whoever are the Naval Officers, in order to be brought up to their several trades as caulkers, ship carpenters, or otherwise" (Admiral Charles Stewart to Navy Board, 11 November 1729;

Baugh 351). He noted that the existing caulkers were "chiefly blacks" and argued that the Crown should buy Negroes for the Navy, because "his Majesty has paid dear" for those "he has been obliged to hire" (Admiral Charles Stewart to Admiralty Secretary, 29 December 1730; Baugh 357). Sometimes the majority of laborers working in West Indian naval yards were black. For instance, in 1749 Admiral Charles Knowles appointed a "Naval Officer and two servants; clerk; gunner and overseer of the Ne-groes; surgeon and servant; four shipwrights; six caulkers; two house car-penters; four watchmen; thirty-three King's Negroes" to work in the naval yard at Port Antonio (Order issued by Admiral Charles Knowles to Richard James, 11 April 1749; Baugh 394). African laborers were indis-pensable because the problem of manning ships "was always acute in the West Indies, where the demand for European seaman was very high" (Rodger 245–46). Adding to the demand and expense was the high mor-tality rate of white sailors, especially those engaged in the slave trade.

The Seven Years War (1756–1763), which was called the French and Indian War in North America, was in many ways the first world war—that is to say, a global struggle between European powers who were vying for control of colonies around the world. The central rivalry was between France and England, and the Spanish allied with the French in 1762. Dur-ing the last three years of the war—the period during which Brace was impressed into service—"the British shifted their military effort to the West Indies, where Martinique, Guadeloupe, and Havana in Cuba fell in turn to amphibious attack" (Shy 305). At the beginning of chapter 7, Brace describes his participation in the English capture of Havana in the sum-mer of 1762. A strategic port that was the center of Spanish power in the Caribbean, Havana was more strongly fortified than any other American port. The British decided to attack it in January 1762, and appointed Lieutenant-General George Keppel, the Earl of Albemarle, to command the land forces and Vice-Admiral Sir George Pocock to command the naval forces. The British planned to assemble a sea-borne army of more than 20,000 men in the West Indies, including at least 500 free blacks and 2,000 slaves from Jamaica (Syrett xiv). Albemarle's force arrived in Barba-dos on April 20, 1762 and began to rendezvous with other ships. The day after his arrival, Albemarle described to Major General Robert Monck-ton the critical role that he expected blacks to play in the expedition. He was dismayed to find that free blacks in Jamaica "would not enlist in the army, for they knew that if they were taken prisoner, the enemy would enslave them," and that the Governor of Jamaica, William Henry Lyttelton, had difficulty obtaining slaves due "great opposition from the planters, who feared economic loss if their slaves were killed or wounded" (Syrett xviii).[17] Albemarle emphasized to Monckton: "As this is an article of the most serious nature, upon which (considering the violent heats) the health of the soldiery and even the success of the expedition may greatly depend, I must recommend it to you very strongly to consider if by any means we can be furnished with a number of blacks from Martinique" (Albemarle to Monckton, 21 April 1762; Syrett 94). A month later he explained to the British Secretary of State for the Southern Department: "The great utility of slaves to Major-General Monckton's army at the reduction of Martinique (I believe he had near 3000 from His Majesty's islands), and the great uncertainty of my receiving any from Jamaica as that island has been so much alarmed for some time past, induced me to take every measure I could think of to procure a number that I might be sure of some assistance to the troops, as the soldiers and sailors cannot possibly work in this country. I purchased near 100 blacks at Martinique, and . . . [from Antigua and St. Kitts] . . . I have got near 500 more, some of them purchased, the rest hired" (Albemarle to Egremont, 27 May 1762; Syrett 136). Albemarle proceeded to mention thirty slaves obtained from Jamaica and fifty free Negroes promised to him from another source. With European soldiers dying in droves from heat and disease, Albemarle continued for the duration of the war to obtain as many slaves and free blacks as he could buy or hire to perform the heavy labor necessary to the expedition. His continuous fretting that "the troops will suffer greatly for the want of them" indicates how crucial African men were to his campaign (Albemarle to Egremont, 27 May 1762; Syrett 136). The Spanish also used a regiment of "Mulattoes" and a regiment of "Negroes" in their forces in Havana (Syrett 147). Thus Brace was one of thousands of African men involved in this battle.

Following the chronology provided by Brace, it appears that Captain Mills set out to join Pocock's fleet early in 1762, but due to a thick fog, his vessel "lost sight of the guide ship, . . . got windbound and could not find the fleet" (chapter 6). They got involved in a battle with a Spanish vessel, during which Brace received five wounds. Mills bestowed the name "Jeffrey" upon him because he, like Jeffrey Amherst, "possessed rather more courage than prudence" (chapter 7). After towing the captured Spanish vessel to Savannah, Georgia, Mills's ship sailed once again for Havana.

Brace mentions that their ship "remained about two months" before the
fortress at Havana, and this fits precisely with the historical time-frame.
The British assault began on June 8, and after a horrific siege in which hundreds of soldiers died from combat while thousands died from heat, yellow fever, malaria, gastrointestinal disorders, and scarcity of drinking water, the Spanish commandant formally surrendered on August 14, 1762.[18]

Slavery in Colonial Connecticut

After the war, Captain Mills returned to trading and sailed with his
crew to Dublin, Ireland and to many North American ports, including
Halifax, Nova Scotia; St. Augustine, Florida; Savannah, Georgia; New York
City; Newport, Rhode Island; and Boston, Massachusetts. Like Equiano
and tens of thousands of other contemporaneous Africans, Jeffrey Brace
was becoming, through no choice of his own, a world traveler and a cultural hybrid. He liked Boston, where he spent about two months and was
"indulged by my master, who allowed me to go about the town" (chapter
7). Discovering a community of "free African descendants, who appeared
to be well contented in their situation" and who showered him with questions and attention, Brace found himself "extremely anxious to remain" in
Boston. One of New England's chief ports for the slave trade and an important site for antislavery agitation, the city retained a significant African
population, despite its prevalent racism. In 1765, Boston's total population was estimated at 15,520, which included 811 Negroes and mulattoes,
about sixty of whom were free (Greene 85; Nash 5). This was a small per-
centage compared to Barbados, but Boston's "colored" community, located primarily in the North End, included many intellectually and politically active free men, slaves, and fugitives (Cromwell 27).[19] Since Africans
in Massachusetts often intermarried with Indians (as they did in every
other colony on the eastern seaboard), Boston's "colored" population had
multi-continental roots. Brace may have encountered Briton Hammon,
whose short memoir, *The Narrative of the Uncommon Sufferings and
Surprising Deliverance of Briton Hammon, a Negro Man*, was printed in
Boston 1760. Although Hammon represented himself as a loyal slave, his
publication of a memoir (which is widely regarded as the first African
American slave narrative) contradicted the racist stereotypes on which
slavery depended, and Brace may well have heard about it. Belinda, the
African woman described above, was one of several black Bostonians who

petitioned the legislature during the 1770s and 1780s, with demands rang-
ing from compensation for their labor to the abolition of slavery. A young
African girl, Phyllis Wheatley (c. 1753–1784), the mother-to-be of African
American literature, was sold on the auction block in Boston on July 11,
1761, about a year before Brace's sojourn there, and her poems would begin appearing in print in 1767. An adolescent Chloe Spear (c. 1750–1815),
whose life was celebrated in an 1832 booklet, *Memoir of Mrs. Chloe Spear,
a Native of Africa,* arrived in Boston around the same time as Brace, having been captured in Africa at the age of twelve and sold to a Boston merchant. Freed around 1783, she would prosper financially through indus-
trious domestic labor and would gain recognition as an inspiring speaker
and a member of Boston's Second Baptist Church, which had accepted
black members since the 1740s (see Minardi 46–50). Crispus Attacks, a
fugitive "mulatto fellow" who may have had either Indian or African ancestry (or both), lived in Boston while Brace was there and would gain
fame posthumously as the first "martyr" of the American Revolution.[20]
Prince Hall (1748–1807), who was born in Bridgetown, Barbados to "an
Englishman, Thomas Prince Hall, a leather worker, and a free colored
woman of French extraction" (Cromwell 31), arrived in Boston in 1765, a
few years after Brace. Initially a steward on ships that sailed between
Boston and England, Hall fought in the Revolutionary War[21] and afterwards gained prominence as a tradesman, abolitionist, agitator for black
citizenship and education, Methodist minister, and founder of the first
black Masonic lodge in Boston (Cromwell 31–32). In short, Boston was a
lively metropolitan port that, despite its embedded legal and social racism,
offered economic as well as intellectual opportunities to Africans and
African Americans in the eighteenth century. Their activism laid the foundation on which more famous abolitionists later built (e.g., David Walker
in the 1820s and William Lloyd Garrison in the 1830s).

Late in 1763 Brace was transported against his will to New Haven,
Connecticut, where Captain Mills sold him to a Yankee Puritan from Milford, Mills's home town. Brace praises Mills as "a kind and humane man"
who was "loved, respected, and revered" by the ship's crew, yet Mills did
not scruple to sell his wounded slave at his convenience. Around the time
that Mills sold Brace in New Haven, he formed a partnership with two
other Milford men, Edward Allen and Thomas Gibb, to purchase a new
54-ton sloop that was built in Connecticut in 1763 and registered in New
Haven on Feb. 17, 1763. The co-owners named the sloop *The Seaflower,*

and early in 1764 Captain Mills and six other men loaded it with typical New England products (beef, pork, and tallow) and sailed from New Haven to the West Indies.[22]

New England Puritans did not hold a large number of slaves in bondage within their households, but they engaged actively in the slave trade and eventually dominated it within North America. In the 1750s and early 1760s approximately 150 slaves per year were imported into Connecticut for sale, and nearly every town in Connecticut had some slaves (Yang 82, 122–23). Sales were sometimes announced in newspaper advertisements such as the one below, which appeared in the *Connecticut Courant* on December 16, 1764:

> To be sold by
> Thomas Mayhew,
> At Hartford.
> A Very Likely Negro Fellow, about 18 or
> 19 years of age; also, a Negro Wo-
> man, about 24, with a girl about 5 years old,
> for which he would take produce.

Compared to the thriving international ports Brace had visited, New Haven was a small conservative town. It was situated at the head of a harbor on the Long Island sound, one hundred forty miles from Boston and seventy-six miles from New York City. At the time of Brace's arrival, New Haven with its farms and outlying villages had a population of about 5,300 whites and 160 blacks. The village proper was organized around the town green, where Brace would have seen three churches, four Yale College buildings, the courthouse, a jail and the Hopkins' Grammar School. The town, which included more than two hundred houses, dozens of stores, a post office, and a custom house, shared the seat of government with Hartford. Primary businesses in New Haven included agriculture, fishing, and the West India trade.[23]

The New England society that Brace entered was only about two percent black, while in Barbados, Brace had encountered a population that was eighty-five percent black. Indentured servitude of poor Europeans had always been a central source of labor for the English colonies, and enslavement of Africans had been practiced in Anglo-America since 1619 when a Dutch vessel delivered twenty Africans to Jamestown, Virginia. All of the New England colonies legalized slavery between the years 1641

(Massachusetts) and 1714 (New Hampshire), codifying it as an inherited, racial status. However, slavery did not flourish in New England the way it did in southern colonies. While most slaves in the West Indies and many in the South worked on large plantations, "few Yankee masters held more than one or two bondsmen" (Pierson 3).

Impoverished white people, children, and immigrants were routinely sold into indentured servitude and Africans into slavery in New Haven. A typical announcement in *The Connecticut Gazette* stated: "Samuel Willis of Middletown will sell several African boys and girls" (Aug. 22, 1761, Scott 109). The lack of denigrating language in the simple announcement that "boys and girls" were for sale testifies to a society well-versed in the exploitation of children as well as Africans. In the months following Brace's arrival the *Connecticut Gazette* announced the sale of "a likely *Negro wench* and *child*" on June 15, 1763; the binding out of poor adults and children on July 4, 1763; and the sale of "a parcel of Irish Servants ["Just Imported from Dublin"] both Men and Women, to be sold cheap" (Barber 165–66). As Robert J. Cottrol observes,

Racial distinctions in colonial America were less pronounced than they would become. This was not because early America had a high regard for black bondsmen but rather because many whites were also in bondage. Recruited from the British lower classes, frequently the Irish, whites held in various forms of servitude often lived lives that were little different from those of black slaves. Indentured servants, apprentices, and seamen worked at the same occupations that slaves did, were sold on auction blocks alongside imported Africans, and were flogged and maimed for many of the same offenses for which blacks were punished. Newspapers in colonial America often carried advertisements for both runaway blacks and runaway whites. (12)

In Connecticut Brace encountered attitudes among the whites that ranged from proslavery to abolitionist and from rabidly racist to mildly egalitarian. People of African descent struggled to assert some agency over their lives. In 1761 the New Haven newspaper, *The Connecticut Gazette,* published eight announcements about runaway slaves. The description of a runaway named Cyrus reveals the ideological contradictions intrinsic to slavery: "Cyrus—a Negro servant, age c. 25 years, runaway from John Lloyd of Stanford; said servant is very clever and is a good butcher and he was wearing an iron collar around his neck at the time of his escape" (17 Oct. 1761). Since Cyrus was both intelligent and skilled as a butcher, qualities that obviously signal a humanity beneficial to society, the barbarism of enchaining him in an iron collar must surely have struck some readers, especially those who were chafing against their own far less injurious "bondage" to the British. Yet severe corporal punishment—including branding, whipping, and execution—of blacks, Indians, and poor whites was not unusual. The colonial newspapers calmly reported torture, calling it "punishment." For example, on November 6, 1767 the *Connecticut Journal and New-Haven Post-Boy* stated: "At a Special Superior Court held here on Tuesday the 27th of October, one James Haning, a transient Person, was convicted of Burglary, and was sentenced to be whipt 15 Stripes, to have his right Ear cut off, and to be branded with the Letter B on his Forehead: and last Monday, he received his Punishment accordingly" (No. 3, p. 3).

Brace describes in a plainspoken manner the sadistic treatment he received at the hands of Yankee Puritans. About twenty-one years old, Brace was still suffering from the five wounds inflicted on him during the Seven Years War when he was purchased by John Burwell of Milford. A small town near New Haven, Milford in 1762 counted 1661 white residents and 134 blacks ("List" 1). Slavery was becoming increasingly controversial throughout Connecticut, and some of the black residents of Milford had been freed, although they were still subjected to legal restrictions placed on nonwhite persons. By 1790 the white population of Milford had grown to more than two thousand people, while the black population remained relatively constant, consisting of 64 slaves, 57 free "Negroes" living in households of their own, and eleven free nonwhites living in white households (*Heads of Household*, first U.S. Census, 1790).

The sixth oldest town in Connecticut, Milford was built in meadows and woodlands bordering the Long Island Sound, in an area formerly occupied by Pequots and Paugussets. The land was fertile, game was plentiful, and the Sound and the East River abounded with clams, oysters, blue crabs, lobsters, and many varieties of fish. Histories written by whites state that the town founders purchased the lands in the 1630s from "Ansantawae, a sachem of the Paugusset Indians who had a village on the banks of the river. The price was six coats, ten blankets, twelve hatchets, twelve hoes, two dozen knives, and a dozen small mirrors" (*History of Milford* 4). White settlement was begun in 1639 by followers of the Reverend Peter Prudden, an immigrant from Hertfordshire, England, who recruited followers when he preached in towns in England and New England (*History of Milford* 3). When Prudden died in 1656, Cotton Mather, a passionate believer in social hierarchy, praised Prudden's "faculty to sweeten, compose, and qualify exasperated spirits, and stop or heal all contentions— whence it was that his Town of Milford enjoyed peace with truth all his days" (*History of Milford* 29).

At the time of Brace's arrival in a frosty October, Milford was a bustling little place with two churches, three taverns, two small church-run libraries, and four schools, as well as many houses and businesses. Shipbuilding was an important industry from 1690 to 1820; many ocean-going ships, including slave ships, were built in Milford shipyards, located on a "well-protected harbor [that] was navigable for the good-sized vessels which tied up at the wharf to load and unload" (*History of Milford* 38). Captain Jonas Green, who held Jeffrey Brace in slavery for a short period in the 1760s, built and launched a 35-ton schooner named the *Sarah Ann* in 1762 (*History of Milford* 38). Milford's earliest merchants built their wealth on the fur trade, a trade that grew ever more active through the eighteenth century. Indeed, Peter Pond (1740–1807), an adventurer and soldier from Milford, was one of the founders of the "powerful Northwest Fur Company, comparable to the East India Company in financial strength and influence" (*History of Milford* 41). Milford merchants prospered by exchanging "horses, cattle, pork, beef, mutton, flour, and corn meal, as well as furs obtained in Indian trade," for "sugar, rum, and molasses from the West Indies, manufactured goods from England, and wines from France" (*History of Milford* 38). Almost one in ten residents of Milford was enslaved. Brace's narrative corroborates Connecticut historian Guocon Yang's finding that "[s]lave ownership corresponded closely with the level of wealth. The richer the people, the more likely they owned slaves" (126–27). Yang notes that although "the overwhelming majority of the Connecticut residents, over 95 percent, were not slave-owners at any given time," 70% of Connecticut's wealthy merchants owned slaves in the 18th century, as did 50% of wealthy farmers, justices, officers, captains, deputies, ministers, and deacons (126–27). In short, slavery was created by and for the religious, governmental, military, legal, financial, and agricultural ruling class, the same elite that exploited the labor of white indentured servants.

In the household of John Burwell (1719–1784), Brace lived with Burwell's cruel second wife, Esther Whiting, and three male children, who ranged in age from eight to twelve. It was common in New England "for

white owners and black servants to work side by side during the day" and
to "retire to the same house at night" (Pierson 3), but in the Burwell
household the white family slept in beds while Brace was forced to sleep
on a "naked hearth" without so much as a blanket. John Burwell descended from a planter named John Burwell of Hemel Hampstead, England, who followed Peter Prudden to Milford in 1639. The Burwells lived
in an area known as Burwell's Farms, located near Prudden's Point, west
of the Oyster River. Encountering snow for the first time, Brace had nothing to wear but a thin linen jacket and a pair of sailor's kilts. Given no shoes,
he was forced to labor outdoors in bare feet. The wounds he had received
at sea "broke out newly," and he "almost perished with cold and hunger"
(chapter 7).

Brace describes Burwell as "a professed puritan" who "would read the
bible and pray both night and morning, for all mankind," while starving,
beating, and torturing the man he held in bondage (chapter 7). Brace's
juxtaposition of Burwell's religious piety with his savage inhumanity antic-
ipates the motif of Christian hypocrisy that would become central to the
antebellum slave narrative. Embracing a contradictory worldview that
combined distaste for tyranny with Calvinist theology, Puritans gravitated
toward a theocratic "social organization led by God's chosen, the
Elect. . . . Connecticut's founding fathers erected their system of government on the proposition that the mass of mankind, the non-Elect, was evil,
corrupt, and hardly fit for political participation" (Roth 39, 40). Women,
children, apprentices, indentured servants, slaves, blacks, Indians, religious dissenters, and many white men were excluded from the political
process; indeed, "as late as the 1760s only twenty-five percent of the adult
males in New Haven took part in town meetings" (Roth 41). Church at-
tendance and observation of the Sabbath, fast days, and religious holidays
were mandatory; those who neglected these religious duties were sometimes prosecuted and fined. The Congregational Church, to which the
Burwell family belonged throughout the eighteenth century, was the
colony's official church, and it collected taxes from all taxpayers, regard-
less of their religious persuasion. The First Congregational Church in Milford was an impressive three-story building with a ninety-foot clock tower
and spire that dominated the architectural landscape. The church disseminated mixed views about slavery and "race." While many Christian
denominations sought to bar slaves from conversion and membership
in the Christian community,[24] Congregationalist ministers as prominent

as Cotton Mather had argued for slave conversions in the seventeenth century. Mather disseminated "a catechism intended especially for slaves," and as early as 1693 he "organized a Society of Negroes, chiefly made up of slaves who had been permitted by their owners to meet for worship and instruction" (Bruce 9). Like whites, blacks in eighteenth-century Connecticut were required to attend church. In most churches "the seating in the church reflected the social hierarchy. The social elite occupied the most prominent seats. Being the lowest in social rank, blacks were assigned to the 'Negro corners' or 'Negro pews,'" which were set in the back or in balconies (Yang 246).

The church's divergent views about slavery were echoed in conflicts that developed around Brace in Milford. Brace describes an occasion when, after being abused by Burwell, he was lying bleeding in a wood-pile, and "Mr. Samuel Eals came and took me up, and very charitably led me into the house, [and] told Burrell that such abuse was inhuman and unchristian" (chapter 7). Samuel Eells Sr. (1698–1789) was married to John Burwell's cousin, Deborah Burwell (1697–1775).[25] Like the Bur-wells, the Eells had lived in Milford since the mid-seventeenth century. The family's progenitor, Captain Samuel Eells, had been Milford's town clerk and the custom master for New Haven County, as well as one of three partners who built a fulling mill on Beaver Brook in 1689. Granted 200 acres of land for service in King Phillip's War, he built a house on Wharf Street around 1700, which is the oldest house still standing in Mil-ford (*Families of Early Milford* 243).[26] The Eells family was prominent in the affairs of both Milford and New Haven. Brace tells us that Samuel Eells was so outraged by Burwell's treatment of him that he clothed him and brought him to his own home, where he nursed him back to health. The conflict between Burwell and Eells illustrates the variety of views of "race" and slavery that existed at the time; members of the same class, cul-ture, and family system were often at odds on the issues. Although not op-posed to slavery per se, Eells was sufficiently appalled by Burwell's treat-ment of Brace to risk a breach in family relations.

As soon as Brace was able to work, he was sold once again, this time to Peter Prudden, a sadistic descendant of Milford's founding preacher, who whipped him for crying at night. Brace found himself passed from one ex-ceedingly cruel Milford master to another, including a merchant named John Gibbs (a relative of Captain Mills's business partner, Thomas Gibbs), Phineas Baldwin Sr. (Mills's father-in-law), Phineas Baldwin Jr. (Mills's brother-in-law), Captain Jonas Green, and a tanner named Murrier. Brace devotes little space to describing the work he was compelled to perform, but the duties he does mention include feeding pigs, foddering other animals, gathering turnips, harvesting crops, chopping wood, and fetching water. Baldwin Jr. used him primarily to tend his two small children, while Green may have put him to work in a shipyard, and Murrier may have required his assistance in tanning hides.

In describing the whippings and abuse he received, Brace makes it clear that he was not a passive victim. He criticizes not only the sadism, but also the appearance, the voices, the management style, the irrationality, and the religious hypocrisy of his masters. In one case he tells us that when Gibbs's young son "began whipping me & chirping to me, as would a driver to his horse," he (Brace) "designedly pushed" him down the stairs (chapter 8). As punishment for attempting to maintain some dignity, he was pushed downstairs himself and given fifty lashes with a horsewhip. The fact that Brace was usually sold within a few months of his purchase suggests that he was determined not to make peace with masters whom he despised.

In a September around 1768 Brace was purchased by Widow Mary Stiles, who lived in Woodbury, a rural town about twenty miles northwest of New Haven.[27] In the brief two paragraphs devoted to the sixteen years he was enslaved by the Stiles family, Brace asserts that the years he spent with Mary Stiles were "a glorious era in my life, as widow Stiles was one of the finest women in the world; she possessed every christian virtue" (chapter 8). While this tribute echoes conventional eighteenth-century praise of "godly women," it is unique in Brace's narrative. He was not usually one to withhold criticism. His affection for Widow Stiles makes psychological sense when one considers the torment that he had endured for several years. As Pierson observes, "In their terrible loneliness and dislocation, most of these slave immigrants were eager to reestablish human contacts and reconnect to social order" (145). With the trauma of the Middle Passage compounded by almost unrelenting atrocities in Barbados, life-threatening skirmishes at sea, and brutal treatment by a series of Yankee slaveholders, Brace desperately needed to experience at least the illusion of kindness and stability. Mary Stiles won his affection by teaching him to read, helping him to improve his English-speaking skills, and treating him with a modicum of grandmotherly affection. It is significant that he never stayed long with a master until he found one who was tolerable. But who was Mary Stiles? What made her, in the view of her slave, "one of the finest women in the world"? Examining the particularities of Mary Stiles's life may help illuminate the forces that shaped Brace's life in Woodbury.

The oldest of six siblings, Mary Stiles (née Johnson) was born in Stratford, Connecticut on October 15, 1695, nine months after her father, George Johnson of Woburn, Massachusetts, married her mother, Hannah Dorman of Stratford (Orcutt 1227). Stratford, a small coastal town about five miles west of Milford on the Housatonic River, was built by English Puritans, who in 1638 began settling on land taken from Pequannocks (Orcutt 6). During Mary's childhood, a Congregational meeting house, a public school, stores, businesses, and over a hundred houses lined the two central streets, Main and Elm. The settlers planted crops on fields that the Pequannocks had cleared and cultivated, and their surplus produce was shipped to Boston, New York, Barbados, and other West Indian islands. The Puritan world was an austere patriarchy ruled by an elite of like-minded white men who demanded obedience, discipline, and control from their subordinates. Insubordinate, unruly, or peculiar women were subjected to enormous social pressure to conform. The harshest form of pressure came in the form of the spectre of witchcraft, which provided an ideological justification for "systematic violence against women" (Karlsen xii).[28] This reality must have struck home with the young Mary Johnson, since she was born a mere three years after the 1692 outbreaks of witchcraft hysteria in Salem, Massachusetts and Fairfield, Connecticut. The young Mary may have been aware that another Connecticut woman bearing her name, Mary Johnson of Wethersfield, had in 1648 become the first woman in New England to be executed for witchcraft (Hall 23). In childhood, Mary and other local youth were told stories about an area of Stratford known as "Gallows Brook" or "Gallows Swamp," where Goody Bassett was hanged for witchcraft in 1651 (Orcutt 147–48). Although the magnitude of the Salem outbreak (185 people were accused of witchcraft and 19 were executed) ended up discrediting witchcraft in the minds of many members of the ruling class after 1692, women (especially servants and the poor) who challenged religious, secular, or familial authority continued to be accused of witchcraft throughout Mary Johnson Stiles's lifetime. Long after executions for witchcraft ceased, women accused of witchcraft were still reviled and persecuted.

On September 21, 1709, shortly before her fourteenth birthday, Mary Johnson married Francis Stiles of Woodbury, a rural village founded as a result of religious conflict among residents of Stratford. Advised by Governor John Winthrop to remove from Stratford due to their disagreements with other Puritan church members, the Rev. Zechariah Walker and fifteen families were granted land in 1672 by the colonial government in valleys where Pootatuck Indians had cultivated crops of corn, beans, and tobacco for many generations. The settlers primarily cultivated wheat, peas, and pork and hunted for other meat and fur. The Woodbury town fathers agreed that "all [read: all white male Congregationalists who were not indentured] were to enjoy equal privileges, both civil and religious," and they placed "a restriction as to the quantity of land which a proprietor might have. No one could have more than twenty-five acres for his home-lot, and the poorest among them was entitled to ten; so that a few rich men could not control the township" (Cothren 4). At the same time that they strove to achieve greater social equality than they had known in England, many of the early settlers owned slaves and exploited the labor of indentured servants. William Cothren, the voluminous antebellum historian of Woodbury, wrote in 1854: "It will be difficult for a portion of our community to believe, that the sainted Walker, Stoddard, and Marshall, those men of God, those lights to the people in this wilderness for so many years, were slaveholders; and yet such is the fact. All the leading men and men of property, in the early days, owned slaves. . . . The various records show, that a considerable proportion of the personal estate of the more opulent of the inhabitants consisted of negro servants" (Cothren 319). The original fifteen families included the Stileses, Curtisses, and Hinmans, whose patriarchs chose home-lots in an area dubbed *White Oak* in honor of a large white oak tree under which the first whites who explored the region encamped (Cothren 37). Their intermarried descendants continued to own slaves until the end of the eighteenth century.

The Puritans of Woodbury, like Puritans throughout New England, strove mightily to forge a mono-culture based on a hierarchy of religion, gender, and race out of the multicultural realities that they faced. The year before the newly married Mary Johnson Stiles arrived in Woodbury, the behavior of the slaveholding Reverend Anthony Stoddard illustrated the violence that often characterized Puritan intercultural relations. One Sabbath evening in 1708 Stoddard was walking in his garden after the conclusion of evening services when he "discovered an Indian skulking in the bushes. He quietly re-entered his house, and took his gun. After watching for a while, Mr. Stoddard obtained a fair view of him, fired, and the Indian fell. He dared not investigate further that night. Early in the morning he discovered another red foe near his companion, whom he also dispatched" (*History of Litchfield County* 696). The Puritans' fear of "savagery," intolerance of difference, and desire for domination made their world a violent place. The circumstances leading to Woodbury's first divorce, which was granted to Jonathan Taylor in the same year that Stoddard shot his "red foe," must have confirmed the Puritan men's worst fears. The General Court granted Taylor a divorce on the grounds that his wife had attempted "to take his life by her violence, deserting him, and living with Joseph Allen, a negro, at Sackett's Farm, N.Y." (*History of Litchfield County* 696). The Puritan intolerance of any sexual "deviation" led to extraordinary excesses; one could be executed in colonial Connecticut for "adultery, sodomy, lesbianism, harlotry, rape, incest, bestiality, and withdrawal as a form of birth control" (Roth 55). Few women were able to escape the way Mrs. Taylor did.

By marrying young[29] and bearing many children, Mary Stiles stepped into roles expected of her. In English law all women were "understood either married or to bee married," as a 1632 legal treatise proclaimed (Norton 25). Sir William Blackstone articulated a long-standing definition of women's status in his famous 1760 statement: "By marriage, the husband and wife are one person in law: that is, the very being of legal existence of the woman is suspended during the marriage, or at least is incorporated and consolidated into that of the husband, under whose wing, protection, and *cover*, she performs everything" (qtd. in Norton 26). Whatever bonds of affection may or may not have bound Mary Stiles to her husband, she was legally subject to his will in virtually all matters of everyday life.

Through quirks in genealogy, Francis Stiles (II) was destined to inherit a great deal of wealth. His grandfather, Francis Stiles (I), had been the steward of an aristocrat in Windsor, England before he immigrated with his three brothers to the Connecticut colony in 1634.[30] He and his wife had four sons and two daughters, but only one of their sons (Benjamin) produced a male heir—Francis (II), who was born around 1690.[31] Thus Francis II inherited the lion's share of his extended family's estate, including his father's estate, the estate of his childless uncle, Thomas Stiles, and possibly a portion of the estates of his other two uncles, who had daughters but no sons. Mary Stiles gave birth to her first child, Francis (III), on July 23, 1710, ten months after the wedding, and the baby died within hours. She gave birth to six more children over the next eighteen years, including four daughters (Sarah, Mabel, Eunice, and Mary), all of whom survived into adulthood and married men from prominent local slave-holding families; a second son Benjamin, who married his second cousin, Ruth Judson of Stratford; and a third son, David, who died at the age of two.[32] Mary Stiles witnessed the births of many grandchildren, at least five of whom died before the age of six, while at least eleven survived into adulthood.

Although no stranger to tragedy, the family of Mary Stiles steadily increased its wealth and prominence within the community's inbred upper crust. In addition to cultivating their land, Francis and Mary engaged in various business, military, and governmental activities. In 1733 Francis was commissioned by Connecticut's General Assembly to be "Lieutenant of the south company or train-band in the town of Woodbury" (*Public Records* 1726–1735, 431). The Stileses also were involved in the West India trade. New York shipping records indicate that a sloop named the *Francis*, co-owned by Captain Benjamin Stiles, Mary Stiles, and George Gibbs, traveled between Bermuda and New York in 1730s, with one Negro slave aboard (Donnan, III, 503). Women rarely were listed as co-owners of boats, so Mary Stiles may have either possessed unusual business acumen and/or commanded an unusual degree of respect within her marriage and community. Her son Benjamin graduated from Yale in 1740 and became Woodbury's first lawyer. While he developed an illustrious public career, Mary's youngest daughter, Mary Jr., married one of the most powerful men in the county, Col. Benjamin Hinman, Esq.

Lieutenant Francis Stiles died on Sept. 9, 1748, leaving Mary a widow after 39 years of marriage. Widows were legally defined as "relicts"—the remnants of departed men. "By law, a widow usually inherited at least a third of the household goods, and she was entitled to use or to receive income from a third of the real estate until she died or remarried. If she had minor children, she might retain practical control of the entire estate until her sons came of age, but the final disposition of family property would not be determined by her but by court order or her husband's will. A widow was ensured maintenance at whatever level the estate allowed, but only rarely did she retain full control of her house and yard or even the assembly of pots, beds, and cows which had once been her domain" (Ulrich 7). In this legal and economic situation, whatever power Widow Stiles held derived from the force of her personality and the esteem her son held for her.

Shortly after Francis Stiles died, Benjamin and Ruth Stiles had their first son and named him Francis after his grandfather. Witnessing her new grandson, Mary Stiles must have recalled the birth and death of her own first son, Francis. In subsequent years, births and deaths were often interlinked in her extended family. Meanwhile, the breakup of a marriage in Woodbury in 1753 indicated that accusations of witchcraft could still be deployed to justify and maintain white male dominance. A blacksmith named Adam Cramer was reputed to work hard to keep his wife, Moll, "in good temper and spirits," because "whenever he was so unlucky as to fall under her ire, everything went wrong with him" (Cothren 159). In order to maintain his Christian reputation among his neighbors, he felt obliged to declare Moll a witch and drive her from his house. The Widow Stiles may have felt uneasy at this turn of events, given her childhood proximity to the violence of witch hunts. The neighborhood watched while Moll Cramer took her young son, "who was believed to have been bewitched by her, and could not be separated from her," and built a flimsy cabin on a hill for shelter. She supported herself and her son "by begging from the much annoyed neighborhood" (Cothren 160). The neighbors reportedly gave her food out of fear that she would bewitch them if they refused.

By the mid-1760s Widow Stiles had become a seventy-year-old grandmother in need of domestic assistance. Perhaps an earlier slave had died or an indentured servant had come of age. Benjamin may have encouraged his mother to purchase a new slave to assist her in the maintenance of her household. The regional rivers and valleys enabled the Stileses to travel with relative ease to visit their friends and relatives in Stratford and Milford, and Mary may have gone to Milford to visit her younger sister, Elizabeth (1701–1797), who had been married to James Pritchard (1698–1749), the grandson of Roger Pritchard, one of Milford's original settlers, and Elizabeth Prudden of the famous Prudden family described above. The two sisters were widowed around the same time. In any case, whether through an auction or through a sale arranged by family and friends, Mary Stiles purchased Jeffrey Brace from his Milford owner and brought him home to Woodbury with her.

The Southbury parish, where Mary Stiles lived in proximity to her children and grandchildren, was situated in a hilly, fertile landscape. The main street, built over an old Indian trail, featured a Congregational Church, a school, some stores, businesses, and houses. The Stileses' home property, delineated by a stone fence, was located about a half mile from the church, while the land that they farmed was located away from the center of town. Brace probably was introduced to a typical prosperous New England home, which would have included bedrooms, a parlor, a kitchen, cellars, pantries, brewhouses, milkhouses, washhouses, butteries, a pigpen, a garden, a henhouse, and a small orchard (Ulrich 13). The settlers buried their dead nearby, in an ancient Pootatuck burial ground (Cothren 109). The Pomperaug River, named after a distinguished Pootatuck sagamore, passed through the village center, and the townspeople fished in nearby Quassapaug Lake. While the town prohibited "Barbadoes liquors" (that is, rum), the residents enjoyed fruit and beverages produced from abundant apple orchards (Cothren 949). In Milford, John Burwell's wife knocked Brace down "with the distaff" when he attempted to drink "some beer or cider" that the family was drinking, but in Southbury Brace most likely drank and helped to make hard cider. "Fall was . . . the season for cider-making. The mildly alcoholic beverage produced by natural fermentation of apple juice was a staple of the New England diet and was practically the only method of preserving the fruit harvest" (Ulrich 23). Brace's recollections of his life with the Stileses suggests that, like most slaves in New England, he was largely confined to the family's circle of domesticity, agriculture, and errands. Since the condition of domestic servitude was intensely intimate (in contrast to plantation slavery), the kindliness or cruelty of family members made an enormous difference in his daily life. While the Burwells had thrown him scraps to eat and treated him like a dog, Mary Stiles most likely permitted him to eat at her table, as many Connecticut slaveholders did, for the sake of efficiency if not civility.

At the same time, the contours of Brace's life were shaped by large social and legal forces. In 1762 the census of Woodbury counted 3514 whites, 53 blacks, and no Indians. Although the census was not fully reliable—it erased Indians and may have undercounted Africans—it shows that Brace lived near dozens of people of African descent. In 1774 the census counted 5, 224 whites, 89 blacks, and 9 Indians (Cothren 698). Only a few remnants of Pootatuck families remained visible in the area. White people sometimes wanted to believe that Indians had disappeared altogether, but examination of Connecticut's Public Records indicates that Indians maintained an oppressed and repressed presence in Woodbury at least until the 1790s. Some Indians were neighbors of the Stileses.[33] Connecticut's enslaved population, which peaked at 5,101 people in 1774,

consisted of 1.3 males for each female, making it impossible for many enslaved men to find partners (Yang 129–30). Indian women, whose numbers exceeded those of Indian men in southern New England, often married African men, but according to his memoir, Brace never formed
a romantic liaison during his years in slavery. Although Connecticut law
permitted slaves to marry, many Yankee masters discouraged their slaves
from forming sexual attachments, as they did not want to deal with children and did not want their slaves' attention diverted from the demands
of the white household. All blacks, enslaved or free, were required to carry
"a pass from the authorities or masters whenever they left home" (Yang
136–37). Blacks and Indians were banned from engaging in trade or huck-
stering, economic activities that enabled some free people of color to
claim a (meager) share in the economy in places like Barbados. Slaves in
Connecticut were subjected to a nine o'clock curfew and could be publicly
whipped if they "were convicted of being in the street without special
permits from their masters or mistresses" (Yang 46). It was illegal for white
families to entertain "blacks, mulattoes, or Indians, unless they were sent
on business" (Yang 47). Furthermore, "licensed shopkeepers and tavern-
keepers were forbidden to entertain any 'man's sons, apprentices, servants, or Negroes' with any drink without 'special order or allowance' from
respective parents or masters" (Yang 41). If people of color were convicted
of a crime, they received punishments exceeding those given to whites.
For example, when convicted for selling or receiving stolen property,
whites received twenty lashes; blacks received thirty (Yang 43).

Brace's memoir suggests that what he valued most during his Woodbury years was Mary Stiles's determination to educate him. Connecticut
Puritans regarded the education of children as one of their primary social
responsibilities, and in Woodbury almost all white people were educated
"in the first rudiments of knowledge. Few could be found who could not
read and write" (Cothren 147). Educators strove to discipline sinful children and train them in the ways of the Lord. "Academic subjects were
taught through rote memorization, and all education was based on limit-
ing self-expression and promoting uniformity" (Roth 58). Throughout
New England, "[s]ome whites pressed for the education of slaves at least
in reading and writing as an aid to their civilization, Christianization, 'de-
Africanization,' and ultimately as a means for controlling them. Although
advocates of education argued that basic education contributed to the
ability of slaves to use the English language effectively, creating more

reliable and obedient servants, this was always a controversial issue" (Horton 19). In Connecticut, debates about the education of black people grew increasingly heated with the passage of time. Mary Stiles decided to send Brace to the local school. However, in a scene that would become frequently repeated in African American life and literature, the schoolmaster reacted to Brace with hostility and violence. The scene took an unusual twist when Brace decided not to accept a whipping and "walked out instead of sitting down." He tells us: "I had expected he would follow me, and had determined in my own mind to give him a whipping, as I verily believed the task would be easy. Anger prompted me to this determination; but he did not follow me" (chapter 8). A tall, muscular young man, Brace apparently intimidated the choleric schoolmaster. In narrating the scene, Brace assumes intellectual and moral as well as physical superiority, noting "[p]rudence kept him [from following me], and vengeance melted me into pity, for I pitied his want of discernment and just judgment" (chapter 8).

Despite this triumph of sorts, a frustrated and emotionally hurt Brace "became a child again . . . and shed tears." He may have been aware of one of the most outrageous pieces of racist legislation in Connecticut, the 1708 Defamation Act, which stated, "if any Negro or mulatto servant or slave disturb the peace, or shall offer to strike any white person, and be thereof convicted, such Negro or mulatto servant or slave shall be punished by whipping, at the discretion of the court, assistant, or justice of the peace that shall have cognizance thereof, not exceeding thirty stripes for one offence" (qtd. in Yang 43–44). In 1730 this law was amended to make it illegal for "any blacks, mulattos, or Indians to utter, publish, or speak 'actionable' words" (Yang 51). Thus white people could taunt, insult, threaten, and attack black people with virtual impunity, knowing that any black person who defended him- or herself risked violent punishment at the hands of "justice." Although slaves were sometimes permitted to offer evidence in self-defense, the courts were never color-blind.

Brace was comforted in his distress when Widow Stiles decided to teach him how to read and speak English herself. Like a significant minority of Christian mistresses who were willing to break social convention and even the law in order "to build the kind of intellectual foundation upon which, in their view, religion had to rest" (Bruce 14), Mary Stiles saw it as her religious duty to enable her slave to read the Bible. The Congregational Church welcomed her to "sign the covenant," but expected women to remain silent in church and forbade them to preach. Thus, teaching Brace and discussing theology with him gave Stiles a rare opportunity to exercise her intelligence and display her knowledge. Brace observes, "She was indefatigable until I could read in the bible and expound the scriptures" (chapter 8).

After Mary's death in 1773, Brace "descended like real estate, in fee simple" to her son Benjamin.[34] Mary Stiles probably had little control over this inheritance because "[u]nless her husband were willing to sign a special contract prior to marriage [which the 13-year-old Mary Johnson would not have been likely to request], a wife could neither own nor acquire property, nor could she enter into a contract or write a will" (Ulrich 7). Brace spent the rest of his period of enslavement in the household of Benjamin and Ruth Stiles and their nine children, some of whom Brace had known since birth and helped to raise. Benjamin Stiles practiced law in Woodbury from the time of his graduation from Yale in 1740 until his death in 1797. He filled many governmental positions between 1749 and 1775, including county land surveyor, county auditor, justice of the peace, and Captain of the north company in his parish. Elected to serve as a representative of Woodbury in Connecticut's General Assembly in 1754–56, 1762, and 1769–71, Benjamin traveled twice yearly to sessions that alternated between Hartford and New Haven.

As mentioned above, Benjamin's youngest sister, Mary, had married Colonel Benjamin Hinman, who like her brother was a lawyer and politician. Hinman represented Woodbury in the General Assembly in 1757, 1759–60, 1768, and 1777–80, and he worked with his brother-in-law, Benjamin Stiles, on various legal commissions and county committees over the years. The Hinmans were among the earliest seventeenth-century English settlers of Southbury, and the family was heavily invested in slavery. Indeed, by 1790 when all of the Southbury Stileses had ceased owning slaves, four of the twenty-five Hinman households in Southbury still had slaves.[35] Benjamin Stiles's nephew, Amos Hicock (the son of Sarah Stiles and Deacon Benjamin Hicock) and his wife Phebe (née Curtiss), also retained a slave. Brace most likely knew most of the black people in Woodbury, including the twenty-five slaves who chose, like Brace, to enlist in the Continental Army in hopes of gaining their manumission (Cothren 319). He also crossed paths with many indentured servants, including Matthew Lyon (1749–1822), an immigrant from a poor family in Wicklow, Ireland, who ran away to America at the age of thirteen after his father

died. He arrived in Woodbury about the same time as Brace and worked
in the home of Jabez Bacon (1731–1806), a tanner, currier, and merchant
(Cothren 320, 517). Lyon, who later became a United States Congressman, played an inspirational role in Brace's life when they reconnected in
Vermont in the 1790s.

In 1774 the reputation of Brace's owner, Benjamin Stiles, began to fal-
ter. He was accused by the inhabitants of the town of Darby of an "error
in a judgment" in a Superior Court that benefited him financially while
costing the inhabitants of Darby. The Assembly declared Stiles's judgment
"erroneous" and reversed it. As a slaveholder, Stiles faced mounting antislavery sentiment. While Connecticut's enslaved population reached its
peak of 5,101 people, the General Assembly passed an act in 1774 pro-
hibiting the importation of any Indian, Negro, or mulatto slave into Connecticut, and within a decade it would begin the process of gradual emancipation. The times were contentious in ways that interwove personal
feuds with global politics. Stiles's public career came to a virtual halt in October of 1775 when he was charged with contempt of government for his
statement that the "'three Colony representatives in the Continental Congress were three good-for-nothing dogs, and no more fit for the place than
his sick negro Jeff'" (Cothren 395). His remarks were personal as well as
political, since the three delegates were his colleagues Roger Sherman,
Eliphalet Dyer, and Silas Deane. Stiles had known the imposing Sherman
for decades. A stern six-foot man with flint blue eyes, Roger Sherman was,
according to John Adams, an "old Puritan" who rarely exhibited compassion or warmth. Before Sherman assumed national prominence, he and
Stiles had had relatively parallel careers. In the 1750s they established
themselves as lawyers in the Litchfield County Court. The Connecticut
bar at the time consisted of a small circle of largely amateur practitioners
who were simultaneously employed in other activities. In 1762 Stiles and
Sherman were appointed to a three-person highway committee, and over
the years they worked side by side as Litchfield County Justices of the
Peace, land surveyors (a lucrative craft that involved selling Indians'
lands), and representatives in the General Assembly. While Stiles may
have felt jealousy and snobbery toward Sherman, an ambitious self-taught
man who, despite his lack of a prestigious genealogy, became one of the
wealthiest men and largest landowners in the region, his remarks reveal
an even deeper contempt for Jeffrey Brace. That contempt contrasts
starkly with the respect that Brace exhibits for Stiles in his memoir when

he asserts that Stiles's "illustrious character is rewarded in the heart of every person living who knew him" (chapter 8).

The General Assembly held a cooler view of Stiles than Brace did. Accusing him of having "publickly and contemptuously uttered and spoken many things against the qualifications of the three delegates," the Assembly declared that Stiles had "openly shewed his inimical temper of mind and unfriendly disposition against the measures taken and pursued for a union of defence in the American cause" (*Public Records 1775–1776*, 157–58). He was cited to appear at the next session to answer to these allegations; however, by 1776 the Revolutionary government was fighting for its life. The royalist faction, which had always been strong in New Haven, was gaining power, and the Connecticut General Court "neglected to enforce and finally repealed, in December 1776, an act requiring an oath of allegiance to the Revolutionary government. In some cases men accused of being outright Tories were elected to office; suspicion fell on certain prominent citizens who were accused of seeking from General Howe 'protections' in case the patriot cause should collapse" (Boardman 169). Stiles avoided prosecution, but he never again was elected to the General Assembly. Meanwhile, his "sick negro Jeff" enlisted in the Revolutionary Army, not to overthrow British tyranny but to escape enslavement by "Connecticut's leaders [who] were devoted Congregationalists, often Yale graduates, tended to come from the families with the largest landholdings, and frequently were active in law and business" (Roth 41).

Fighting for Freedom in the Revolutionary War

When Brace first arrived in Connecticut, sentiment against the British was mounting in the American colonies. Influenced by the ideas of the Enlightenment, colonists increasingly believed that the English king was an arbitrary (as opposed to God-ordained) ruler who threatened their "natural rights" to life, liberty, and property. Brace must have had many occasions to hear and reflect on the rhetoric of freedom and inalienable human rights between 1763 and 1776, when tightening imperial regulations aroused the colonists' resentment and rebellion. "On the eve of the war, among the population of two million six hundred thousand were five hundred thousand Negroes, both free and slave. With almost one of every six Americans being black, they were of interest to both sides in the conflict" (Bull 67). When Brace enlisted in the continental army, he was not slow to recognize the irony of fighting for American "freedom": "I also entered the banners of freedom. Alas! Poor African Slave, to liberate freemen, my tyrants" (156). As David Walker would put it in 1829: "Now Americans, I ask you candidly, [were] your sufferings under Great Britain one hundredth part as cruel and tyrannical as you have rendered ours under you?" (142). Brace tells us that before the Revolution he had considered direct revenge: "I had contemplated going to Barbadoes to avenge myself and my country, in which I justified myself by Samson's prayer, when he prayed God to give him strength that he might avenge himself upon the Philistines, and God gave him the strength he prayed for" (156). In this passage, as in dozens of others throughout his memoir, Brace uses the religion of his oppressors to attack rather than to submit to their racial ideology. Employing violent revolutionary imagery—a risky rhetorical act—Brace casts slaveholders as Philistines and himself as a Samson whose desire for revenge is justified. But he wisely abandoned his unfeasible revenge fantasy to achieve personal liberation and to work for the abolition of slavery.

Before the Revolutionary War, the general policy in the British colonies was to forbid the arming of slaves. However, in times of need, exceptions were made. For instance, between 1715 and 1720 the South Carolina Assembly, feeling threatened by Indians, "ordered that in time of danger masters were to make available to militia officers the services of trusted slaves from ages sixteen to sixty" (Quarles, *Black Mosaic* 31). Slaves who killed or captured an enemy would receive ten pounds. In 1739, when the Spanish garrison was threatening South Carolina, the colony authorized the enlistment of "recommended" slaves and approved a variety of rewards for fighting well, including manumission for "killing an enemy, taking him alive, or capturing his colors" (Quarles 31). However, two slave uprisings in the following few months led the Assembly to reverse their position and refuse to arm blacks. Despite white misgivings, "in colonial America official attitudes toward arming the Negro did not always mirror actual practice" (Quarles 33). Throughout the eighteenth century, some black men in both southern and northern colonies enlisted, and many of them procured their freedom, especially in the New England colonies.

On November 7, 1775, the British Crown's Governor of Virginia, John Murray, Earl of Dunmore, declared that all indentured servants and Negroes who were "able and willing to bear arms" and who joined His Majesty's Troops would be freed (Quarles 35). The British followed this policy throughout the Revolutionary War, promising blacks their freedom in exchange for fighting. Although the American military largely excluded blacks during the early stages of the war, by 1779 the northern colonies and Maryland "decided to enlist blacks whatever the risks" and to offer freedom in exchange for military service (Quarles 55). The rebels were desperate to induce men to enlist. In general, "Americans were so provincial or so indifferent to the war that troops could be obtained only by offering large land bounties for enlistment and cutting the term of service to three months" (Billington 61). Even with these inducements to both white and black men, General George Washington could never gather more than 19,000 soldiers, and perhaps as many as 5,000 of them were black (White 7). White as well as black soldiers often fought without adequate guns, ammunition, clothing, or food.

African American soldiers, sailors, laborers, spies, and guides played a significant role in the Revolutionary War. As William C. Nell notes in his 1855 *The Colored Patriots of the American Revolution,* Crispus Attucks, an ex-slave who had run away from his Massachusetts master in 1750, was "the first martyr of the American Revolution" (14). He was killed in the Boston Massacre of 1770, and Crispus Attucks Day was a patriotic holiday until the Fourth of July was established as a national holiday in 1783. Black soldiers fought valiantly, despite the fact that they and their families were subjected to what Nell calls "the spirit of color-phobia, then rampant in New England" (33). As Ralph Ellison notes in *Invisible Man,* "historically most of this nation's conflicts of arms have been—at least for Afro-Americans— wars-within-wars" (xii). From Jeffrey Brace in the Revolutionary War to Ellison himself in the Merchant Marines during World War II, African American soldiers placed white Americans in what Ellison calls "an archetypal American dilemma: How could you treat a Negro as equal in war and then deny him equality during times of peace?" (*Invisible Man* xiii).

Black soldiers, some free and some enslaved, constituted about two percent (300 to 400 men) of Connecticut's Revolutionary troops (White 8). They enlisted for a variety of reasons. Free blacks were motivated by political conviction, desire for adventure, and/or economic promises. Slaves were motivated primarily by promises of manumission, although not all slaves who survived were freed. Some blacks were hired or forced to serve as substitutes for their masters or other white men. During and after the war their fates varied widely. Some died on the battlefield; others were wounded; some died from disease, cold, hunger, and hardship;

others were court-martialed and whipped for absence from duty; many were manumitted; a few were honored; some were re-enslaved; some were awarded pensions, and some died in destitution.[36] Historical markers commemorating the sacrifices of Revolutionary veterans often placed the names of black soldiers last, if at all. A contemporary observer noted: "a blank space is left between them and the whites; in genuine keeping with the 'Negro Pew' distinction—setting them not only below all others, but by themselves, even after that. And it is difficult to say why. They were not last in the fight" (qtd. in Nell 136).

According to William Cothren, twenty-five slaves from Woodbury, motivated more by hopes of obtaining manumission from slavery than by dreams of freedom from British rule, "enlisted at various periods of the war, and made good soldiers, fighting valiantly for the liberties of the country. Several of these, having survived the perils of the war, returned and resided in Woodbury, and received pensions from the general government, in common with others, for their military services" (319). Most of these black soldiers have disappeared from historical records. Those who are named in archival documents include Cummy, Jem, Peter, Tite, Tony, and Robin, whose surnames were recorded simply as "Negro," as well as James Liberty and Jeffrey Liberty, who had been enslaved in Woodbury by Jonathan Ferrand (White 59–62). Like Brace, Jeffrey Liberty fought for many years in the Revolution and was manumitted after the war.[37] He chose to remain in Woodbury and was eventually buried in the Judea Cemetery, where his gravestone reads "Jeff Liberty and his Colored Patriots" (White 27). Despite Liberty's heroism, his former slaveholder's daughter, Esther Ferrand, and her husband, Simeon Mitchell, continued to practice slavery (Cothren 544).

Brace also was joined in combat by many slaves from Milford, including at least one (Peter Gibbs) who bore the surname of one of Brace's former masters. Milford's other black soldiers included Job Caesar, Pomp Cyrus, Jube Freeman, William Sowers, Congo Zado, and many others whose names have been lost to history (White 57–64).

Brace had difficulty recalling the exact dates of his service in the Revolutionary War, but his memoir in conjunction with military records indicates that he completed more than five years of duty between 1777 and 1783. Some uncertainty remains because record keeping during the Revolutionary War was far from a precise science, especially regarding African Americans, who were often given or adopted repetitious nicknames such as "Pomp Liberty," "Cuff Liberty," "Sampson Cuff," and "Dick Freedom." Complicating the matter is the coincidence that three Connecticut slaves by the name of Jeffrey (two from Woodbury and one from East Haven) enlisted around the same time. Brace most likely knew Jeffrey Liberty, as mentioned above. In February 1777, a slave named Jeffrey Sill enlisted in New Haven as a private (*Rolls and Lists* 109). Sill was enslaved by Samuel Hemingway, Esquire, one of the largest slaveholders in East Haven, Connecticut, who at the time of the 1790 census still owned four slaves. Hemingway allowed Sill to enlist "with the understanding that he would return to slavery again after the war. However, Sill re-enlisted at the end of his first three year term without Hemingway's approval. Hemingway petitioned the General Assembly and proposed manumitting Sill, provided the state compensate him for the loss of his slave, and as he had already obtained a substitute for himself in the army, to allow Sill's enlistment to act as a substitute for another man, Argariah Bradley. The Assembly voted in the negative on both requests" (White 27–28). It appears from extant records that on May 26, 1777, Jeffrey Stiles (as Brace was then known) enlisted in the regiment of Colonel Return Jonathan Meigs. Jeffrey Stiles's dates of service and pattern of re-enlistment were similar to Sill's, and it is not always clear which man is referred to in the records.

Brace's memoir confirms the historical evidence that blacks and whites often served side by side in the Continental Army. In *Observations of the Physical, Intellectual, and Moral Qualities of Our Colored Population,* which was published in New Haven in 1834, Ebenezer Baldwin asserted that "in the opening as [in] the closing scene of the American revolution, African blood was freely poured out, and mingled with that of the more favored white man on the altar of liberty. I should not omit to mention . . . the company of Africans attached to Meigs' regiment raised for continental service in New Haven and its vicinity. . . . The regiment . . . was one of the most efficient in the continental line" (31). Brace spent much of the war in integrated units, but he may have spent some time in Connecticut's black or non-white companies as well. The first non-white Connecticut company was formed with eleven black soldiers and five Indians in 1780 in Colonel Durkee's Fourth Regiment (White 32). In 1781 a company consisting forty-eight black privates was formed as Connecticut's Second Company of the Fourth Regiment. Both Jeffrey Liberty and Jeffrey Sill (or Jeffrey Stiles) served in this company (White 33). According to William Nell, "some objections were made, on the part of officers, to accepting the command of the colored troops. In this exigency, Capt. Humphreys, who was attached to the family of Gen. Washington, volunteered his services. His patriotism was rewarded, and his fellow officers were afterwards as desirous to obtain appointments in that corps as they had previously been to avoid them" (133). Humphreys, who was later promoted to colonel and then to general, "never actually commanded the unit, since he was an aide-de-camp to General Washington from 1781–1783, the entire time that it was active. All of the officers and noncommissioned officers in the company were white, and all of the privates were black" (White 32). Brace's representation of his military duties and his interactions with fellow soldiers confirms David White's finding that most black soldiers "appear to have been soldiers on the same footing with whites" (29).

Brace tells us that at the time he enlisted, Mary Stiles's "two sons, Benjamin and David, were drafted to fight in the revolution." However, military records indicate that it was her grandsons, Nathan and David, ages 18 and 26, who were drafted. Mary's son Benjamin, who had served as a Captain in his parish in the 1760s, was 56 years old in 1777, and her son David had died at the age of two. Benjamin's sons enlisted in the Continental Army in Woodbury, Connecticut on June 18, 1777. They arrived in camp together on August 16, 1777, and were paid at the rate of two pounds per month for service in "Captain Amos Heicok's Company in the 13 Regiment of Militia from the State of Connecticut, commanded by Benjamin Hinman, Esqr., from the day of their arrival in New York to the day of discharge and allow one day to every 20 miles travel to and from camp." Captain Amos Hicock was the cousin of the young enlistees, and Col. Benjamin Hinman was their uncle, which may help to explain why their military service amounted to the merest token.[38] Whether Hicock and Hinman were attempting to protect their relations or were unimpressed by their military potential, Nathan was discharged on September 4, having served for only 29 days, including the ten days allotted for travel, and David Stiles was discharged on September 13, having served for one month and seven days, "including 10 days to go and come from camp" (Nathan Stiles Card No. 37087439; David Stiles Card No. 37087433). Jeffrey Brace, in his mid-thirties, was already an accomplished soldier and a veteran of a major world war; he served in the Revolution for more than five years.

Meanwhile, Benjamin Stiles Jr. apparently performed no military duty, although he was between his brothers David and Nathan in age. Turning 20 in 1776, he followed in his father's footsteps by attending Yale, studying law (with his father), and working as a lawyer, justice of the peace, and politician. He served as representative for Southbury in Connecticut's General Assembly from 1792 to 1795, where he was forced to reflect on the issue of slavery during fierce debates in May 1794. The lower house passed a bill for the abolition of slavery, which declared: "The practice of enslaving Negroes and people of Colour, which has been gradually introduced into this State is found by experience to have a direct and necessary tendency to keep their minds in Ignorance, is productive of immorality, degrading to the dignity of human nature, and destructive of the natural Rights which every member of an equal and just Government ought to enjoy" (*Public Records, 1793–1796,* xix). Although there is no record of how Stiles voted on this bill (which was not approved by the Council of Assistants, which had veto power over the lower house), his family was directly implicated in what his colleagues called the immoral, degrading, and destructive institution of slavery.

While Stiles Jr. was anticipating an illustrious career and avoiding military service, his father's slave was fighting, quite literally, for freedom. Although some white men brought their slaves to the war with them to serve as their servants as well as soldiers (for example, George Washington's slave, William Lee, served in the war as Washington's servant and was not manumitted until his master's death), Brace did not serve alongside the Stiles boys; rather, he served as a private in various companies of infantry for the duration of the war. In contrast to his relatively serious treatment of the Seven Years War, Brace's representation of the Revolution is notably irreverent, often comic, and sometimes satirical. His memoir achieves one of its greatest moments of rhetorical credibility when he describes an occasion when he lied successfully to his commanding officer, Colonel Return Jonathan Meigs. Brace recalls that a group of soldiers led by Samuel Shaw, "a brave soldier but as complete a petty thief as ever graced a camp," stole a pig from a Tory farmer. The hostility between "patriots" (or Whigs) and Loyalists (or Tories) ran deep. As Billington explains, "Most of the Tories were from the upper class, including officials, Anglican clergymen, and wealthier merchants whose dislike of the 'rabble' inclined them toward monarchy. The loyalists were so mistreated by patriot mobs that thousands fled to the West Indies, Canada, or England" (61). Shaw and his buddies brought the stolen pig back to camp, and the Tory farmer came looking for it, furious about the theft. Col. Meigs questioned the troops to find out how they obtained the pig. Brace claimed that the owner had brought it for sale but the soldiers suspected him of being a Tory spy and so they determined to keep the pig until the officers could question him. He relates: "My fellow soldiers were glad of the opportunity of confirming the truth of my assertion—which . . . completely satisfied the Col. of our innocence" (chapter 8). This story reveals Brace's wit and effectiveness as a storyteller while also illuminating the sense of camaraderie and empowerment he found as a soldier in his unit.

Several decades after the war, a Captain Jonathan Brooks, who knew Brace in Woodbury, recalled that Brace served two tours of duty, one for eight months and another for eighteen months, after which he returned to Woodbury and "challenged [for] his freedom." Although many inhabitants of Woodbury "were in favor of Jeffery[,] his master contended that he was still his slave." To obtain his freedom, Brace decided to re-enlist and to fight for the duration of the war (Seth Wetmore to Samuel C. Crafts, 28 Dec. 1819; see appendix B). Brace does not mention this conflict with Benjamin Stiles in his memoir, nor does he mention that in the summer of 1783 he was given an honorable discharge with a badge of merit. He tells us that his leg was wounded during one battle and part of one finger was chopped off by a British soldier whom he afterwards killed. We learn from Samuel C. Booge, a lieutenant who knew him, that "Jeffery Brace was a faithful Soldier and . . . there was no better Soldier in the Army" (Sworn deposition of April 4, 1818).

"Freedom" in Vermont

After the war, Brace returned to Woodbury, Connecticut, where he lived with his former master, Benjamin Stiles, for one year. He tells us that after this year Stiles "consented that I might go where I pleased and seek my fortune" (chapter 5). He does not mention Stiles's earlier unwillingness to manumit him. Stiles had little choice but to consent for three reasons: Brace had been legally manumitted as a result of his military service, many inhabitants of Woodbury supported his cause, and the State of Connecticut had passed (in 1784) an act for gradual emancipation. Brace contemplated the economic options available to an African man in New England, and like hundreds of white folk from Connecticut, he chose to head for Vermont, having heard "flattering accounts of the new state" (chapter

9). The "flattering accounts" included the fact that Vermont was the first state to abolish slavery. Established as the fourteenth state, Vermont's 1777 constitution states:

THAT all men are born equally free and independent, and have certain natural, inherent and unalienable rights, amongst which are the enjoying and defending life and liberty; acquiring, possessing and protecting property, and pursuing and obtaining happiness and safety. Therefore, no male person, born in this country, or brought from overseas, ought to be holden by law to serve any person as a servant, slave or apprentice, after he arrives to the age of twenty-one years, nor female in like manner, after she arrives to the age of eighteen years, unless they are bound by their own consent after they arrive to such age, or bound by law for the payment of debts, damages, fines, costs, or the like.

The "second precedent-shattering grant to the people at large was made in the establishment of universal manhood suffrage" (Newton 76).

Brace set out for Vermont in 1784, stopping in Lennox, Massachusetts, for one month en route, where "for the first time I made a bargain as a freeman for labor" (Chap. 9). After earning five dollars, Brace moved to Poultney, in southern Vermont. From a white perspective, Vermont at the time was a frontier wilderness. Nathan Perkins, a white pastor from Hartford, Connecticut who kept a diary of his six week journey through Vermont in 1789, emphasized the poverty and obscurity of Vermont life. He noted the prevalence of starvation and disease and complained that the state was full of "deists & proper heathen" (26). At the same time, he thought that the landscape, especially the regions near Lake Champlain, offered "the best sort of land . . . & the streams [are] full of small fish" (17). Brace found Vermont rich in promise. He tells us, "I enjoyed the pleasures of a freeman; my food was sweet, my labor pleasure: and one bright gleam of life seemed to shine upon me" (chapter 9). Brace worked hard and often gained success, but periodically he found himself cheated out of promised wages and victimized by broken contracts. Eventually he managed to buy some land in Poultney, and he then went to the neighboring town of Dorset to attempt to earn enough money to start a farm on his land.

In Dorset Brace got a job working for John Manley, one of Dorset's original settlers, who opened a tavern in Dorset in the late 1700s. While working at Manley's tavern, Brace met and married the Widow Susannah (Susan) Dublin, "a native African female, who possessed a reciprocal abhorrence to slavery" (chapter 9). Brace appeared genuinely surprised by "the supreme joy of being united" to a "virtuous, patient, loving, and prudent" woman, so late in his life. He was in his early forties at the time, and his memoir mentions no previous romantic or sexual relationship. Brace's slowness in marrying was not at all unusual for blacks in New England at the time; indeed, "[t]he eighteenth century saw a low rate of natural increase among New England's Negroes" (Pierson 18–19). Brace's trauma at witnessing the pervasive sexual violence of slavery may have made it difficult for him to form intimate relationships, and his slaveholders in New England most likely would have forbidden or frowned upon the formation of such relationships. New England masters usually "did not prize fertility" in their slaves (Pierson 19). When Brace as a free man finally was able to form an intimate bond, he treasured it keenly.

Perhaps the most unfortunate omission in Brace's memoir is his omission of Susan's story. He tells us that her "sufferings had been equal to any that can be delineated by the pen, or endured by the bravest of the human race, whose history I must omit as it will swell these memoirs beyond the bounds of my limits" (chapter 9). Because he provides us with few details about her background, I have found it impossible to discover any supplemental information about her. Most extant slave narratives in the eighteenth and early nineteenth centuries were narrated by men, so we would have much to learn from Susan Dublin Brace's story.

Through hard work and persistence, the Braces achieved significant successes in their life together, but the peace and material comfort they deserved were never fully realized. The most painful problem they encountered stemmed simultaneously from Vermont's pervasive racism and its entrenched practice of exploiting children, especially black children.[39] William Pierson explains, "Since the practice of separating white children from their natural parents to follow training and domestic work in other households had been relatively common practice in seventeenth-century New England, the developing practice of separating black families probably did not seem especially cruel to northern slave owners [or to whites in general]. The binding out of both white and black children as apprentices remained a normal practice of poor relief and guardianship throughout the colonial era" (27). Contributing to this "normal practice" was the idea that Africans were incompetent parents, a concept that was an entrenched part of slave ideology. As early as 1707, Hans Sloane, an English traveler to Jamaica, observed," The *Negroes* are usually thought to be haters of their own Children, and therefore 'tis believ'd that they sell and dispose of them to Strangers, for Money, but this is not true. . . . [T]he parents here, altho their Children are Slaves for ever, yet have so great a love for them, that no Master dare sell or give away one of their little ones, unless they care not whether their Parents hang themselves or no" (112–13). Like the African parents cited by Sloane, the Braces viewed attempts to deprive them of their children with deep rage. Susan had two children from her first marriage: a twelve-year-old boy (not named in the memoir) and a young girl named Bersheba (no age given). Coveting these children, Elizabeth Powell of Manchester and Archibald Dixon of Poultney entered a complaint against Brace. Brace states: "The complaint amounted to this, that I was a black man. The corruption and superstition, mingled with the old Connecticut bigotry and puritanism, made certain people think a Negro had no right to raise their own children" (chapter 9). The Braces protested as forcefully as they could, but Elizabeth Powell was a formidable opponent. She was married to Martin Powell, a former lieutenant in the Continental Army who was a wealthy landowner in Manchester as well as an innkeeper, selectman, town clerk, treasurer, jail keeper, justice of the peace, judge of probate, and a member of the Vermont State Legislature, in which capacity he served on several powerful state committees. Elizabeth and Martin Powell had three children living in their home, and Martin had nine grown children from his first wife, Rhoda Thompson (Bigelow 270–72). Elizabeth Powell and Archibald Dixon succeeded in forcing Jeffrey and Susan Brace to "bind out" Susan's two children as indentured servants. Brace tells us that Mrs. Powell took the girl, and Mr. Dixon took the boy. The U.S. Census confirms that one free person of color was living in the Powell household in Manchester, and another was living in the Dixon household in Poultney in 1790. Although Mrs. Powell promised to teach Bersheba to read and to give her a feather bed when she was freed at the age of eighteen, she failed to do so. Brace attempted to sue her, but he could not find a lawyer "who would undertake the cause of an old African Negro" (chapter 9).

Meanwhile, Jeffrey and Susan began having children together. Although Brace does not tell us how many children they had, the 1790 lists five free people of color in the Poultney household of Jeffrey Bran [*sic*], which suggests that they had three children by 1790. Around 1795 they returned to Poultney to clear the land that Jeffrey had bought some years earlier. Like most land in Vermont, their land was rocky, full of trees, and difficult to farm. Compounding their hardships was a jealous, spiteful neighbor, Jery Gorham, who coveted their land, turned his cattle loose in their crops, tapped their maple trees, and harassed them in every way he could imagine. Gorham tried to bind out the Brace children, but Brace declared that "while I lived, no authority should bind out my children" (91). After seven years of strife, Brace contemplated ways to find a better life.

One option he considered was going to Kentucky with his old friend, Matthew Lyon, who had had a colorful career in national politics since his teenage days as an indentured servant in Woodbury, Connecticut. Brace was not alone in being attracted to Lyon, who was a courageous writer, an independent thinker, and a generous soul who "instead of looking out for himself alone . . . was always ambitious to build up prosperity around him" (Ullery 132). Lyon had moved to Vermont in the 1770s. He married Beulah Galusha, a daughter of Governor Chittenden, whom he met while working on the governor's farm. He became a captain and colonel of the militia, and was one of the original grantees in Fair Haven, Vermont, where he established a saw mill, an iron mill, and a paper mill. Like Ethan Allen, another Woodbury resident who moved to Vermont, Lyon was a heavy drinker who was sometimes regarded as vulgar, but was also widely loved. Lyon became an outspoken local politician and in 1793 was elected to the United States Congress. In 1798 he was indicted under the newly passed Alien and Sedition Laws for printing "scurrilous, scandalous, malicious, and defamatory language" about President John Adams and was sentenced to four months imprisonment and a $1,000 fine—a sentence that transformed him into a popular hero among like-minded Vermonters. While in jail, he was once again nominated for Congress by the local Democratic party. Men who could vote flooded to the polls, including a seriously ill French Vermonter named Stephen D. Maranville who had to be carried three miles to the polls to cast his vote for Lyon. According to legend, a political opponent exclaimed, "What! Uncle Steve! Are you able to be out?" "Able," said the old man; "yes; and strong enough to carry a *Lyon* in my hand!" (Joslin 52). Lyon's prosecution increased his popularity but ruined him financially, so when his term in Congress expired (ca. 1802), he decided to move to Kentucky.

Brace decided against joining Lyon because he was afraid that being in the slave state of Kentucky would make him vulnerable to reenslavement. Ironically referring to Lyon's persecution for his exercise of free speech, Brace stated: "I did not know that . . . I should say something which would cause me to be prosecuted and punished as a seditious person" (chapter 10). The friendship between Brace and Lyon indicates that indentured servants sometimes recognized a kinship with slaves, while their divergent paths in life suggest that Lyon's whiteness helped him overcome barriers that Brace would never be able to surmount.

After deciding not to join Lyon, Brace sold his farm and moved with his family to Sheldon, a small village in northern Vermont near the Canadian border. Situated in gently rolling mountains and divided by the Missisquoi River, Sheldon already had ten nonwhite residents before the Brace family arrived in 1802—two in the household of Samuel B. Sheldon and eight in the household of Elnathan Keys (1800 U.S. Census). The Braces settled initially on land belonging to Major Jedediah Clark, who had been a neighbor of the Stileses in Woodbury, Connecticut. Jeffrey Brace also was acquainted with the town's leading family, the Sheldons, after whom the town was named. Elisha Sheldon, a lawyer and judge from Litchfield County, had served alongside Benjamin Stiles in Connecticut's General Assembly, and his elder son, Colonel Elisha Sheldon, had commanded the Second Regiment of Light Dragoon in the Continental Army (*History of Litchfield County* 122; Aldrich 617). After living and working on Clark's land for two years, Brace was able to obtain fifty acres of land from Major Samuel B. Sheldon, a younger son of Elisha Sheldon. Brace states: "I paid him down in cash twenty dollar, and he was to wait six years for the reminder, the price being five dollars per Acre" (chapter 10). The deed recorded in Sheldon in May 1804 named a different price, asserting that Samuel B. Sheldon "granted bargained and sold" Brace fifty acres "for and in consideration of friendship" (appendix C). Whether the price was friendship or five dollars an acre, Sheldon reneged on the agreement a year later. Brace states: "I cleared about ten acres fit for corn; but there came a man, and wanted the whole lot; his name was Crocker, and Shelden sold him the whole lot, and told me he would pay me for the betterments, and let me have a lot near the middle of town, which was never performed: yet I have that charity for the memory of Major Shelden, that if he had lived, he would have amply satisfied me" (chapter 10). A second deed, recorded in Sheldon in June 1805, indicates that Brace remembered the original price accurately (fifty acres at five dollars an acre). It states: "Know all men by these presents the I, Jefre Brace, of Sheldon . . . for and in consideration of two hundred and fifty dollars, received in full

to my satisfaction of Saml. B. Sheldon . . . do foever quitclaim . . . the
same land which said Samuel B. Sheldon deeded to me on the 5th day of
May, 1804" (appendix C). Brace's account suggests that the money was
merely promised, not delivered. Sheldon died suddenly of a severe cold
in 1807 at the age of 47.

Disappointed in Sheldon, Brace and his son-in-law bought some land
in Georgia, a farming community near St. Albans on the fertile shores of
Lake Champlain. They cleared a farm and temporarily prospered. On
March 8, 1807 Susan Brace grew ill; on March 19 she died. Brace observed:
"Short was the warning, but heavy the blow . . . . I was left without an
earthly companion, to linger out the remainder of my days" (chapter 10).

The 1810 Publication of *The Blind African Slave*

In 1810 Brace, who was blind[40] and in his late sixties, narrated his life
story to Benjamin Prentiss, a white lawyer who, despite his education, was
poor and obscure. Unlike the typical white editors of antebellum slave narratives, Prentiss may have been even less financially secure than his black
subject. The copyright, filed on June 20, 1810, identifies Benjamin Franklin
Prentiss as a St. Albans lawyer. The *Blind African Slave* was the first book
ever published in the small town of St. Albans. It was printed by a young
newspaper publisher named Harry Whitney, who advertised it weekly between July and October 1810 in his short-lived newspaper, the *Franklin
County Advertiser.* On October 18, 1810, the newspaper announced that
the book would be "ready for delivery on Wednesday next" and could be
obtained from either Prentiss or Whitney, whose paper was located at the
new brick store on the southwest corner of the court house square. The
newspaper ceased publication the next week, and Whitney moved on,
printing newspapers in various Vermont towns until August 1817, when
he filed for bankruptcy. He died the next year, around the age of thirty.

The Blind African Slave gives no indication of how Jeffrey Brace and
his amanuensis-editor Benjamin Prentiss met or why they agreed to col-
laborate on the memoir. Admitted to the Franklin County Bar in August
1808, Prentiss apparently made almost as little money as a lawyer as he did
from sales of the book. On June 5, 1811, he was residing in the household
of Luther Whitcomb in Milton, a small town south of St. Albans, when the
town selectmen directed the constable to warn him and his family, along
with Whitcomb and five other families, to leave town (Milton Town Meet-

ing Records, Vol. 3). Jeffrey Brace was warned out of the same town fifteen months later, on September 1, 1812. "Warnings out" were a method approved by an 1801 Act of the State of Vermont whereby town selectmen, at their discretion, could issue warrants to new arrivals warning them that the town would not support them should they become welfare cases (Rollins Vol. 1, 6). Benjamin Prentiss thus appears to have been a young man with little social or financial support in the 1810s, and thereafter he disappears from the historical record. What the book itself reveals about Prentiss is that he was a lucid, eloquent man who viewed slavery as a barbarous institution.[41]

Although Prentiss owned the copyright as "author," Brace hoped to gain some royalties from sales of the book. He explains his determination to narrate his story as arising primarily out of his sense of "my duty to myself, to all Africans, who can read, to the Church, in short to all mankind, to thus publish these my Memoirs, that all may see how poor Africans have been and perhaps now are abused by a christian and enlightened people. Being old and blind, almost destitute of property, it may bring me something to make me comfortable in my declining days, but above all, it is my anxious wish that this simple narrative may be the means of opening the hearts of those who hold slaves and move them to consent to give them that freedom which they themselves enjoy, and which all mankind have an equal right to possess" (chapter 11). The hasty disappearance of *The Blind African Slave* most likely left Brace disappointed both in his hope of opening the hearts of slaveholders and in his hope of gaining material comfort from book sales, but his influence on history may be glimpsed in the fact that through storytelling and moral suasion he helped shape the political climate of Vermont, which by the mid-nineteenth century became "the most antislavery state in the Union" (Roth 291).

A Narrative of Conversion and Christian Community

The concluding chapter of Brace's memoir describes his religious conversion and testifies to the piety that has been on display since the first chapter's profuse biblical citations. This conversion cannot be adequately understood outside of its political context. Like most European Americans, white Vermonters were generally uncomfortable with the concept of religious freedom. While Vermont's constitution assured all men of their right to worship God according to the dictates of their conscience, until 1793 it contradicted itself by adding "nor can any man *who professes the Protestant religion* be justly deprived or abridged of any civil right as a citizen on account of his religious sentiment" (qtd. in Newton 76; my emphasis). Although Vermont's laws changed, people who did not publicly embrace Protestant Christianity continued to find their civil rights threatened.

In *Roll, Jordan, Roll: The World the Slaves Made*, Eugene Genovese observes: "The religion of Afro-American slaves, like all religion, grew as a way of ordering the world and of providing a vantage point from which to judge it. Like all religion it laid down a basis for moral conduct and an explanation for the existence of evil and injustice" (162). William Pierson notes: "Only a tiny elite of black Yankees became practicing Christians; but those who did used their faith as a philosophy of resistance that promised an end to slavery and a reordering of society in line with the principles of justice" (149). Brace was keenly aware that Christianity provided an avenue to education, oratory, and empowerment. In chapter 7, he points out that the differences between "the Ethiopian, Turk, Indian, Chinese, Tartar or Englishmen" stem not from color but from levels of access to education and to power. As proof of his argument, he points out: "Even in this country, where the African is degraded and disgraced; his heart broken, his hope destroyed, and almost generally deprived of education, do you not see some geniuses burst forth and rise above the tyranny and oppression they are under, and stand as monuments of admiration? Behold some of your ministers of the gospel! Go to the African churches, in the cities of New York and Philadelphia, see their devout attachment to the religion of their Savior. Hear the pathetic and persuasive eloquence of their preachers" (chapter 7). Brace understood that although Christianity was a tool of empire and subjugation, it also paradoxically "allowed for the possibility of an entrance by black people into an intellectual setting, a realm of thought, and a world of skills that might otherwise have been defined as exclusively white. Giving a place to the black voice, it challenged any definition of intellectuality and intellectual authority based on color. Providing for at least one kind of community in which a black voice could be heard, it placed at least a measure of such authority in the hands of people of African descent, even slaves" (Bruce 17).

Christianity has been historically both on the side of bondage and on the side of liberation, a tool of empire and a tool of revolution. Its ideals of love and equality contradict its advocacy of hierarchy, subordination, and submission. A man of extraordinary intellectual acumen, Brace searched the Bible, the only text readily available to him, for ways to make sense of his brutal life experiences and to find a culturally salient language in which to voice his protest and to prophesy destruction to the oppressor. He used biblical quotations both to create meaning from his suffering and to indict the people who inflicted it upon him. He found authority to speak in passages such as Ezekiel 2.6–7: "And thou, son of man, be not afraid of them, neither be afraid of their words. . . . And thou shall speak my words unto them, whether they will hear, or whether they will forbear; for they are most rebellious." His rhetorical use of biblical language connects Brace to the American jeremiad tradition as well as to the history of African American abolitionist oratory.

Brace remained an impoverished farmer and laborer, but as a devout Christian and eloquent abolitionist he grew to hold a respected place in an emerging mixed-race abolitionist matrix in Vermont. The 1800 U.S. Census counted 557 people of African descent in Vermont, a number that included several noteworthy literary and religious figures. Lucy Terry Prince (1732–1821), the African-born author of the first known African American poem ("Bars Fight"), had moved with her prosperous free black husband, Abijiah Prince, from Massachusetts to Guilford, Vermont, a small town about thirty miles southeast of Poultney, in 1760. She educated her six children, agitated (unsuccessfully) for her oldest son to be admitted to Williams College, and gained a significant local reputation as a storyteller and orator. Alexander Twilight (1795–1857), the first African American in the United States to graduate from college, was born on a Vermont farm in 1795 to a white or fair-skinned mother and a "mulatto" father who, like Brace, had served as a private in the American Revolution. From the ages of eight to twenty-one, Twilight was forced to work as an indentured servant on a farm neighboring his parents' farm. Nonetheless, he managed to graduate from Middlebury College in 1823, and he became a preacher and teacher known for his piety, temperance, and love of knowledge. Elected to the Vermont House in 1836, Twilight was "the first African-American to serve in a state legislature in the United States" (Hahn 39). Brace most likely crossed paths with the famous black theologian, essayist, and preacher, Lemuel Haynes (1753–1833), who was born in Connecticut and accepted a pulpit in a predominantly white Congregational Church in Rutland, Vermont, in 1788, four years after Brace's arrival in the neighboring town of Poultney. Although religiously orthodox, Haynes was passionately antislavery. Like Brace, he had served in the

Revolutionary War, and he traveled widely in Vermont preaching in Congregational churches and remote northern regions in the late eighteenth and early nineteenth centuries.[42]

The most important evidence of Brace's involvement in a Vermont Christian abolitionist community comes from an obscure 1852 biography written by a black church elder, John W. Lewis, about Charles Bowles, another black Vermont preacher.[43] Born in Boston in 1761 to a black father and a white mother, Bowles fought in the Revolution as a teenager, underwent a religious conversion in New Hampshire, and settled in Vermont. Lewis's description of Bowles's career as a traveling preacher reveals that a lively, multiracial, antislavery religious network existed in Vermont from the 1780s through the nineteenth century, and that Jeffrey Brace was an important part of that matrix. Lewis tells us that Bowles was not the only "colored man" in Vermont whose influence helped to "revolutioniz[e] the public sentiment of the State, against the abomination of American slavery" and to destroy "prejudice against color" because "contemporary with him was another colored man in the State, of remarkable influence as a christian, and a bible scholar, although he was once a slave. . . . I allude to brother Jeffrey Brace. I am acquainted with several brethren, in whose hearts were planted the seeds of Abolitionism, by the simple tale of that man's wrongs, inflicted by the cruel slave power. Said one brother, to hear Elder Bowles preach, and brother Jeffrey Brace talk, was enough to make abolitionists of a whole community" (190). Lewis follows this testament to Brace's rhetorical power with a summary of Brace's memoir, which he calls "a book once published, giving a minute history of that man" (191). Lewis assumes that many of his readers would have read Brace's book, but his error-ridden synopsis suggests that he himself gave it a cursory reading at best. Nonetheless, Lewis provides us with a rare glimpse into the critical reception of Brace among his contemporaries.

Benjamin Prentiss, perhaps recognizing that long Bible passages detracted from the book's narrative interest, makes it clear in his "Apology" at the end of The Blind African Slave that the "scripture is inserted by the request of the narrator, and under his immediate direction." This suggests that the aged, blind Brace dictated his choice of scriptures to Prentiss word for word. One of Brace's rare twentieth-century readers, Susan Willis, asserts that Brace's "appeals to Scripture, which occur unexpectedly throughout the text, are given as data, juxtaposed, rather than integrated in the narration" (202). While this may be true for readers, for

Brace the Bible permeated his life and consciousness. Biblical images, stories, oratory, and poetry undergirded his ability to articulate meaning in English on multiple emotional and intellectual registers. He concludes his life story elegiacally, citing Jeremiah 9.1 to express his enduring grief: "Oh that my head were waters, and mine eyes a fountain of tears, that I might weep day and night for the slain daughter of my people."

Pension Application and Death

On March 18, 1818, thirty-five years after the end of the Revolutionary War, the United States Congress passed an act to provide pensions for eligible veterans. Under the administration of President James Monroe (1817–1825), the War Department, which reviewed pension applications, was headed by Secretary of War, John C. Calhoun, an ambitious South Carolina statesman who would become the country's most influential proslavery philosopher. When he took charge in October 1817, the War Department was in disarray, both in terms of personnel and finances, including $40,000,000 of unsettled accounts (Capers 63). Calhoun was an efficient administrator, but he was also militaristic and racist. One of his pet projects was the subjugation and "civilization" of Indians, who, he argued in 1820, "must be brought gradually under our authority and laws, or they will insensibly waste away in vice and misery" (Calhoun, "Report" 70). In a conversation with the antislavery New Englander John Quincy Adams, Calhoun stated that slavery was a social necessity for the South, not only because blacks were inherently servile, but also because slavery "was the best guarantee of equality among the whites" (qtd. in Capers 71).

Despite the prevalence of racism in the War Department, many black veterans were awarded pensions. On April 4, 1818, Jeffrey Brace filed his application in the Franklin County court to receive the eight dollars per month to which he was entitled under the new law. The War Department's Pension Office initially rejected his claim on the grounds that it could not find a record of service under his name. Brace had forgotten that he had enlisted under the name of "Stiles." James L. Edwards, the Pension Office administrator, asserted that there was "a strong belief that [Brace's claims] are not founded on truth" (see appendix B). While the pension judges' suspicions about Brace may have had a racist inflection, they routinely rejected applications for a variety of reasons. My perusal of the papers of Samuel C. Crafts, the Vermont congressman at the time, revealed that he was asked to get involved in more than thirty contested pension applications between 1818 and 1820. Fortunately for Brace, the Franklin County Judge of Probate, Seth Wetmore, became his impassioned advocate. The reasons for Wetmore's personal interest in Brace's case are somewhat enigmatic,[44] but he told Crafts that he had known Brace and his children for more than twelve years. Wetmore devoted himself to the just resolution of Brace's case. He actively gathered depositions from soldiers who had known Brace during Revolution, and he wrote multiple letters to the War Department and to Congressman Crafts on Brace's behalf. He told Crafts that Brace "has always sustained a good character. No one can suspect that he has wilfully made any false statement—He is a member of a respectable Baptist Church in Georgia." He pled: "Now Sir at the request of sundry respected inhabitants of Georgia I write this & their request is that you would call at the Secretary Office. . . . Jeffery is poor: dependant on his children for support, & his children are also poor—Your attention will oblige the cause of humanity" (Wetmore to Crafts, Dec. 28, 1819; appendix B).

The court records paint a picture of an elderly Jeffery Brace who was destitute of property and dependent on his children and the charity of friends. Wetmore told Crafts that Brace's children were anxious about their father's prospects and inquired frequently at his office. The depositions reveal that, despite his poverty, the aged Brace was a respected member of his community. His pension claim was supported by friends, county officials, and former comrades in war who testified forcefully on his behalf. Finally, on July 11, 1821, Brace received the pension due him, including arrears, which totaled $328.23. This money was most likely sufficient to make his final six years of life materially comfortable.[45]

Jeffrey Brace died in Georgia, Vermont, on April 20, 1827. He was memorialized in his old town of Poultney, where the local newspaper departed from its usual one-line obituary to publish the following tribute to him:

DIED

In Georgia, Vt., Jeffrey Brace, an African, well known by the appellation of "Old Jeff," supposed to be nearly 100 years old. He was taken from Africa by a party of white kidnappers, when about 16 years old—was with Gen. Wolfe at the siege of Quebec,[46] and served in the American Revolutionary Army, for which we believe he received a pension from our government. He had for many years been totally blind, yet his mental powers appeared to be hardly impaired. The powers of his memory were frequently tested by repeating whole chapters of the scriptures nearly verbatim. He was formerly a resident of this town. (*Northern Spectator* 4.18, Wed. May 9, 1827)

By mid-century the power of Brace's memory had achieved legendary status within Vermont's abolitionist community. John W. Lewis, who did not know him personally but who heard stories about him from many of his contemporaries, asserted in 1852 that Brace's

noble pious character had a powerful influence on the public mind in Vermont. He had a powerful and wonderful memory, a trait characteristic of the African race, and although for many years during the latter part of his life, he was perfectly blind, he had the bible so completely committed to his memory, that he could repeat it chapter and verse from Genesis to Revelations, with an accuracy truly astonishing. One might sit down with him and open the bible in any place, and commence reading in any chapter or verse following, and so continue to do. It has been said of him, that if the bible was lost, and not a copy to be found on earth, if a good writer should sit down with him, he could repeat from memory so that a complete copy could again be produced. At Camp, Quarterly, or Yearly Meetings, Conferences, or associations of all denominations, an interview with brother Jeffrey, was eagerly sought and enjoyed, by ministers and people. Now, kind reader, be assured that two such kindred spirits [Brace and Bowles] could not be without their influence in shaping the mind of the community in Vermont. . . . Brother Jeffrey Brace in life, was useful, and in death was happy. It may truly be said of him, "His record is on high" (196).

Autobiography and "Authenticity"

John W. Lewis's hyperbolic praise of Brace's memory hardly seems exaggerated to this biographer after the years I have spent discovering the factual accuracy of Brace's memoir. The success of autobiographers depends largely on their ability to persuade readers of their truthfulness, yet autobiographical persuasiveness, like persuasiveness in any genre, is largely a matter of rhetorical performance. As William L. Andrews has shown, nineteenth-century black autobiographers learned to recognize that "their great challenge was much more than just telling the truth; they had to *sound* truthful doing it, or else risk the failure of their rhetorical enterprise" ("Dialogue" 89). Historians and literary critics have demonstrated "preference for and confidence in the plain style over most forms of

imaginative expression in antebellum [and earlier] black autobiography"
("Dialogue" 90). The few critics who have mentioned Brace's memoir
often have found it unpersuasive, yet historical research validates its accuracy to an extent unusual to the genre of autobiography.[47] As editor,
Prentiss sometimes used literary embellishments, such as ornate speeches
inserted at implausible moments, in ways that disrupt the reader's ability
to view the memoir as a simple account of personal experience. In *To Tell
a Free Story,* Andrews describes the need for and the difficulties of writing black autobiographies in the eighteenth and nineteenth centuries:
"For the Afro-American and his white sponsors, autobiography answered
a felt need for a rhetorical mode that would conduct the battle against
racism and slavery on grounds other than those already occupied by pro-
and antislavery polemics. . . . Next to the Bible itself, autobiography was
the script—the sanctified record and the directing text—that the victims
of the African diaspora in America needed most to sustain them during
their tribulation and to explain to them the reasons for their suffering" (5,
14). Writing at the dawn of the genre, Prentiss and Brace searched with
little guidance for narrative forms, images, and metaphors "through which
the unknown within the self and the unspeakable within slavery might be
expressed" (Andrews, *To Tell* 9). Although Prentiss was unable to master
those techniques of novelistic discourse that foster the illusion that texts
are windows to unmediated reality, Brace's verifiable accuracy in recol-
lecting historical detail should encourage readers to attend seriously to his
account of slavery and "freedom."

In his voluminous work, *The Origins of African American Literature,
1680–1865,* Dickson Bruce correctly observes that *The Blind African
Slave* is "one of the most remarkable efforts to create an efficacious black
voice" between 1800 and 1816 (98). However, since Bruce did no archival
research on the memoir, he discredits it as "Benjamin Prentiss's purported
autobiography of Boyrereau Brinch," and suggests that "the narrative was
in most ways a compendium of earlier works, repeating stories others had
told" (98)—a peculiar assertion given the paucity of antislavery stories
published before 1810. While it is true that Brace's memoir is similar to
Equiano's in that it forms a collage of genres and draws on multiple literary traditions, including travel literature, spiritual autobiography, sea adventure, war story, picaresque novel, and poetry, many parts of Brace's
memoir are unprecedented. In its totality the book is unique. Brace an-
ticipates Harriet Wilson's analysis of New England bondage in *Our Nig*
(1859), as well as Richard Wright's analysis of northern racism in *Black*

Boy (1945), yet among all of the slave narratives that have been written and discovered in the past two centuries, some of Brace's stories are unparalleled.

Bruce accurately notes that Brace's memoir shares several features with Olaudah Equiano's 1789 book, *The Interesting Narrative of the Life of Olaudah Equiano, Written by Himself,* and Venture Smith's 1798 work, *A Narrative of the Life and Adventures of Venture, A Native of Africa.* All three narrators were born in Africa and captured by slave traders as children, Smith at the age of eight around 1737, Equiano at the age of eleven in 1756, and Brace at the age of sixteen around 1758. During these decades, approximately 53,000 Africans were transported to slavery in the Americas each year (Allison 197). All three captives were taken first to Barbados, which in the eighteenth century was a common destination for British slave-trading ships.[48] While all three narrators describe their families, cultures, and native landscapes in respectful terms, their backgrounds were distinct and varied. In brief, Smith recounts witnessing his father being tortured to death during a large scale war with an African enemy that was "instigated by some white nation who equipped and sent them to subdue and possess the country" (8). Smith was shackled with hundreds of other captives and put on a ship bound for Barbados. He describes the Middle Passage as "an ordinary passage, except great mortality by the small pox" (13). Sold into slavery first in New York and then in Connecticut, Smith managed through extraordinary exertions to procure enough money to purchase his freedom. He later purchased his wife, his children, and some other slaves whom he manumitted. As a free man in New England, he both prospered and suffered. His narrative attends with approximately equal interest to the indignities of slavery and the means by which he earned money. Religion plays little role in his story.

Equiano's and Brace's much longer narratives describe their native cultures in detail. Equiano recalls three Africans capturing his sister and him, while Brace describes English slave traders surrounding him and a group of boys while they were swimming. Both narrators describe the horrors of the Middle Passage, both were transported to Barbados, and both worked as enslaved sailors during the Seven Years War aboard English vessels that engaged in skirmishes with the French and Spanish. Like Smith, Equiano bought his freedom, whereas Brace was manumitted as a reward for his service in the Revolutionary War. Equiano developed a primarily British identity and became an active abolitionist with international recognition, whereas Brace became a Vermont farmer and laborer

whose abolitionist voice gained some local currency. Both men converted
to Christianity, the principles of which they cite forcefully to condemn
slavery and the Christian society that promoted it.

What I mean to emphasize in these brief synopses is that the memoirs
of three contemporary Africans whose lives were shaped by the trans-
atlantic slave trade will inevitably share some commonalities. What also
emerges from each text is a distinctive choir of voices, a resilient personality, and an extraordinary life. Brace's autobiography is episodic; it does
not present a unified, coherent life, and its form exceeds what would become the standard plot (slavery to freedom) of the antebellum slave narrative. A hybrid, collaborative text that reflects Prentiss's biases and interests as well as Brace's, *The Blind African Slave* highlights the sufferings
and accomplishments of a person who is simultaneously extraordinary and
common; unique and representative; tribal and modern. Brace's life was
characterized by violence, disruption, dislocation, disenfranchisement,
alienation, struggle, perseverance, and stubborn affirmation of love and
hope. Brace and Prentiss do not bestow a graceful narrative shape on this
life; rather, the book is bound together by a political philosophy that is abolitionist, anti-racist, and humane.

Our knowledge of history and our understanding of ourselves are shaped
as much by omission and erasure as they are by the stories told to us. Like
Equiano, Brace became, against his will, a quintessentially modern man,
a displaced person who was routed through and grew roots in Africa, the
West Indies, and New England. Jeffery Brace and Susannah Dublin were
among Vermont's earliest, most cosmopolitan, and most extraordinary non-
Indian settlers, and they bequeathed the world a prolific line of descendants, many of whom still live in St. Albans and the surrounding stretches
of northern Vermont. In the nineteenth century the Brace family of St.
Albans included farmers, laborers, craftsmen, and at least one fiddler.[49]
Peter Brace (1848–1913) followed in his great grandfather's footsteps by
joining the Company E. 54, Massachusetts Infantry, the black Civil War
regiment celebrated in the Hollywood film *Glory*. The book left to us by
Jeffrey Brace and Benjamin Prentiss offers us the possibility of reclaiming
a muted legacy of Africans, West Indians, and Americans. It is my hope
that this new edition of *The Blind African Slave* will write Jeffrey Brace
back into history and will uproot some of our former certainties about slavery, social history, and American literature.

Jeffrey S. Brace's gravestone.

Peter Brace's gravestone.

Notes

1. Apparently relying on incomplete notes, Prentiss's form of citation ranges from naming author and title to citing "a periodical of 1804" to crediting "a very learned writer" and "some writers." His sources on Africa include relatively reputable works by Jedidiah Morse, Friedrich Horneman, Thomas Shaw, and William Guthrie, as well as *Travels in the Interior of Africa,* a fraudulent travelogue published in 1801 by the pseudonymous Christian Frederick Damberger. Although not explicitly cited, Mungo Park's popular 1799 memoir, *Travels in the Interior Districts of Africa,* may have influenced this section as well. Park's appeal to Vermonters was evident in the St. Albans weekly newspaper, the *Franklin County Advertiser,* which on July 26, 1810, ran an article about Park as well as an advertisement for *The Blind African Slave.* Harry Whitney was the publisher of both the newspaper and Brace's memoir.

2. In 1999 Vincent Carretta breathed new life into the old scholarly convention of questioning the authenticity of slave narratives by suggesting that Olaudah Equiano may have been born in South Carolina rather than in Africa. He provides evidence that Equiano was most likely "younger than he admits when he left Africa," but produces no definitive evidence that Equiano was born in South Carolina; rather, he concludes merely that the "evidence regarding his place and date of birth is clearly contradictory and will probably remain tantalizingly so" ("Olaudah Equiano" 102, 103). Since slave traders almost never recorded the names of the African people they bought and sold, it is impossible in most cases to document the place and time of a particular slave's African origin. Whatever the vagaries of Equiano's case, Brace's offers no similar ambiguity. Equiano was an internationally renowned public figure—an abolitionist orator and writer— whose African roots were questioned in his own day, whereas Brace was a farmer and laborer whose abolitionist agitation was known only within a portion of New England. None of his contemporaries questioned Brace's African origin in any of the extant documents; on the contrary, everyone mentioned it as a matter-of-fact. The question is not if Brace came from Africa, but where in Africa he came from.

3. It is important to place this "high-born" convention in context by noting that because African and European societies were intensely class-conscious (indeed, the slave trade depended on powerful Africans identifying with the class interests of powerful Europeans rather than with their fellow Africans as "racial" compatriots), much of the early protest against slavery emerged from a sense that the wrong sorts of Africans were being enslaved. For instance, in 1688 Aphra Behn published a novel about the abuses of slavery in Surinam entitled *Oroonoko; or, The Royal Slave,* which is arguably the first English novel ever published. The primary outrage that Behn connected to slavery was its ability to undermine class hierarchies by juxtaposing "royal" with "slave." Many freed people as well as

slaves understood the advantage that might accrue to them if they appealed to class values to combat the racism in which they were trapped.

4. Brace often comments on the presence of racism in American society, locating it in the reader and in white society, not in himself, as in this direct address to the reader: "Now, although I am a poor, despised black wretch, in the sight of man, permit me, kind reader, to offer some ideas of mine, and do not despise them because they come from an African negro, who are, by white men considered an inferior race of beings" (31). Although Brace describes his consternation at being surrounded by a "pale race of white Vultures" when he is kidnapped, and he sometimes employs the language of racial dichotomies into which he was thrust, much of the time he resists the language of "race." He maintains an open attitude toward the particular individualities of the people he encounters, despite the fact that he would have been well-justified in arguing, as David Walker did in his revolutionary 1829 "Appeal to the Colored Citizens of the World," that "whites have always been an unjust, unmerciful, avaricious and blood thirsty set of beings, always seeking after power and authority" (135). Brace typically satirizes his oppressors with terms such as *"humane christians,"* "civilized society," and "puritans," words that, ironically, "whites" use to construct their alleged superiority to "blacks."

5. After chapter 2 Prentiss limits his editorial intrusions to occasional citations of popular antislavery poems and appears to allow Brace to tell his own story, largely in his own voice.

6. Equiano adopts a similar view: "I cannot forbear suggesting what has long struck me very forcibly, namely, the strong analogy which . . . appears to prevail in the manners and customs of my countrymen, and those of the Jews, before they reached the Land of Promise, and particularly the patriarchs, while they were yet in that pastoral state which is described in Genesis" (43).

7. An estimated 279,100 African slaves arrived in the British American colonies between 1766 and 1775 (including 32,800 transported to Barbados), compared to approximately 152,600 in 1720–1729 and 242,100 in 1795–1804 (Richardson 456).

8. Quobna Ottobah Cugoano describes a similar form of kidnapping in his 1787 narrative: "I was early snatched away from my native country, with about eighteen or twenty more boys and girls, as we were playing in a field" (147).

9. Rawley suggests an overall mortality rate of 10 percent during the Middle Passage, but some catastrophic voyages recorded much higher rates. For example, three voyages in the mid-eighteenth century "together lost 58 per cent of their cargo" (Rawley 290). Slaves who were held in captivity for significant periods of time before embarking for the Americas died at a higher rate than those who embarked quickly. Levels of drought, famine, and epidemics in Africa also affected mortality rates. The diseases that killed slaves and crew in large numbers

included fevers, yaws, scurvy, smallpox, measles, intestinal worms, and especially dysentery (which was called "the flux").

10. *The Connecticut Gazette* announced on 24 May 1755 that Captain Isaac Mills (or "Miles") of New Haven had arrived at the small island of St. Eustatia and announced on 31 May 1755 that he was preparing to depart from Antigua. Mills's later partner in the shipping business, Captain Edward Allen, was sailing between New Haven and the West Indies at the same time (Scott 4, 5).

11. Baptisms began to be recorded in Barbados in 1637. In an October between 1637 and 1642 (the year was not recorded precisely) an "Edward son of James and Margaret Welch" was baptized in Christ Church Parish (Sanders, *Baptisms* 251). The Welch line grew during the seventeenth century and by the early eighteenth century became racially diverse. Welches of every hue still live in Barbados in the twenty-first century.

12. Handler reports: "In 1748, the first year for which statistics on Barbadian freedmen are available, only 107 were reported, and in the 1770s, there were barely about 500—in both cases a minute fraction of Barbados's total population" (Handler et al, *Freedmen* i). I believe that more careful scrutiny of the data would show that the freed population has been undercounted.

13. For example, on January 2, 1819 a free colored woman named Jessey Welch borrowed 25 pounds from a white moneylender (Welch and Goodridge 96). In 1823 three Welches (Frederick, James Payne, and Venture) were among the 373 freedmen who signed a Counter-Address to the Governor demanding various civil rights. In 1825 a free black woman named Maria Welch of St. Michael Parish who was wealthy enough to own slaves ordered in her will that one slave should be sold to pay for her funeral and the balance of her estate should go to a friend (Handler et al, *Freedmen* 56).

14. "In the St. Michael parish register for 4 December 1685, for example, a marriage is entered between 'Peter Perkins, a negro, and Jane Long, a white woman'" (Beckles, *Centering Woman* 68).

15. Captain Isaac Mills (or "Miles") was born in Milford, Connecticut, on 8 May 1728. He married Katherine Baldwin of Milford in 1751 and captained ships that were active in the West India trade from at least 1755, when he sailed from New Haven to Antigua and St. Eustatius, to 1764, when he sailed from New Haven to Barbados and Tortuga (Scott 155, "A List of Ships").

16. William Burke, the son of William and Mary Burke, was baptized in St. Philip Parish on May 18, 1697 (Sanders, *Baptisms* 463). His wife-to-be, Margaret Lord, the daughter of James and Ann Lord, was baptized in the same parish in July 1703 (Sanders, *Baptisms* 464). The Burke and the Lord families had been in Barbados since the beginning of British colonization in the mid-seventeenth century. Not among the major land-owning families, they were likely either small farmers

or indentured servants. William became a mariner and moved to St. Michael Parish, where he and Margaret were married on May 27, 1727. The Marriage Register identifies Burke as a "mariner" and Lord as a "spinster" (BDA RL1/2/291). They had one child, Edward, who was born on August 14, 1729 and died at the age of twelve (BDA *Burials* RL1/3/32). William Burke was buried in St. Michael Parish on July 22, 1788 at the ripe old age of 91. His burial record describes him as "William, son of William Burke of the 49th Rgmt" (BDA *Burials* RL1/5/466).

17. The British had hoped to entice free blacks to enlist with a policy that "the corps of Negroes to be raised in Jamaica . . . should have an equal share in all booty gained from the enemy" (*Admiralty to Pocock,* 18 February 1762; Syrett 46).

18. Syrett says that in Havana between 7 June and 9 October, 1762 the British navy lost more than 1200 seamen and marines to disease and only 86 to combat, while between 7 June and 18 October the British army lost 4,708 to disease and 658 to combat. "In addition, large numbers of soldiers were sick at the end of the campaign, and many of these later died or were physically incapacitated for months" (xxxv). Colonizing the West Indies exacted a high price, even from the "victorious" colonizers. Syrett concludes, "The British took Havana and gained the Floridas, but at the cost of an army, and perhaps unknowingly set the stage for the loss of an empire" (xxxv).

19. Cromwell observes that after 1800 many blacks moved to Boston's West End.

20. In his 1865 book, *The Black Man,* the fugitive slave author William Wells Brown quotes the description of Attucks from the *Boston Gazette* (November 20, 1750):

> Ran away from his master William Brouno Framingham, on the 30th of Sept., last, a Molatto Fellow, about 27 years of Age named Crispus, well set, six feet 2 inches high, short curl'd Hair, knees nearer together than common; had on a light coloured Bearskin Coat, brown Fustian jacket, new Buckskin Breeches, blew yarn Stockins and Checkered Shirt. Whoever shall take up said Run-away and convey him to his above said Master at Framingham, shall have Ten Pounds, old Tenor Reward and all necessary Charges paid. (107–8)

21. Other black Bostonians who fought in the Revolution include Primus Hall, Cato Howe, Primus Jacobs, Brazillai Lew, Peter Salem, and Salem Poor (Cromwell 30–32).

22. *The Seaflower,* commanded by Mills, stopped in Antigua early in February 1764 (Scott 155), then continued on to Bridgetown, where it arrived in late February or early March ("A List of Ships"). Mills departed shortly thereafter, naming his destination as Tortuga, a small island off the northern coast of Haiti which was famous as a base for privateers ("A List of Such Ships"). In 1767 the *Seaflower* was still engaged in the West India trade, sailing between New Haven and Kingston, Jamaica, but under the command of a Capt. Olds (Scott 210). In the

1770s Mills served on town committees in Milford and in 1776, 1777, and 1778 was elected to represent Milford as "a deputy of the freemen" in the Connecticut General Assembly. Supplied with arms during the Revolutionary War, Mills died in Milford on 15 November 1780 (Scott 196, 460; *Public Records of the State of Connecticut*).

23. At the time of Brace's arrival in Connecticut, "New London newspapers during 1760 and 1761 convey some idea of the colony's shipping. These show more clearances for the Caribbean than for any other area—36 percent. New York City ranked second with 30 percent and Boston a poor third with 12 percent" (Main 304–5).

24. Fear of converting slaves stemmed not only from racism but also from a centuries-old belief that the Bible permitted enslavement of infidels but barred enslavement of fellow Christians.

25. Alternatively, Brace may have been referring to Samuel Eells Jr. (1730–1804).

26. The Eells-Stow house is preserved by the Milford Historical Society and can be viewed on their website, www.milforded.org/schools/orange/mvirtualtour/milfordhistorictour.htm.

27. The area where the Stileses lived was part of the town of Woodbury until 1786, when it was incorporated as the town of Southbury.

28. "No one knows exactly how many people died in Europe and America during the witch-hunting years—estimates range from tens of thousands into the millions—and few authors attempt to calculate the proportion of women to men among them. Four-fifths is a conservative estimate" (Karlsen xii). The English Parliament made witchcraft a capital offense in 1542, and there were periodic outbreaks of massive violence, most of which was directed against women. Between 1645 and 1647, for instance, "several hundred people had been hanged in the wake of England's most serious witchcraft outbreak. More than 90 percent of these English witches were women" (Karlsen 2). In New England, at least "344 persons were accused of witchcraft . . . between 1620 and 1725. Of the 342 who can be identified by sex, 267 (78 percent) were female" (Karlsen 47). Most of the male victims were relatives or public supporters of the accused women.

29. Mary Stiles married younger than was normal in Connecticut at the time. In New Haven the "median age of those [women] who married during 1700–1709 was 22 and 30 years later it was 21½" (Main 18n. 32) In northern New England between 1650 and 1750 "on the average, women married somewhere between the ages of 20 and 22 . Husbands were four or five years older" (Ulrich 6). Francis Stiles was born around 1690 (the precise date is unknown), so he would have been about twenty years old at the time of the wedding.

30. Among the earliest English settlers in Connecticut, the Stileses prolifer-ated throughout the English colonies. Their most famous descendant, Ezra Stiles

(1727–1795), was not only a Congregational minister and President of Yale College, but also one of the leading slaveholders in New England. Like his distant relative, Mary Stiles, Ezra Stiles supported the education and religious indoctrination of slaves.

31. Francis (II) was the fifth child of Benjamin Stiles of Woodbury and Elizabeth Rogers of Milford. The eldest son of Francis I, Ephraim, had three daughters. Francis I's second son, Samuel, died childless. Francis I's third son, Benjamin, had two sons, but the first disappeared from the record and apparently died in childhood. Francis I's fourth son, Thomas, died childless.

32. Cothren's *History of Ancient Woodbury* provides details for the following biographical sketches of the children of Francis and Mary Stiles. The first child, Francis Jr., was born and died on July 23, 1710.

Their oldest daughter, Sarah (b. October 21, 1711), married Deacon Benjamin Hicock the Second in Woodbury on February 28, 1733. Sarah and Benjamin Hicock faced a series of personal tragedies: their daughter Olive died at the age of three months on January 22, 1735; their son, Simeon, died at 11 months, on September 22, 1746; and their daughter Patience died at the age of 6 on September 30, 1752. Sarah died on October 4, 1772, and Benjamin followed her to the grave within two years, dying on October 23, 1774 at the age of sixty-three (Cothren 505).

Mabel (b. May 9, 1714) married Andrew Hinman on the same day as her older sister's wedding (February 28, 1733).

Eunice (b. August 18, 1717) married David Curtiss (1718–1782) of Woodbury. They had five children between 1743 and 1752 (Cothren 533–34).

Benjamin (b. February 11, 1720) married his second cousin, Ruth Judson (b. April 26, 1726), on April 26, 1747. Ruth was the daughter of Captain David Judson and Phebe Stiles, the daughter of Ephraim Stiles (Orcutt 1230). Benjamin and Ruth had nine children: Francis (b. 1748), Phebe (b. 1749), David (b. 1751), Ephraim (b. 1753), Benjamin (b. 1756), Abel (b. 1758), Nathan (1759), Judson (birthday unknown), Phebe (b. 1764). The second child died young, but the rest survived into adulthood (Cothren 699; Cothren supplies the wrong year for Nathan's birth).

David (b. April 8, 1725) died before his second birthday, on March 31, 1727.

Mary, born 7 January 1728, married Colonel Benjamin Hinman, Esq. of Woodbury. Their three-year-old son Sherman died in 1752. Mary died at the age of fifty-five in 1783. Colonel Hinman was married a second time, to a woman named Sarah who was twenty-two years his junior. He lived until March 1810, when he died at the ripe old age of ninety-one. Sarah followed him to the grave nine months later (Dec. 1810).

34. In 1792 three Indians—Joseph Marvee, Jemima Sucanux, and Daniel Sucanux—petitioned the General Assembly for permission to sell their thirty-three acres of land that bordered the estate of Nathan Stiles, Mary's grandson (*Public*

Records, 1789–1792, 523–24). The next year Nathan and Judson Stiles described to the Assembly various problems that arose from the inability of seven Indians with whom they were "Tenants in Common" to partition their land. The Assembly appointed a white man "with full Power to agree upon and make Partition for and in behalf of said Indians" (*Public Records, 1793–1796,* 122).

34. I have not found any record that confirms the date of Mary Stiles's death. Brace says that she died about four years before her [grand]sons enlisted in the Revolution, which would place her death in 1773.

35. The Stileses' neighbor, Captain Timothy Hinman, held one person in bondage, as did Truman Hinman and John Hinman. Edward Hinman or "Lawyer Ned," an influential Litchfield County lawyer and justice of the peace known as "one of the most corpulent men of his day," and his wife Ann (née Curtiss) Hinman enslaved six people (Cothren 369). The other remaining slaveholders in Southbury were Asa Coggwell, who enslaved five people, Edward Allen, who enslaved three; Esther Thomson, who enslaved two, and Simeon and Esther Mitchell, who enslaved one. The 1790 Census listed one free person of color living in a household headed by a white person, and four households headed by free people of color in Southbury: Peter Galloway's household of two, Dolphin Philips' household of four, Joab Sharp's household of five, and Robin Starr's household of two. Galloway fought in the Revolution in 1778, and Starr fought for the duration (1777 to 1783). Originally from Danbury, Starr moved to Woodbury shortly after the war and received a military pension (White 62).

36. For specific examples, see William Nell and David O. White. Much remains to be written about African American soldiers in the Revolution.

37. David White found records of manumissions of twenty-three slaves in Connecticut due to their service in the Revolutionary War, but he suggests that "undoubtedly there were numerous others" (20).

38. In addition to a successful career in law and politics, Benjamin Hinman (1720–1810) had a long record of military service, receiving his first commission to fight with British forces against the French in Quebec in 1751 and climbing the military hierarchy until he was commissioned colonel in 1771. In 1775 "he was appointed colonel of the fourth regiment of enlisted and assembled troops for the defense of the colony" (Cothren 372).

39. Elise Guyette found that one third of the black servants in Vermont, listed in the 1820 census "were children thirteen years old or under, probably indentured by parents unable to care for them. Two thirds of these young servants were girls" (98). Brace's account reveals that parents were often rendered "unable" to care for their children by the coercion of white neighbors. Guyette continues: "In 1830 one fifth of Vermont's black servants were nine years old or under, two thirds of them girls. These youngsters were generally the only black living in the household" (98). For another powerful dramatization of the ways race, class, and gender

82 INTRODUCTION

oppressions converged to victimize a young child in New England, see Harriet Wilson's *Our Nig*.

40. Although the book's title calls attention to Brace's blindness and the book's "as-told-to" form is mandated by the fact that Brace could no longer see to read and write, Brace's lack of sight does not appear in the text to loom large in his consciousness. Rawley provides a possible source of Brace's blindness: "The inflammation of the eye called ophthalmia, contagious and a cause of blindness, afflicted Africans in great numbers" (293). When a case of ophthalmia broke out on a French slave ship in 1819, the "thirty-nine slaves who remained sightless were thrown into the sea; the captain expecting to recover his losses from the underwriters" (293).

41. On September 1, 1812, the Milton selectmen directed the constable "to summon Jeffery Brace now residing in Milton to depart said town" (Milton Town Meeting Records, Vol. 3, p. 35). Being warned out did not necessarily make people leave. Prentisses and Braces continue to appear in Milton town records throughout the nineteenth century. It is possible that Benjamin Prentiss was related to Samuel Prentiss, who was born in Connecticut in 1772, moved to Vermont at about the same time Brace did, and was admitted to the bar around 1792. After practicing law in Montpelier, the state capital, for three decades, he was appointed Chief Justice of the Vermont Supreme Court in 1829 and elected to the U.S. Senate in 1830, in which position he advocated the abolition of slavery.

42. For more information on the Princes and Haynes, see Zirblis 154, 240.

43. John W. Lewis (1810–1861) was a "Freewill Baptist minister, antislavery and temperance lecturer, denominational historian, and champion of black nationalism and Haitian immigration." Born in Rhode Island, he "settled in St. Albans about 1850, and became a traveling agent for *Frederick Douglass' Paper* in Vermont.

44. Perhaps Seth Wetmore's own experience of unjust imprisonment cultivated a sense of compassion for victims of social injustice. Around 1810 he was appointed sheriff at a time when "it was hazardous to be sheriff on account of the scarcity of money, the difficulty of collecting debts by process of law, and the general demoralization of the people" (Hemenway 314). Trusting people's promises to pay their debts, he was forced to default on "an execution for a large amount in favor of the Vermont State Bank, and was confined to the jail limits for some time" (314). He resolved this issue by selling the property of the debtors, but he remained in financial straits for the rest of his life. He served as Judge of Probate from 1817 until his death in 1830 and was generally viewed as "a useful citizen in all matters that concerned the welfare and prosperity of the community, and his opinion and advice was much relied on in all concerns of the village" (Hemenway 314).

45. On 8 September 1831 the St. Albans Probate Court appointed a J. L. Chandler to administer the estate of Jeffrey Brace, who had died intestate, "leaving goods, chattel, rights, credits, and estate." A handwritten note in the margin mentions his pension. This document indicates that by the time of his death Brace had built an estate significant enough to be the source of possible contention and legal interest. (See appendix C.)

46. The incorrect statement that Brace was with Wolfe in Quebec apparently grew out of a misreading of his description of being named after Jeffrey Amherst, who was commander-in-chief of the forces that fought in Quebec. (It was Wolfe who won the battle there.)

47. For example, after I called *The Blind African Slave* to his attention, Jerome Handler wrote: "I am greatly suspicious of the veracity of these pages, and suspect a fabrication" ("Survivors" 54).

48. Most African slaves transported by the British were brought to ports in the Caribbean before being distributed to other colonies. (For distribution chart, see Richardson 456.) Pierson explains some of the reasons why few Northerners obtained their slaves directly from Africa:

> Northern merchants had little need to gamble cruelly on purchasing large cargoes of African slaves with their high mortality rates; it was more convenient and economical to purchase from the West Indies and the continental colonies small retail lots of mixed slaves better suited to northern markets. This northern trade in slaves was noted as early as 1679 by Connecticut's Governor William Leete, who explained, "As for blacks, there comes sometimes three or four in a year from Barbados." Except for an increase in the size of cargoes, conditions changed little during the next century. (3)

49. Jeffrey and Susan Brace had at least one daughter and two sons. Brace purchased land with the daughter's husband in Georgia, Vermont. Archival sources suggest that the two sons, Jeff and Ishmael, were born before 1790. Ishmael appears in three notices in the *St. Albans Adviser* in January 1809. Jeff married a woman named Diana and apparently died before 1830, when the U.S. census lists Diana Brace as a head of household in St. Albans. They had at least one child, Theodore (1816–1864), who became a laborer and a fiddler. He married Sally Prince of Swanton, with whom he had at least six sons, two of whom died young— one at four and the other at nineteen. An outline of lives of those who survived into adulthood provides some clues about life for African Americans in nineteenth-century Vermont.

Jeffrey S. (1844–1895), worked as a laborer, car cleaner, and mechanic. In 1863 he married a "colored" woman, Mary E. Phelps, who gave birth to a daughter who died in infancy. The next year she had a son, Orrison, who survived, but she died of consumption a year later, at twenty-one. More than twenty years passed before Jeffrey remarried. In 1889, he married Anna Jackson of Ellenburgh, with whom he had at least three children.

Peter (1848–1913) fought for the Union in the first Massachusetts 54th and was wounded in the Battle of Honey Hills. He married Louisa Woodbeck of St. Albans, with whom he had at least six children. After losing Louisa to death or divorce, Peter at age thirty-six married Rebecca Johnson, with whom he lived at 12 Lasell St. in St. Albans.

Wyron (1854–?) became a laborer and married Ellen Day of Missisquoi Bay or Philipsburg, Canada in 1875. Ellen was likely a French Canadian or Abenaki. It was Wyron Brace's first marriage; he was twenty, and Day was twenty-two. They had two daughters who died before the age of two, followed by a son named Wyron. The U.S. Census places Wyron the elder in the "household" of the Windsor State Prison in southern Vermont in 1880. Described in the census as a "laborer," he was either a prison inmate or a poor-farm boarder. Named after Jeffrey Brace's father Whyrn, Wyron appears proud of his African roots; he told prison officials or census takers that his father was born in Africa and his mother in Vermont. During these years, Wyron and Ellen Day divorced. Wyron (also known as "Toney") returned to St. Albans in the early 1880s, where on April 14, 1885, he married Mary Turner of Williston, Milton, Georgia, or Essex (also known as Marie Letoureau of Williamstown), with whom he had already had a child. Vital records list Mary/Marie as "colored," and her constantly changing story of origins suggests that she, like Ellen Day, may have been an Abenaki or a mixed race Quebecois. Wyron and Mary lived on Lasell St. and had at least thirteen children, seven of whom were born dead or died in infancy.

Ethan (1859–?) became a laborer and married Ellen Day, his brother Wyron's ex-wife, in 1884. One birth certificate states that Ellen had given birth to eleven children, including four with Ethan. In 1886 Ethan and his family were living on Water St. near Lasell; in 1891 they were living on Lasell St. near elm in St. Albans.

A Note on the Text

This edition follows the original 1810 edition. For the ease of the reader, I have silently corrected some of the obvious printing, punctuation, subject-verb agreement and spelling errors that appear to me to have no meaning or relation to either the conscious authorial intentions or the unconscious attitudes of Prentiss or Brace. For example, "accordding" is corrected to "according," "preparitory" to "preparatory," "monkies" to "monkeys," and so on. I have not corrected syntax or changed archaic or unusual spellings that Prentiss uses consistently (e.g., I have not replaced "Barbadoes" with "Barbados" or "christian" with "Christian"). I have changed the archaic long "S" to the lowercase "s" in the manuscripts transcribed in the appendixes.

In the eighteenth and early nineteenth centuries, the spelling of proper names often was not standardized, and variations occur frequently even in official records. In *The Blind African Slave*, spellings of names depended not only on Brace's memory, but also on Prentiss's transcription of what he heard Brace say. When quoting from published sources, Prentiss spelled authors' names inconsistently. In all cases, I have let proper names stand in Prentiss's original spelling within the text of *The Blind African Slave* but have used a more standard spelling—that is to say, the variant found most often in external documents such as birth, marriage, and death records—in my introduction and annotations.

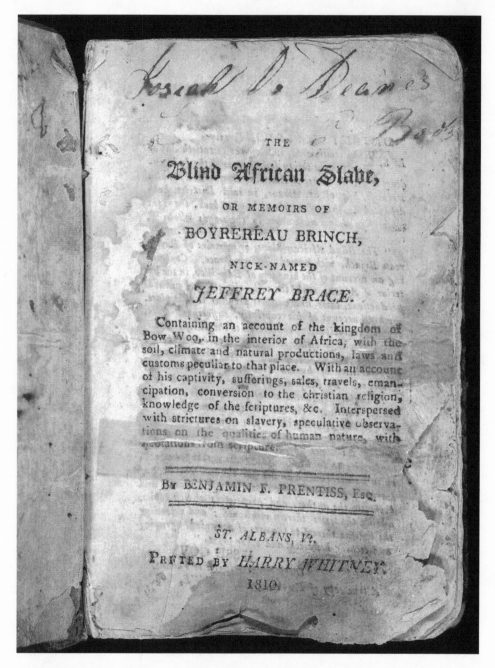

THE

Blind African Slave,

OR MEMOIRS OF

BOYREREAU BRINCH,

NICK-NAMED

JEFFREY BRACE.

Containing an account of the kingdom of
Bow Woo, in the interior of Africa; with the
soil, climate and natural productions, laws and
customs peculiar to that place. With an account
of his captivity, sufferings, sales, travels, emancipation, conversion to the christian religion,
knowledge of the scriptures, &c. Interspersed
with strictures on slavery, speculative observations on the qualities of human nature, with
quotations from scripture.

BY BENJAMIN F. PRENTISS, Esq.

ST. ALBANS, Vt.

PRINTED BY HARRY WHITNEY.

1810.

Title page of *The Blind African Slave*, 1821 edition. *Crafts Family Papers, Special Collections, University of Vermont Library.*

The Blind African Slave;
Or, Memoirs of Boyrereau Brinch,
Nicknamed Jeffrey Brace

Introduction

To the Public

The following sheets contain a general narrative of an African slave; some account of his ancestors, the kingdom of Bow-woo situated on the river Neboah or Niger in the interior of Africa; a description of the soil, climate, vegetables, animals, fowls, fishes, inhabitants, population, government, religion, manners, customs, & c. With a detail of the manner in which he was kidnapped by the English; a brief account of the custom of civilized nations in luring the innocent natives of Africa into the net of slavery; and a regular narrative from his own mouth of his captivity, together with many of his native brethren, their sufferings in the prison, or house of subjection, his adventures in the British navy, travels, sufferings, sales, abuses, education, service in the American war, emancipation, conversion to the christian religion, knowledge of the scriptures, memory, and blindness.

While we regret that one innocent man should be held in chains of bondage by another, at any period of time, we must spurn with indignation any idea of the propriety of christian nations, with no other excuse than lust of lucre and difference of religion, holding as slaves the whole African people, because they are not civilized or bear not the same complexion, having no other crime, save credulity or innocence.

When we look at the custom of European and American nations of purchasing, stealing, and decoying into the chains of bondage the negroes of Africa, and the custom sanctioned by the laws of the several governments; that public and private sales are legal; that they are bartered, sold, and used as beasts of the field, to the disgrace of civilization, civil liberty, and christianity; each manly feeling swells with indignation at the horrid spectacle, and whoever has witnessed the miserable and degraded situation to which these unfortunate mortals are reduced, in the West Indies

and southern states of United America, must irresistibly be led to ask—
Does not civilization produce barbarity? Liberty legalize tyranny? And
christianity deny the humanity it professes?

This simple narrative of an individual *African* cannot possibly compass
all the objections to slavery; yet we hope that the extraordinary features
and simplicity of the facts, with the novelty of this publication, will induce
many to read and learn the abuses of their fellow beings. If the miserable
owner of human blood is not moved to acknowledge the iniquity of his
possession, and thereby emancipate his slaves, he will at least alleviate
their sufferings.

Within the last century, many sentiments of barbarity and superstition
have been done away, "and pure and holy freedom" seems to be verging
towards perfection. The Parliament of G. Britain have emancipated their
Catholic brethren, the advocates of *African freedom* have caused the walls
of the House of Commons to reverberate the thunder of their eloquence,
and a partial emancipation has been effected in their foreign dominions.
In *America,* that spirit of liberty, which stimulated us to shake off a foreign
yoke and become an independent nation, has caused the New-England
states to emancipate their slaves, and there is but one blot to tarnish the
lustre of the *American* name, which is permitting slavery under a constitution, which declares that "all mankind are naturally and of right ought to
be free."

Whoever wishes to preserve the constitution of our general government, to keep sacred the enviable and inestimable principles, by which we
are governed, and to enjoy the natural liberty of man, must embark in the
great work of exterminating slavery and promoting general emancipation.

THE AUTHOR
St. Albans, Vt. August, 1810.

Chapter 1

General observations—account of the river Neboah or Niger—of an English vessel engaged in the slave trade—general account of the kingdom of Bow-woo—description of Deauyah, the capital—king's palace—face of the country—soil—climate—laws and customs, peculiar to this country—crimes how punished—mode of the creation of nobility—war feast—brief account of Boyrereau's ancestors—father, mother, brothers, sisters, & c.—speculative observations—scriptures.

Few indeed have been the travellers who have penetrated into the interior of Africa, as far as the kingdom of Bow-woo, which is situated between the 10th and 20th degrees of north latitude, and between the 6th and 10th of west longitude; and these few have been of that class of travellers, who are either incapable of, or have other pursuits than, communicating to the world that useful information, which has so long been sought in vain. We have indeed obtained some knowledge of the river Neboah of Niger, which runs throu' this fertile dominion. According to the account in Morse's Universal Geography,[1] this river is one of the longest in the world. It is said to be navigable for ships of any size, upwards of 1500 miles.

1. A popular reference work compiled by Jedidiah Morse (1761–1826). Usually referred to as the "American Universal Geography," its full title is *The American Geography; or, A View of the Present Situation of the United States of America: Containing Astronomical Geography.—Geographical Definitions, Discovery, and General Description . . . With a Particular Description of Kentucky, the Western Territory, and Vermont . . . To Which Is Added, An Abridgement of the Geography of the British, Spanish, French and Dutch Dominions in America and the West Indies.–of Europe, Asia, and Africa.* 2nd Ed. London: John Stockdale, Piccadilly, 1792. It went through multiple editions in the late eighteenth and early nineteenth centuries, and I have not yet located the page that Prentiss quotes or paraphrases.

"The Niger, according to the latest accounts, rises near Sankaria, longitude 6 degrees 20 minutes west, latitude 11 deg. north, thence running northerly to Knia-bia, thence Northeast to Bammako, thence generally a northeast course to Sego and Jennu, thence, after forming the island of Janbala 90 or 100 miles in length, it leaves Tombuctoo to the north, passes east by Houssa and is lost in the low lands and lakes of Ghana and Wangara; or if we can credit the accounts of Mr. Horneman,[2] it continues its course easterly to the north of the mountains of the Moon; thence northeasterly until it falls into Bahriel Arrak, which by some has been considered the Nile, from Abyssinia, thence passing Nubia, Sennaar, and Dongolia, it divides Egypt into two parts, pursuing a northerly course, and falls into the Mediterranean by several mouths." But in examining the latest and most approved maps of Africa we cannot find such a river described and it is therefore believed that no historian or engraver has been able to delineate exactly the source or direction of this river. Yet certain it is, that its source is north of the equator, and it is navigable for boats as far as the town of Deauyah, the capital of the kingdom of Bow-woo, which is situated in the county of Hughlough, about three miles from the river on an extensive plain, fertilized by the most luxuriant bounties of nature, peculiar to that clime. According to some writers, "this river has its source in the lake Bernu, and runs directly west, enters the Atlantic, or Western Ocean at Senegal, after a course of 2800 miles. It increases and decreases like the Nile, fertilizes the country, and has grains of gold in many parts of it. The Gambia and Senegal are only branches of this river."

In the year 1758, an English vessel, engaged in the slave trade, sailed up this river to the head of navigation and came to anchor before the town of Yellow Bonga. The hurricane months having commenced, they made their peace with the natives, the crew went on shore, and remained through the rainy season, which commences in May and continues until September.[3] After this season of the year was past and during the time of high water, it appears that they continued their passage up the river about 70 miles farther, leaving the Captain, Supercargo, and some other officers and gentlemen to riot in the luxury of the land, with the chief inhabitants, whom their intrigue and apparent affability, the Europeans had induced

2. *The Journal of Friedrich Hornemann's Travels, From Cairo to Mourzouk, the Capital of the Kingdom of Fezzan, in Africa.* By Friedrich Hornemann (1772–1800), James Rennell, William Marsden et. al. London: G. and W. Nicol, 1802.

3. In northern West Africa "the rains start in May and end in September" (Udo 12).

to become friends. While the vessel lay at anchor in a kind of lake formed in the river, they sent out their boats to steal the innocent natives and succeeded but too well.

Here we will leave these dealers in human flesh and blood, and give some account of the kingdom of Bow-woo, before mentioned. This kingdom, or principality lies about, or the capital stands about, 280 miles above the town of Yellow Bonga—and here the account is taken from the narrator's own mouth who was only 15 or 16 years of age when he was taken and borne away from prosperity, affluence and ease into ignominious slavery.

This he considers to be a province or colony of the Empire of Morocco,[4] the extent of its boundaries he is unable to ascertain, nor can he tell accurately the number of its inhabitants. But the city of Deauyah, the capital and residence of the king, also the native place of Boyrereau, the narrator, is situated on the bank of a small river, about six rods wide, which empties into the Niger, three miles below the town, which is between five and six miles in length, along the east side of said river, and is built in a manner peculiar to that country—the houses are placed in rows, & are joined, only where broken off or intersected by cross streets. This town, besides public buildings, contains nine rows of houses, which are long and low, none more than one story high, except the King's Palace. They are generally built of a kind of clay, made into a cement, which is strengthened by being bound together by small sticks of timber in the body of the walls, so that the face of the same upon both sides is made perfectly smooth and painted, or rather colored white, red, blue, green, purple, or black, according to the fancy of the possessor, which variety renders the view very picturesque and really diverting to the beholder.

The King's palace is situated near the north part of that city, and is composed of about thirty buildings of a very diversified appearance, many of them are in some degree elegant, and this palace includes all the public buildings of the city, except a market and two places of public worship. The country adjacent, for many miles around, appears like a perfect plain, and thinly inhabited, except where there are villages, which are to be met

4. Under Sultan Ahmad al-Mansur, Morocco invaded the area that is now Mali in 1591 and established a sub-Saharan empire that subsided gradually in the seventeenth century. Moroccan expatriate military governors (known as the *Arma*) maintained significant influence in the Niger bend region until at least 1737 (Shillington 181–83). Morocco controlled a trade route through the Sahara desert, and Brace's account suggests that the Kingdom of Bow-woo continued trading with Morocco through the mid-eighteenth century.

once in about two leagues, generally, in every part of the kingdom, except in the mountainous part, of which he has but little knowledge.—The climate, as may naturally be supposed, is uniformly hot, except in the rainy seasons (which is called in their language *vauzier*). As a very learned writer observes, "The natives in these scorching regions would as soon expect that marble should melt, and flow in liquid streams, as that water, by freezing, should loose its fluidity, be arrested by cold, and ceasing to flow, become like the solid rock."

Laws & Customs peculiar to this Country

The King is absolute and enjoys unlimited authority over his people; he has, properly speaking, no ministers. The first grade of nobility perform the office of councilors of state and are properly governors or first magistrates in counties or small districts; and on important occasions are summoned to sit in grand council before the King.

Petty offences are punished with whipping. Adultery is considered as a capital offence, and the offenders are both tried in grand council before the King, and if clearly proved guilty by at least two witnesses, both the adulterer and adulteress are buried alive, with their heads above ground, which are shot into pieces and left exposed to view for the terror of others. Murder and Treason are adjudged and punished in the following manner: at the close of a war in which the King in person is commander in chief, he assembles all of his chief officers to what is called the grand War Feast, as a preparatory step to the banquet. He causes a strict inquiry to be made into the conduct of every officer and soldier. Those who have been guilty of any offence, also those who have signalized themselves, are indiscriminately called before him and his council, on a full, fair and candid investigation. If it does clearly appear that any officer or soldier have been guilty of cowardice, they are banished from the kingdom, with this condition, that if they engage in any foreign service and are once distinguished for their bravery, they are again restored to the privileges of citizenship, but if they return without thus retrieving their characters, they are shot as traitors, who are on a fair conviction by two witnesses before the king, in grand council in the foregoing manner, sentenced to be shot by twelve of their ablest archers. Murderers are punished in the same way.

But those who have signalized themselves in battle or by extraordinary feats of military skill and bravery or wisdom in the war council are invited to partake of the feast with the King himself and created, if old men, members of the council; if young men, are made members of the king's life guards, which consists of seventy or eighty young noblemen. This ceremony is performed in the following manner: twelve young virgins of noble birth are arrayed in blue silk robes and adorned with gold caps, bracelets of gold upon their right arms and ankles; the hero is seated on a kind of second throne. A maid approaches him with a bowl of water and a white linen cloth, another with a flask of oil, they wash and anoint his feet, he then has a wreath of honor placed upon his head, which is a gold laced cap, with two globes of solid gold on each side, which are for the purpose of fastening in and supporting plumes by way of ornament; then he is allowed to kiss the queen's hand, and be seated in the proper seat according to his grade of nobility. Thus at the close of a war with the Vough Boo nation, the grand father of Boyrereau, on the father's side, was honored with the title of councillor and governor of the country of Hugh Lough. His name was Yarrah Brinch—Here we must observe, that titles in some degree are hereditary as his son, the father of the present narrator, succeeded to the title of governor of said county, whose name was Whryn Brinch; he was also Captain of the king's Life Guards, which as before stated, consisted of seventy or eighty men, honored according to the foregoing custom or descended by right of nobility to this station. His mother's name was Whryn Douden. Wrogan had living, when last he received a father's blessing or beheld a mother's tender anxiety, three Brothers and four Sisters, to whom the pure and unsullied love of artless simplicity and fraternal affection rendered thrice dear, as nature unshackled by artifice was the principle guide of their tender youthful minds; the mention of whose names calls from a heart almost subdued by grief one sad tear of fraternal remembrance consecrated to religious resignation. The eldest brother's name was Cressee, 2d Deeyee, 3d Yarrah; the eldest sister's name Desang, 2d Bang, 3d Nabough, 4th Dolacella. Boyrereau descended from Crassee Youghgon, grandfather on the mother's side, who was a distinguished officer in a former war, and after a glorious campaign, he returned with the trophies of victory, covered with wounds to the capital, amid the acclamations of a grateful people, was created first Judge of petty offences and civil differences in the county of Voah-Goah. Boyrereau was the third son and seventh child of an ancient and honorable family in the kingdom of

Bow-woo, situated in that part of Africa called Ethiopia,[5] and of that race of people denominated negroes, whom we as a civilized christian and enlightened people presume to call heathen savages, and hold them in chains of bondage, who are our fellow mortals and children of the same grandparent of the universe. These reflections bring to his mind the following scripture:—

Ezekiel, chap. 2, ver. 1—And he said unto me, Son of man, stand upon thy feet, and I will speak unto thee.

2. And the spirit entered into me when he spake unto me, and set me upon my feet, that I heard him that spake unto me.

3. And he said unto me, Son of man, I send thee to the children of Israel, to a rebellious nation that hath rebelled against me: they and their fathers have transgressed against me, even unto this very day.

4. For they are impudent children and stiff-hearted. I do send thee unto them; and thou shalt say unto them, Thus saith the Lord God.

5. And they, whether they will hear, or whether they will forbear, (for they are a rebellious house) yet shall know that there hath been a prophet among them.

6. And thou, son of man, be not afraid of them, neither be afraid of their words, though briars and thorns be with thee, and thou dost dwell among scorpions; be not afraid of their words, nor be dismayed at their looks, though they be a rebellious house.

7. And thou shall speak my words unto them, whether they will hear, or whether they will forbear; for they are most rebellious.

8. But thou, son of man, hear what I say unto thee, Be not thou rebellious, like that rebellious house: open thy mouth, and eat that I give thee.

Deuteronomy, chap. 28, ver. 64.—And the Lord shall scatter thee among all people, from the one end of the earth even unto the other; and there thou shalt serve other gods, which neither thou nor thy fathers have known, even wood and stone.

65. And among these nations shalt thou find no ease, neither shall the sole of thy foot have rest; but the Lord shall give thee there a trembling heart, and failing of eyes, and sorrow of mind.

66. And thy life shall hang in doubt before thee; and thou shalt fear day and night, and shalt have none assurance of thy life.

67. In the morning thou shalt say, would God it were even! and at even thou shalt say, Would God it were morning! For the fear of thine heart wherewith thou shalt fear, and for the sight of thine eyes which thou shalt see.

5. Prentiss is confused about African geography. Brace most likely came from Mali in West Africa. See introduction.

68. And the Lord shall bring thee into Egypt again with ships, by the way whereof I spake unto thee, Thou shalt see it no more again: and there ye shall be sold unto your enemies for bondmen & bondwomen, & no man shall buy you.

Exodus, chap. 22, ver. 20—He that sacrificeth to any god, save unto the lord only, he shall be utterly destroyed.

21. Thou shalt neither vex a stranger, nor oppress him: for ye were strangers in the land of Egypt.

22. Ye shall not afflict any widow, or fatherless child.

23. If thou afflict them in any wise, and they cry at all unto me, I will surely hear their cry;

24. And my wrath shall wax hot, and I will kill you with the sword; and your wives shall be widows and your children fatherless.

Chapter 2

Soil—vegetables and animal productions by sea and land of the Barbary states—
a sketch of the history of these states—timber peculiar to the kingdom of Bow-
woo—palm wine and oil—some customs—various kinds of fruit &c.— produc-
tion of the country by cultivation—animals, such as cows, oxen, sheep, goats,
horses, hens, geese, turkeys of the domestic kind, with wild beasts peculiar in that
country—quadrupeds—fowls &c.—with 3 of the psalms of David.

That the reader may have some idea of the productions of this most luxuriant part of the world, it is thought proper to give an account in this chapter of the various bounties of nature peculiar to this kingdom, which with
some small variation is applicable to the whole empire of Morocco and
Barbary states,[1] and whoever is in the least acquainted with the history or
geography of this quarter of the globe will at once see that what is here
recorded is undoubtedly true, although it is principally taken from the
narrator, and he dependant upon his own memory, and only in the sixteenth year of his age when he was taken, and in order to demonstrate the
strength of his mind and the correctness of his memory, it is thought ex-
pedient here to quote from a late modern writer upon the soil, vegetable
and animal productions by sea and land, in the states of Barbary. "These
states, under the Roman empire, were justly denominated the garden of
the world; and to have a residence there was considered as the highest
state of luxury. The produce of their soil, formed those magazines, which
furnished all Italy, and great part of the Roman empire, with corn, wine
and oil. Tho' the lands are now uncultivated, through the oppression and

1. The Barbary States included the North African states of Tripolitania, Tunisia, Alge-
ria, and Morocco, which were led in the sixteenth century by the Turkish corsair Barbarossa.

barbarity of their government, yet they are still fertile, not only in the above mentioned commodities, but in dates, figs, raisins, almonds, apples, pears, cherries, plums, citrons, lemons, oranges, pomegranates, with plenty of roots and herbs in their kitchen gardens. Excellent hemp and flax grow on their plains; and by the report of Europeans, who have lived there for some time, the country abounds with all that can add to the pleasures of life; for their great people find means to evade the sobriety prescribed by the Mahometan Law, and make free with excellent wines, and spirits of their own growth and manufacture. Algiers produces salt-petre and great quantities of excellent salt: and lead and iron have been found in several places in Barbary. Neither the Elephant nor the Rhinoceros are to be found in the states of Barbary; but their deserts abound with lions, tigers, leopards, hyenas and monstrous serpents. The Barbary horses were formerly very valuable, and thought equal to the Arabian, though their breed is said now to be decayed, yet some very fine ones are occasionally imported into England. Camels, dromedaries, asses, mules, and also kum-rahs, a most serviceable creature, begot by an ass upon a cow, are their beasts of burden. Their cows are but small and barren of milk, their sheep yield indifferent fleeces, but are generally as large as their goats. Bears, porcupines, foxes, apes, hares, rabbits, ferrets, weasels, moles, chameleons, and all kinds of reptiles are found here, besides vermin" (says Dr. Shaw, speaking of his travels through Barbary[2]). "The apprehension we are under, in some parts at least of this country, of being bitten or stung by the scorpion, the viper, or the venomous spider, rarely fail to interrupt our repose, a refreshment so grateful and really necessary to the weary traveller. Partridges, quails, eagles, hawks, and all kinds of wild fowls are found on this coast, And of the smaller birds, the capsa-sparrow is remarkable for its beauty and the sweetness of its notes, which is thought to exceed that of any bird; but it cannot live out of its own climate. The seas and bays of Barbary abound with the finest and most delicious fish of every kind, and were preferred by the ancients to those of Europe."

2. Thomas Shaw (1694–1751), *Travels; Or, Observations Relating to Several Parts of Barbary and Levant.* Oxford: The Theatre, 1738. Prentiss's "quotation" is either a collage of paraphrases and quotations from Shaw or a passage from an edition of Shaw that I have not yet located. Shaw's 1738 *Travels* contains the phrase "the Apprehensions we are under, of being bit or stung by the Scorpion, Viper, or Venemous-Spider, rarely fails, in some Parts of these Countries, to interrupt the Rest, that is so grateful and necessary to a weary Traveller" (v), but his description of Barbary's fish is less rosy than Prentiss's version: "Neither is there any great Variety or Plenty of Shell Fish [or other fish] upon the Barbary Coast" (260).

Here it may not be improper to digress so far from the narrative as to give a short sketch of the history of these states, although the kingdom of Bow-woo does not partake much of the general history of them, as it is placed so far in the interior, and bordering upon the negroland, which lies south of this kingdom, therefore it is altogether probable that this part of Africa was never much effected by foreign wars or European conquests, yet as they are now subjects of the empire of Morocco and must be included among the Barbary states, I think it may be useful to insert the following sketch of the general history of those states, which is quoted from Guthrie's "Geographical, Historical and Commercial Grammar."[3] There perhaps is no problem in history so unaccountable as the decadence of the splendor, power and glory of the states of Barbary, which, when Rome was mistress of the world, "formed the fairest jewel in the imperial diadem. It was not until the seventh century that, after these states had been by turns in possession of the Vandals and Greek emperors, the caliphs or Saracens of Bagdad conquered them, and from thence became masters of almost all Spain, from whence their posterity was totally driven, about the year 1492, when the exiles settled among their friends and countrymen on the Barbary coast. This naturally begot a perpetual war between them and the Spaniards, who pressed them so hard, that they called to their assistance the two famous brothers, Barbarossa, who were admirals of the Turkish fleet, and who, after breaking the Spanish yoke, imposed upon the inhabitants, of all those states, excepting Morocco, their own laws. Some attempts were made by the emperor Charles V, to redeem Algiers and Tunis, but were unsuccessful; and as observed, the inhabitants have in fact shaken off the Turkish yoke likewise.

"The emperors or kings of Morocco are the successors of those sovereigns of that country who are called sheriffs, and whose power resembled that of the caliphate of the Saracens. They have been, in general, a set of bloody tyrants; though they have had among them some able princes, particularly Muley Moluc, who defeated and killed Don Sebastian, king of Portugal. They have lived in almost a continual state of warfare with the kings of Spain and other Christian princes ever since: nor does the crown of Great Britain sometimes disdain, as in the year 1769, to purchase their friendship with presents."[4]

3. William Guthrie (1708–1770), *A New Geographical, Historical, and Commercial Grammar: and Present State of the Several Kingdoms of the World.* 1st American ed. improved. Philadelphia: Johnson & Warner, 1809.
4. The quotation is from Guthrie 205.

In giving an account of the timber peculiar to this kingdom, we shall mention the name both in the English and Bow-woo languages, that the reader (if a scientific person) may form a correct idea of the key, or principle, of their tongue; and in tracing some words back to their origin (Hebrew), from which the narrator considers their language derived, will find him correct; as in their religious belief they have a tradition which has been handed down from time almost immemorial, that all the Ethiopian nations, in short that all Africans descended from Jethro, the priest of Midean.—But more of this hereafter.

The word *tree* in the Bow-woo language is called *Chua* or *Chuah*. Among the names of the trees in his native language, are the *autong,* or what in English is called red-wood tree; the *yahoo,* or wool tree,[5] which tree is productive of wool, but not exactly in imitation either of cotton-wool or that produced from any kind or breed of sheep known to the narrator. Its qualities, however, are such that it is capable of being manufactured into cloth, and in that country is very useful, and much used in making a kind of cushion for seats and mattresses, or beds for lodging; also for filling or stuffing the sides and bottoms of their sedan chairs, for the use of the nobility. *Naughn chua,* or palm tree, which produces most excellent wine, something as our maple in this country produces sugar or molasses, but with much less labor, as the process is almost as simple, and not much unlike tapping the maple and procuring the sap. The sap or juice of the Palm, when first drawn resembles milk and water, but soon changes its color. Being put into vessels prepared for the purpose, it ferments, and in a few days becomes a most delicious wine. This tree also produces a nut, or fruit, which being pounded, or broken and pressed, makes an oil, which is used as food or rather as sauce to many kinds of food frequently eaten by the natives, and is often exported to Morocco. Their Divines consider it to possess also a kind of sacred quality, and make use of it to anoint their feet, and the feet of all those whom they consecrate to holiness. The *Mahroo-chua,* or cabbage tree, which produces clusters of leaves, that form heads, which in size, shape, taste and color, are almost exactly like our savoy cabbages. The *See-chua,* or Orange tree, grows in abundance in this country. Their variety and quality of oranges exceed those of any other part of the world. *Grossang-chua,* or lemon tree, is found in every part of the kingdom in

5. Possibly the *Bombax buonoponzense* or "Gold Coast bombax," a tropical deciduous tree sometimes referred to as a "silk-cotton-tree" because its fruits contain silky fibers (Graf 977).

great abundance; the produce of which is much superior to any the narrator has seen in any part of the West-Indies. *Ossang-chua,* or Lime tree, is the natural production of the kingdom of Bow-woo, as also of the adjacent country. There is also a tree peculiar to that country, called in their language the *Ahbue-chua,* or Bread tree. This tree resembles the pear tree of this country, and produces a fruit, which, when ripe, resembles a baker's loaf of wheat bread, in color, taste, size, and almost in shape, which would rather compare with a pear or red pepper pod. This fruit in the season of it, is gathered by the poor class of people, dried and stored in their houses, like our corn, until the next harvest.[6] *Augoh chua*—no English name known for this tree, as there is no tree in this country which bears it any resemblance, save only the chestnut. It bears a fruit, or rather a nut, about the size of a common hen's egg, and resembles the chestnut in taste and quality, but it is not encompassed within a burr, and is much larger than the chestnut, burr and all. *Sigua-chua,* or pomegranate tree, is a natural production of this clime, and is produced in abundance in this kingdom. *Douah-chua,* or mandrake tree, is peculiar to this part of the world; the fruit resembles a peach, only when ripe it is as blue as what we call blue berry, and is most exquisitely sweet. The mandrake is considered as a royal fruit, and is frequently carried to Morocco to grace their emperor's royal table; and such is the superstition of the natives that they believe it to be a divine, or sacred fruit, and emblematical of the fruit of good works in that promised land "from whose bourne, no traveller returns."

Never chua, or muskmelon tree, which bears a fruit resembling a large ripe muskmelon in color, shape and size, also in taste, only that it is much sweeter. This fruit is so plenty in the season of it that not one hundredth part of it can be used, and is suffered to fall and rot upon the ground. The tree resembles the white-wood tree of this country, and grows upon moist land, or near the edge of running water; there is also a kind of stalk grows out of the ground, which is about as big at the bottom as a man's leg and grows from four to six feet high, that bears a fruit called *wheih-whah,* or pine-apple. This is thought by some to be a delicious fruit, and a similar kind grows in the West Indies and is frequently plenty in our seaport towns. There is also a tree, or bush, resembling the black alder of Amer-

6. Possibly a mulberry or Moraceae, a family of deciduous trees mostly of pantropical distribution. The breadfruit tree (*Artrocarpous utilis*) is a staple food plant in the West Indies and other tropical regions.

ica, which bears a plum, red as scarlet, about the size of a hen's egg, which is exceedingly palatable, and is said to possess all the qualities of meat, bread, and water, which is frequently a sumptuous repast for the forlorn and wearied traveller.[7]—The name in the language of this kingdom is *Zeahhigh.*

This country, as may well be supposed, produces abundance of grapes; to mention all of them would swell the description of natural productions into a volume. My object and limits will necessarily prescribe me on this, as it does on many points, which might be interesting to the botanic reader. Therefore, I will mention only two kinds, which are most extraordinary and bear no resemblance to the grapes of any of the European countries or those produced in any part of the United States of America.

The most curious kind of wine grape peculiar to this country is the *Whahah,* or blue grape, which grows on vines in the meadows or on the banks of slow meandering rivulets, and do not hang in clusters like the English summer or winter grapes, but hang singly, more in imitation of the plums natural to the wilds of Vermont and many parts of the state of New York; and they are of the size of a common apple, or about two inches in diameter, of a deep blue color, deliciously sweet; the juice is produced in abundance and when first pressed is exquisitely sweet; but after being kept a few days as naturally might be expected ferments, and has a tartness which gives it a pleasant flavor, especially when required by thirst. The operation upon the faculties of men is more like that of the real Turkish opium than any other antidote produced from nature in the eastern or southern quarters of the globe, yet discovered (according to the description we receive of it) or explained by any chemist, ancient or modern. The other kind of grape, which we have promised to mention and which excites our peculiar attention, is called *Otua* and is a deep crimson or red grape,

7. NOTE—Mr. Demberger, in his travels in the interior of Africa, makes mention of a kind of fruit he met with at the foot of a mountain, about 250 miles from the river Niger, which gave him a delicious meal, as he was almost famished for want of food, having traveled upon the mountains for many days, finding little or no refreshment, which he describes as being red as scarlet and about the size of a peach. The writer considers this the same mentioned here. [Prentiss]

In his fabricated and fantastical *Travels through the Interior of Africa* (London and Boston, 1801), the pseudonymous Christian Frederick Damberger describes an evening at the foot of a mountain in "a beautiful wood, where I found all sorts of fruit, particularly the bijong, with which I satisfied my hunger and quenched my thirst." He asserts that the "bijong" has "a red color, sweet taste, and is the size of a hen's egg" (384).

the qualities of which are not so well known to the narrator but its peculiar shape and size excite attention and are so interesting to those who have formed the idea that the very name of grape, in the English language, conveys an idea of a round fruit, produced from a vine, hanging in clusters. The shape of this grape resembles a man's finger; it hangs upon the vine, more like the pods of pole beans, than any thing we can conceive; its color resembles blood, its taste the cranberry, and is frequently preserved, and conveyed to the emperor, to add one more foreign dainty to his imperial, diabolical, and tyrannical luxury. There is also a tree in that country that in leaf, body, shape and size resembles the butternut of this country; its fruit bears some resemblance to the butternut, only its color changes three times; first it is green, next yellow, then when ripe, crimson, and when it begins to decay it becomes a chocolate color, and what is peculiar, there never appears to be any material alteration in the taste or smell.

Thus we end an account of the natural or spontaneous growth of this country. We have only mentioned a few which are in the fresh recollection of the narrator, and those most extraordinary to American people.

The common productions of art, or the cultivation of the soil, are, first, *Morea,* or rice, which is similar to that produced in the southern states of United America, and sold in all parts of our common country.[8] *Pieree,* or corn, which is raised in abundance, almost without the hand of the agriculturalist; as the land is almost completely prepared by nature, and the simple sowing, or planting and gathering, is the chief labour to procure an abundant crop. It more resembles the Virginia, than what we call Indian corn. The *Brofea,* or barley, is also easily raised, without much labor or attention, and resembles the English barley, which is cultivated some in America, but more in Europe, especially in England. *Dra,* or Beans, are also raised plentifully. *Poah,* or pease, are cultivated with ease, and are productive of large crops by being cultivated in the manner they are in America. *Cannau,* or potatoes, are raised but no other kind than what are called sweet potatoes, which are produced only in our southern climes.[9] *Gambreau,* or parsnips, are frequently raised or cultivated rather as an ornament to their gardens, than as a necessary vegetable. *Threa,* or onions,

8. Historian Richard L. Roberts confirms that in the eighteenth century: "Despite the importance of trade, the economy of the Niger valley remained essentially agrarian. From the standpoint of both the gross domestic product and the deep structures of everyday life, cereal production was probably the region's most important economic activity" (25).

9. I.e., yams: starchy vegetables that are botanically distinct from but similar to sweet potatoes. Yams have long been a staple of the West African diet.

are a sauce which is cultivated with great attention and considered among the natives as a signal bounty of their great father the sun.[10] Coffee grows almost spontaneously, but is considered as an object of cultivation, and is called, in the Bow-woo language, *Leuee.*[11]

In mentioning the animals peculiar to this kingdom, we will refer the reader to the natural history of Africa, as it falls not within our limits or design to give a particular description of them, and those peculiar to that quarter of the globe will apply with little, or no variation, to this kingdom. Therefore, we will only give the names in both languages, of such as the narrator can recollect. *Zenamah,* or lion; *Wallah,* or leopard; *Sopeah,* or horse; *Oblea,* or cow, *Douo,* or cattle; *Bleah,* or sheep. There are two kinds of goats to be met here; the one, the large kind, which is called *bowh,* the small goat is called *Auvaun.* It produces milk, although the cow does not; neither do the sheep produce wool. The animal in this country, which is commonly called Orang-Outang, is known by the name of *Yeahoo.* Monkeys are extremely plenty in every part of this dominion, and are called *Auzee.* They are a very imitative animal, but more peculiarly so, in this part of the world, than in any other, as those children of nature give them lessons of imitation, more striking, as more natural, than do the Europeans, where art has almost defaced the beauties, which once adorned a primitive world. The *Auyeury,* or what we call baboons, are met with in abundance in the interior of the country. The camel is called in the Bow-woo Language *Auwolah* and is very useful to the natives, particularly in their wars and journeys to Morocco. The unicorn is a noble animal and a native of that part of the world. They are dangerous in case of resentment and are called by the name of *Beauch.*[12] Among the mountains they frequently find panthers but their name in his native language, the narrator has forgotten. There are several kinds of squirrels in this country, but much smaller in size than the grey or black squirrel of America; none being larger than the red squirrel of Vermont, and are called in their language *esujah.*

10. The Dogon of Mali view Africans as "creatures of light emanating from the fullness of the sun." However, they view the sun as female—the mother, not the father (Griaule 17, 105). Equiano also represents his Ibo people as sun-worshipers: "As to religion, the natives believe that there is one Creator of all things, and that he lives in the sun" (40).

11. The African kola tree (from the Mandingo word "kolo") was cultivated for its bitter, caffeine-containing nuts, which were used to make beverages.

12. Possibly a reference to the northern white rhinoceros, a subspecies of *Ceratotherium simum,* native to West Africa. Unpredictable and dangerous, it charges with great force when irritated. Among land mammals, it is second only to the elephant in size, and its front horn is sometimes more than eighteen inches long.

There are several kinds of amphibious quadrupeds in this country. An animal resembling the North American beaver in shape and size, is frequently met in the low lands and upon the banks of rivers. The Africans call it, *Zoo-row,* it is of a blue color, they make but little account of it, as the fur is indifferent, and the flesh is not used by the natives, but it provides for itself with as much sagacity as the beaver of this country; it fells trees and builds shelters partly above and partly in the water, so as to be capable of shunning an attack, either from sea or land. Thus fortified, he defies the king of the forest, or aquatic foe, unless they, contrary to nature, should enter into a coalition. The *Vro roo* is an amphibious animal, resembling the muskrat, only its adroitness is unequaled by any other animal known in that country. It is said to plunge into the water, on one side of a stream that is ten rods in width, and in ten seconds appears upon the opposite side and seems rather to dart than run, until it is out of reach of the foe. The Vro-roo is a very inoffensive animal and appears to fear every creature that approaches it. There are many frogs, toads, crocodiles, serpents and vipers. The alligators are said to resemble those of South America and are sometimes the destroyers of children. The turtles or terrapins are exceedingly plenty; many are of a monstrous size and are called *Slough-Lough;* they are taken for the purpose of making use of their shells, which are frequently used as boats, or scows, in their small streams.

Fowls are numerous—however my limits will not permit me to mention but few. There is the *Autorouk,* or wild turkey, very numerous and useful. The *Gay,* or Partridge, bears a great likeness to the partridges among us. The *Whetece,* or goose, more resembles the wild goose than our domestic or English goose. The *Proseau,* or hawks, are of various kinds and sizes. The *Soo,* or hen, resembles the guinea-hen frequently seen in America and is undoubtedly of the same species. There are also *Fleuhie,* or eagles, of a monstrous size, that are dangerous to children in many parts of the kingdom. They, however, build their nests upon the mountains among the rocks and seldom, unless driven by hunger or in pursuit of food for their young, descend upon the low lands, where it is thick settled. They have been taken when young and kept as a curiosity, and at two years old weighed 160 pounds. Their backs are a dark blue or black, with white talons and breasts.

It may be said no country abounds with a greater variety of birds, of various kinds, which it is impossible to give a general description of. The aquatic animals, or fishes, peculiar to this country are not very numerous, as none are presumed to inhabit this interior country, only such as came up the river Niger. The name of fish is called *Threa.*—I shall mention only two kinds; the one prized very high by the natives resembles the sturgeons frequently taken in our rivers; they are frequently taken and offered up as sacrifices for the sins of the people.

Also, they always have a dish cooked at the feast of the Passover, which will be mentioned hereafter. There is an excellent fish, which the narrator has forgotten the African name of, yet the English of it signifies gold fish, it is about the size of our salmon, and is covered with scales that are transparent, and the same color of pure gold—they are taken in abundance and sold in the capital by the poorer class of people, many of whom follow fishing for a subsistence.

Here we close our account of the various natural productions of this kingdom; many by design have been omitted, as an account of them might not be amusing to but few readers, and many have been unavoidably left out, as the narrator could not recollect their names in his original tongue or native language. Extraordinary as some facts may appear there can be no doubt of their authenticity, and when we consider that both ancient and modern authors have agreed that, by nature, Africa abounds with more spontaneous luxuries than any other quarter of the globe; which tends to make man indolent and barbarous. Yet the peculiar characteristic of this nation is peace, humanity and courtesy to strangers.

There is a custom that is strictly adhered to in all parts of the kingdom, that is, if a stranger comes among them, of whatever nation or description, and makes inquiry for any person, the person enquired of is obliged to wash and anoint the stranger's feet, give him refreshment, if required, and either go with him to the person, if known to the native, or give him the best directions in his power, and on refusing or neglecting to do the same, on complaint and conviction, the offender must be publicly whipped twenty-five stripes.[13] However absurd or ridiculous this custom may appear to a civilized people, certain it is fraught with courtesy and benevolence; and if we could find the same spirit prevalent among a christian people, what a good thing it would be in the estimation of the stranger who should receive the benefit, and he could exclaim with the Psalmist.

13. Walter E. A. van Beek offers a similar description of Dogon village life: "Hospitality and openness are essential values: each Dogon, it is felt, should be accessible at all times for anyone. . . . [T]he Dogon consider strangers as guests" (14).

Psalm CXXXIII.

The benefit of the communion of Saints.

A song of degrees of David.

1. Behold, how good and how pleasant it is for brethren to dwell together in unity.

2. It is like the precious ointment upon the head, that ran down upon the beard, even Aaron's beard; that went down to the skirts of his garments;

3. As the dew of Hermon, and as the dew that descended upon the mountains of Zion, for there the Lord commanded the blessing, even life forevermore.

Psalm CXXVIII.

The sundry blessings which follow them that fear God.

A song of degrees.

1. Blessed is every one that feareth the Lord; that walketh in his ways.

2. For thou shalt eat the labor of thine hands: happy shalt thou be, and it shall be well with thee.

3. Thy wife shall be as a fruitful vine by the sides of thine house: thy children like olive-plants round about thy table.

4. Behold, that thus shall the man be blessed that feareth the Lord.

5. The Lord shall bless thee out of Zion: and thou shalt see the good of Jerusalem all the days of thy life.

6. Yea, thou shalt see thy children's children, and peace upon Israel.

The narrator feels the full force of the application of the following psalm to himself, and hopes all those who are advocates of a difference in human nature, or for slavery, will read.

Psalm 129.

1. Many a time have they afflicted me from my youth, may Israel now say,

2 Many a time have they afflicted me from my youth; yet they have not prevailed against me.

3. The plowers plowed upon my back: they made long their furrows.

4. The Lord is righteous: he hath cut asunder the cords of the wicked.

5. Let them all be confounded and turned back that hate Zion.

6. Let them be as the grass upon the housetops, which withereth afore it groweth up:

7. Wherewith the mower filleth not his hand, nor he that bindeth sheaves his bosom.

8. Neither do they which go by say, The blessing of the Lord be upon you: we bless you in the name of the Lord.

Chapter 3

Whryn Brinch Capt. of the King's Life-guards attends the King on a tour to visit the Emperor at Morocco—his account of a ship and white people—some account of the feast of the Sun—imitation of Josiah's dedication of the temple—arguments in favor of the equality of human nature—scripture—conclusion of the feast—our hero's departure from his friends and home—his swimming in the Niger—manner he was taken—how confined in the boat.

In the year 1758 Whryn Brinch was summoned to attend the King on a tour to the city of Morocco to visit the Emperor, as was the custom to be performed or a duty imposed upon them each year, this being the first year that Whryn Brinch commanded the King's life guards on a tour to the western or Atlantic ocean; of course had little or no knowledge of such a being as a white man; and had as imperfect an idea of a ship or vessel as he would have of any thing that was in existence.

In this tour the Father of the narrator purchased a pair of pistols and piece of purple silk, and on his return, while enjoying the pleasure of the society of his growing family, all rejoicing at his return from so long and arduous a journey, and their curiosity not a little excited by the articles of European and India manufacture which he had presented them with. While my Father and Mother had some gentle dispute about the quality of the silk (for here the writer takes the language of the narrator) I was busy snapping and observing the beauties of the pistol. As soon as an opportunity offered I asked my father where the pistols came from, and where he had obtained them, he said, they came from the white people, who lived on the waters and came to our shores and landed at Morocco, where he purchased them. White people! said I, what kind of beings are they? How do they get to Morocco, from the great waters? Why, said my father, they have every appearance of men, like our people only they are as pale as the moon and are covered with clothes from head to foot, with large platforms upon their heads; and they float along on high shells like the Slough Barrow,[1] only one shell contains hundreds of them, and it has wings like the Ethelry.[2]

Much more was said, but my attention was so taken up with the pistols that I have forgotten the remainder. The conversation soon turned upon the feast dedicated to the sun (which is performed something in imitation of the feast of the Passover we read of) which was fast approaching and is always celebrated at this season of the year. And here I will observe the king always performs his journey to the Emperor's castle during the rainy season, as in any other season of the year, it is dangerous to pass the great deserts of sand which lie between Deau-Yah and Morocco; and the feast commences immediately on the king's return. While domestic joy gladdened the heart of each individual of our artless and innocent family, and the public mind of the whole nation was occupied with preparations, and the anticipated felicity which would gladden the hearts of every individual of the community; little did I think of my approaching fate. No favorite genius whispered to me impending destruction or years of ignominious slavery; little did I foresee that when I should be raised to the zenith of all earthly enjoyment, that in a moment I should become a slave.

The feast approached, and the preparations were complete on the part of my father, who was to be mounted upon an elegant African horse, clothed in a beautiful scarlet net, which he had procured at Morocco, he to be clothed in a purple silk dress, according to the style of the moors, with his pistols hanging by his sides, fastened to a leather girdle of scarlet; with a cap laced with gold, with two globes of solid gold on each side, large enough to fasten in twelve plumes, by way of ornament. Thus prepared, in the morning my father assembled his whole family, before the rising of the sun, to invoke his blessing. After the usual ceremonies of invocation, homage and adoration, the whole family sat down to breakfast, a frugal repast of milk and fruit, with hearts alive to filial and fraternal affection. Reciprocal pleasure crowned the board with the purest domestic delight.

The king's trumpet sounded; the escort appeared; my father mounted

1. Slough Borrow, is in the English language, Turtle or Terrapin. [Prentiss].

2. Ethelry, Needle or Spindle, have wings and hover or light upon the water at pleasure. [Prentiss].

his steed and was away, to obey the commands of the king and enjoy the pleasure of the feast—which is performed in the following manner.—At sunrise the king and his nobles assemble upon a large plain. The king, queen, and some of the noble ladies of honor are with the high priests ushered into the centre, while the remaining nobility and gentry form a large circle with the king's life guard, between him and the rising sun; then a circle of light-horse is formed, next the armies of the nation, which is completed with the indiscriminate multitude of every sex and age. As soon as bright Sol makes his appearance in the east, the trumpets are sounded from one end of the plain to the other. A solemn dirge is chanted, in the style of a requiem of an old catholic Abby, by the females of honor, together with the priestesses, who hold a conspicuous rank among the nobility. There are certain ceremonies performed in the mean time, by the royal and divine personages, such as offering up sacrifices according to the custom of the jews. Lambs, kids, gold-fishes, mandrakes and scarlet grapes are offered up as sacrifices to their God, the Sun, whom they worship as devoutly as Christians worship the trinity. After this solemn devotion ends, the king, with his life-guards in front, forms a procession; the oldest and highest in rank of his nobility form in next to him, with the divines in front of them, who always hold a conspicuous rank among the favorites of the government, on account of their divinity. Next, the young men of noble birth and titles form. When the armies of the nations are formed in a manner peculiar to this tribe or kingdom, the light dragoons form in front of the armed forces; then the infantry, or footmen, are formed in ranks according to their grades in the field. To close the procession, the multitude of every sex and age are formed on, according to their seniority. The whole procession is abundantly supplied with the best of instrumental music, such as trumpets, drums, fifes, flutes, tambourines, violins and many other instruments peculiar to the country, the African names of which I have forgotten. They march, as formed, in circles, in imitation of the sun, who, in their opinion, passes around them to examine their actions, during which ceremony they play, sing, dance and shout from one end of the procession to the other,[3] which induces me to believe that this people descended from the children of Israel, as when Josiah

3. In the mid-twentieth century a Dogon elder in Mali described a similar liturgical ritual in which "the whole complex of dancers, orchestra, and the place where they dance constitutes a picture of the smithy beating out the rhythm of the movement of the universe" (Griaule 189). The orchestra beats drums and blows bellows. After becoming inflamed with

kept the feast of the Passover, for the dedication of the temple, he caused the chief priests and disciples or principals to form in circles around him, and the multitude formed a large circle around the temple, which in this manner with certain ceremonies was dedicated to the God of Israel.

And having received, through the blessings of divine providence, a partial English education, alto' a poor *African Slave,* who are shunned and despised by a paler race of christian people; I have presumed to read, understand, believe and expound the scriptures, as the oracles of divine inspiration.

We read in sacred writ that Adam was the first man and Eve the first woman, created by God in his own likeness, perfect, and placed in the garden of Eden, from whom descended all human beings, then where is the distinction? Being so placed, they were irresistibly drawn by the involuntary volition of their own wills to partake of the forbidden fruit, for it was God's will, and that was irresistible. They could have no foretaste, or desire, but their maker's, therefore it was involuntary; it was by the lure of the serpent and design of their creator; yet they being perfectly free it must be the volition of their own wills that they did thus partake of the forbidden fruit, which produced the knowledge of good and evil; corrupted the whole human race, and damned all mankind without any possible redemption, save only through the mercy of god himself. Adam, Eve, and their descendants, we have a regular history of, in the four first books of the holy bible, down to the Israelitish nation. Moses, the leader of the children of Israel and the inspired author of the sacred history here mentioned, it appears, married the daughter of Jethro, the priest of Median.

Now, altho I am a poor, despised black wretch, in the sight of man, permit me, kind reader, to offer some ideas of mine, and do not despise them because they come from an African negro, who are, by white men, considered an inferior race of beings. I, altho thus considered of an inferior race, do hope, and verily believe, that I have received that blessing promised to those who have faith in God, and continue to the end in ways of well doing. Therefore, I have occasion to reflect upon the scriptures, according to which I find that there were flags set up to prevent any soul from entering the garden of Eden, after Adam and Eve were driven out; and that

---

heat and overflowing with sweat (which represents "the ancestors' words overflowing"), "the masked dancers with their girdles of red fibres become fragments of the sun. Certain movements imitate those of the sun" (Griaule 188).

they had no children until after that time. And we, in the sacred description of the place, read that there was a river running out of the same, which had four heads. This I understand to be a figurative description of the world, or globe, which is inhabited by man. The first branch of this river is called Pison:

Genesis ii—10.—And a river went out of Eden to water the garden: and from thence it was parted, and became into four heads.

11. The name of the first is Pison: that is it which compasseth the whole land of Havilah, where there is gold.

12. And the gold of that land is good: there is bdellium[4] and the onyx stone.

13. and the name of the second is Gihon: the same is it that compasseth the whole land of Ethiopia.

14. And the name of the third river is Hiddekel: that is it which goeth toward the east of Assyrria. And the fourth river is Euphrates.

Now, as that part of the globe called Africa is productive of much gold, I am led to form this idea, that the river Pison is emblematical of that quarter which is figuratively set forth as the land of Havillah, and being ranked as first in scripture, where do we find a reason to believe the inhabitants are an inferior race of beings? Some of the divine advocates for slavery presume to say that the negroes descended from Cain, who was cursed, and had a mark put upon him; that all his descendants are natural born slaves. Was not the mark to prevent his being hurt, or at least killed; if so, what can our christian readers say to the conduct of slave owners, who whip, scourge and put to death the poor African negro, considering them as descendants of Cain. But pursue this point a little farther:

Genesis, iv—25—And Adam knew his wife again, and she bare a son and called his name Seth: For God, said she, hath appointed me another seed instead of Abel, whom Cain Slew.

26. And to Seth, to him also there was born a son, and he called his name Enos: then began men to call upon the name of the Lord.

From Seth we have a regular genealogy of the Patriarchs, down to Noah, who had three sons, Shem, Ham and Japheth, who took to themselves wives, and entered the ark with their father, and all the rest of the world were drowned in the flood, except Noah and his wife, his three sons

4. Bdellium: a gum resin obtained from various trees in Africa and the East Indies.

and their wives; then where are the descendants of Cain?——Gen. vii—
7—And Noah went in, and his sons, and his wife, and his sons' wives with
him, into the ark, because of the waters of the flood.

21. And all flesh died that moved upon the earth, both of fowl, and of
cattle, and of beast, and of every creeping thing that creepeth upon the earth, and
every man:
22. All in whose nostrils was the breath of life, of all that was in the dry land
died.

Now let the advocates for a distinction in qualities of human nature
ponder well upon the foundation of their arguments, if they believe the
scripture.—But to turn to the feast at Deau-Yah.——The next ceremony
was the feast or banquet which was prepared in a kind of festoon[5] upon
the side of the plain. Where nature had been in the least deficient in the
production of natural shade, art was made use of to supply that deficiency,
and a complete canopy of evergreen shaded all those who were seated at
the banquet. The repast is frugal and chiefly composed of the natural productions of the country with the aid of little or no art in the preparation;
dates, figs, plums, grapes, goat's milk, cream, gold-fish, palm wine and oil
are the chief dishes that compose the sumptuous feast. As soon as they rise
from their refreshment, which seldom detains them more than thirty minutes, the trumpets sound, and they repair, in the before mentioned order,
to the king's palace, where he is seated upon the throne in an open porch
of the palace, fronting the lawn; when all are seated he suffers a gay and
warlike tune to be sung and played by his subjects of all ranks; this is generally in praise of his emperor or of himself. When the music ceases, he
delivers, in person, a speech, during which time the most profound silence
is observed. At the close of which he calls in the aid of a few of his chief
councillors, and appoints all the officers, or governors of towns, counties
and districts; fills all vacancies as far as can be done until the setting of the
sun, at which time all business ceases, solemn music strikes up and lasts
for about five minutes, which closes by the sound of the trumpet, and firing of platoons, at which signal the exercises of the day cease, and all retire to enjoy, without ceremony, such enjoyment as is preferred. Thus the
feast continues from day to day, until all the officers of the government are
appointed and installed, or sworn into office, the pleasures varying from

5. Festoon: a decorative chain hanging between two points.

day to day. One day, combats are performed; next, feats of agility; on another, acts of strength &c. until the feast closes, which continues generally about seven days. There is a tradition which was handed down among us, that this custom was anciently introduced by a great high priest of a foreign land, whose name was Ziphia; and here I will observe that there are certain societies, as I was informed by my Grandmother, Whryn Dooden Wrogan, which had certain oral information communicable to each other on certain obligations being taken, which traced the origin of that people to the days of Noah, who, according to divine history, with his sons, Shem, Ham and Japheth, are the second original fathers of all human beings. Ziphia the high priest in our language, I understand to be Jethro, the priest of Midian, who went and lived in a foreign land, and who was father-in-law to Moses, and O! how my soul has regretted that I was too young to become a member of the before mentioned society, for there, I verily believed, I should learn the origin of all nations; the veil of superstition would be rent in twain. Man in his native elements would be held to view; their origin and descent would be portrayed; each kingdom and nation would be clearly seen and known, if real distinctions are; the proofs would be strong and convincing; if all mankind were naturally equal, we, however sable, if wise and virtuous, should be on a level with all mankind.[6] These things bring to my mind a chapter of sacred scripture which I often repeat, when memory brings me back to my native land; the visions of night cause me to read, while in the arms of Morpheus, the following scripture, which is verified by the ancient customs of my forefathers.

EXODUS, Chap. 18.

1. Jethro bringeth to Moses his wife and two sons: 7. Moses entertaineth him, 13. and accepteth his counsel.

1. When Jethro the priest of Midian, Moses' father-in-law, heard of all that God had done for Moses, and for Israel his people, and that the Lord had brought Israel out of Egypt;

2. Then Jethro, Moses' father-in-law, took Zipporah, Moses' wife, after he had sent her back,

6. By asserting that his people descended from Jethro, who was not only Moses's father-in-law but also his wise counselor, Brace claims a Biblical myth of origins to counter a central tenet of proslavery propaganda, the myth that Africans descended from Ham. Because Ham witnessed his father, Noah, lying naked in a drunken stupor, Noah cursed Ham and his son, Canaan, in Genesis 9.25: "Cursed *be* Canaan; a servant of servants shall he be unto his brethren."

3. And her two sons, of which the name of the one was Gershom; for he said, I have been an alien in a strange land;

4. And the name of the other was Eliezer; for the God of my father, said he, was mine help, and delivered me from the sword of Pharaoh:

5. And Jethro, Moses' father-in-law, came with his sons and his wife unto Moses into the wilderness, where he encamped at the mount of God:

6. And he said unto Moses, I, thy father-in-law Jethro am come unto thee, and thy wife, and her two sons with her.

7. And Moses went out to meet his father-in-law, and did obeisance, and kissed him; and they asked each other of their welfare: and they came into the tent.

8. And Moses told his father-in-law all that the Lord had done unto Pharaoh and to the Egyptians for Israel's sake, and all the travail that had come upon them by the way, and how the Lord delivered them.

9. And Jethro rejoiced for all the goodness which the Lord had done to Israel, whom he had delivered out of the hand of the Egyptians.

10. And Jethro said, Blessed be the Lord, who hath delivered you out of the hand of the Egyptians.[7]

11. Now I know that the Lord is greater than all gods: for in the thing wherein they dealt proudly, he was above them.

12. And Jethro, Moses' father-in-law, took a burnt offering and sacrifices for God: and Aaron came, and all the elders of Israel, to eat bread with Moses' father-in-law before God.

13. And it came to pass on the morrow that Moses sat to judge the people; and the people stood by Moses from the morning unto the evening.

14. And when Moses' father-in-law saw all that he did to the people, he said, What is this thing that thou doest to the people? Why sittest thou thyself alone, and all the people stand by thee from morning unto even?

15. And Moses said unto his father-in-law, Because the people come unto me to inquire of God:

16. When they have a matter, they come unto me, and I judge between one and another; and I do make them know the statutes of God, and his laws.

17. And Moses' father-in-law said unto him, The thing that thou doest is not good.

18. Thou wilt surely wear away, both thou and this people that is with thee: for this thing is too heavy for thee; thou art not able to perform it thyself alone.

19. Hearken now unto my voice, I will give thee counsel, and God shall be

---

7. The second half of the verse is deleted: "and out of the hand of Pharoah, who hath delivered the people from under the hand of the Egyptians."

with thee. Be thou for the people to Godward, that thou mayest bring the causes unto God:

20. And thou shalt teach them ordinances and laws, and shalt shew them the way wherein they must walk, and the work they must do.

21. Moreover thou shalt provide out of all the people, able men, such as fear God, men of truth, hating covetousness; and place such over them, to be rulers of thousands, and rulers of hundreds, rulers of fifties and rulers of tens.

22. And let them judge the people at all seasons: and it shall be, that every great matter they shall bring unto thee; but every small matter they shall judge; so shall it be easier for thyself, and they shall bear the burden with thee.

23. If thou shalt do this thing, and God command thee so, then thou shalt be able to endure, and all this people shall also go to their place in peace.

24. So Moses hearkened to the voice of his father-in-law, and did all that he had said.

25. And Moses chose able men out of all Israel, and made them heads over the people, rulers of thousands, rulers of hundreds, rulers of fifties and rulers of tens.

26. And they judged the people at all seasons: the hard causes they brought unto Moses, but every small matter they judged themselves.

27. And Moses let his father-in-law depart; and he went his way into his own land.

At the close of the feast the boys of the partakers thereof, as is the custom, were allowed to put on some conspicuous ornament of their fathers and go to such amusements as they thought most pleasing to their propensities, bathing in the Neboah or Niger, being considered a useful as well as pleasing amusement. On the close of the feast, myself with thirteen of my comrades, went down to the great Neboah to bathe. This was in the 16th year of my age; my father and mother delighted in my vivacity and agility; on this occasion, every exertion on their part seemed to be made use of, to gratify what they called their youthful boy. As it was almost a league and an half, everything was done for my outset, whether at the time I was convinced, or whether by infatuation I have convinced myself from events, that there was something portentous in my parting from my parents, I am unable to say. But it appears to me now that their whole souls were in ecstasy in thus gratifying their darling boy. All was hilarity, anxiety, and delight; my mother pressed me to her breast and warned me of the dangers of the waters, for she knew no other. My brothers and sisters all assisted to ornament me and give me advice, and wish me much delight. My father with the austerity of a Judge tenderly took me by the hand and said, "My son conduct yourself worthy of me, and here you shall wear my cap." He then put it upon my head, and said, "My dear Boyrereau, do not get drowned, but return before the setting of our great father the sun." My comrades were waiting at the porch of our front door, I flew to the door with a heart lighter than a feather. My brothers and sisters followed my father and mother, standing behind them to observe my departure and agility. O! God that my limbs had refused their office on that fatal day, or I had been laid a corpse on the clay of my native land, before I had been suffered to move from the threshold of my father's dwelling. O! the day that I passed the church for the last time, a whole family following with anxious looks my steps and motion, the well known sportive rivulet, I passed the arch of clay. I, before I descended the hill which shut me from the sight of home forever cast behind me one last and longing look to see if I could catch one pleasing glance of a fond mother; but alas! I could discover no trace of home, only the pleasing and conspicuous views of my native town. When I turned round, I found my companions before me. The anticipated sport caused my heart to leap with joy, I ran down the declivity of the hill, we reached the Neboah; about 10 o'clock in the morning, we went down upon a point or rather elbow of the river, just above the junction of the small river before mentioned with the Niger.

There was a small shade of grape vines under which there was a smooth flat of green grass. We quickly and hastily undressed ourselves and prepared for the consummation of our wishes; kings upon their thrones might envy our felicity, as we could anticipate no greater pleasure and knew no care. A perfect union prevailed; all had a noble emulation to excel in the delightful sport before us; we plunged into the stream, dove, swam, sported and played in the current; all striving to excel in feats of activity, until wearied with the sport, we returned to the shore, put on some of our clothing, began to think about returning to our homes, as fatigue and hunger invited.

When we ascended the bank, to our astonishment we discovered six or seven animals fastening a boat, and immediately made towards us. Consternation sat fixed upon every brow, and fear shook every frame; each member refused its office. However, home invited so urgently that nature began to do her duty, we flew to the wood with precipitation. But Lo! when we had passed the borders and entered the body thereof, to our utter astonishment and dismay, instead of pursuers we found ourselves waylaid by thirty or forty more of the same pale race of white *Vultures*, whom to pass was impossible, we attempted without deliberation to force their ranks. But alas! we were unsuccessful, eleven out of fourteen were made captives, bound instantly, and notwithstanding our unintelligible entreaties, cries & lamentations, were hurried to their boat, and within five minutes were on board, gagged, and carried down the stream like a sluice; fastened down in the boat with cramped jaws, added to a horrid stench occasioned by filth and stinking fish; while all were groaning, crying and praying, but poor creatures to no effect. I after a siege of the most agonizing pains describable, fell into a kind of torpid state of insensibility which continued for some hours. Towards evening I awoke only to horrid consternation, deep wrought misery and woe, which defies language to depict. I was pressed almost to death by the weight of bodies that lay upon me; night approached and for the first time in my life, I was accompanied with gloom and horror.

Thus in the 16th year of my age, I was borne away from native innocence, ease, and luxury, into captivity, by a christian people, who preach humility, charity, and benevolence. "Father! forgive them for they know not what they do."[8]

I remained in this situation about four days. The cords had cut the flesh, I was much bruised in many parts of my body, being most of the time gagged, and having no food only such as those brutes thought was necessary for my existence. Sometimes I courted death, but home would force upon me with all its delights and hope, that soother of all afflictions, taught me to bear with patience my present sufferings.

8. Quoting Christ's cry from the cross, Brace connects himself with Christ's suffering as well as his forgiveness.

Chapter 4

On the fourth day, about four o'clock in the afternoon, we arrived at the
ship and were carefully taken out of the boat and put on board; even this
momentary relief seemed to cheer my desponding spirits, and at least
eased the pains I endured, by relieving me of those galling cords with
which I was bound. I was suffered to walk upon the deck for a few minutes under a strong guard, which gave my blood an opportunity in some
degree to assume its usual circulation. But in a short time I was forced into
the hole, where I found my comrades, with about thirty more poor African
wretches whom the ship's crew had stolen from a neighboring tribe. These
poor creatures were screaming, crying and wringing their hands, with
prayers and ejaculations to the great Father for their deliverance. This
group was composed of men, women and children. Some little girls and
boys, not more than six or seven years of age were shut up in a pen or stye,
crying for food and water and their fathers and mothers. One little boy
about seven years of age told me he went in the evening to drive the goats
for his mother, and they ran after him and caught him, and his mother did
not know where he was, and he was afraid his little brothers and sisters
would starve, as he was the oldest child and there was no one to drive the

goats, as his father was taken away before, therefore there was no one to help her now.

The author has inserted the following lines, taken from a periodical publication of 1804, which he deems pathetic and apropos.

"Help! Oh, help! thou God of Christians!
Save a mother from despair!
Cruel white men steal my children!
God of Christians hear my prayer!

From my arms by force they're sever'd;
Sailors drag them to the sea;
Yonder ship at anchor riding,
Swift will carry them away.

There my son lies stripp'd and bleeding;
Fast with thongs his hands are bound;
See the tyrants how they scourge him;
See his sides a reeking wound!

See his little sister by him;
Quaking, trembling, how she lies!
Drops of blood her face besprinkle;
Tears of anguish fill her eyes.

Now they tear her brother from her,
Down below the deck he's thrown.
Stiff with beating, thro' fear silent,
Save a single death like groan.

Hear the little creature begging;
"Take me white men for your own!
Spare! Oh, spare my darling brother!
He's my mother's only son."

See, upon the shore she's raving,
Down she falls upon the sands:
Now she tears her flesh with madness,
Now she prays with lifted hands.

"I am young, and strong, and hardy,
He's a sick and feeble boy;
Take me, whip me, chain me, starve me,
All my life I'll toil with joy.

Christians, who's the God you worship,
Is he cruel, fierce or good?
Does he take delight in mercy?
Or in spilling human blood?

Ah my poor distracted mother!
Hear her scream upon the shore:"—
Down the savage captain struck her,
Lifeless on the vessel's floor.

Up his sails he quickly hoisted,
To the ocean bent his way;
Headlong plung'd the raving mother,
From a high rock in the sea.[1]

I for a moment forgot my distress and shed one tear for the boy. But sympathy assumed her dominion, and we all wept for one another and ourselves; the children crying for bread and water, and no white soul paid any attention.

Matthew VII——7.

7. Ask, and it shall be given you; seek and ye shall find; knock, and it shall be opened unto you:

8. For every one that asketh, receiveth; he that seeketh findeth; and to him that knocketh it shall be opened.

9. Or what man is there of you, whom, if his son ask bread, will he give him a stone?

10. Or if he ask a fish, will he give him a serpent?

11. If ye then, being evil, know how to give good gifts unto your children, how much more shall your Father which is in heaven give good things to them that ask him?

12. Therefore all things whatsoever ye would that men should do to you, do ye even so to them: for this is the law and the prophets.

1. This poem was published anonymously in the *Boston Weekly Magazine* 25.2 (14 April 1804), with this preface: "The distress which the inhabitants of Africa experience at the loss of their children, which are stolen from them—by persons employed in the barbarous traffic of human flesh, is, perhaps, more thoroughly felt than described. But, as it is a subject to which every person has not attended, the author of the following lines hopes that, possibly he may excite some attention, (while he obtains indulgence) to an attempt to represent the anguish of a mother, whose son and daughter were taken from her by a ship's crew, belonging to a country, where the God of Justice and Mercy is owned and worshipped."

Luke X——25.

25. And, behold, a certain lawyer stood up, and tempted him, saying, Master, what shall I do to inherit eternal life?

26. He said unto him, What is written in the law? how readest thou?

27. And he, answering, said, Thou shalt love the lord thy God with all thy heart, and with all thy soul, and with all thy strength, and with all thy mind; and thy neighbor as thyself.

28. And he said unto him, Thou hast answered right: this do, and thou shalt live.

29. But he, willing to justify himself, said unto Jesus, And who is my neighbour?

30. And Jesus answering, said, A certain man went down from Jerusalem to Jericho, and fell among thieves, which stripped him of his raiment, and wounded him, and departed, leaving him half dead.

31. And by chance there came down a certain priest that way; and when he saw him he passed by on the other side.

32. And likewise a Levite, when he was at the place, came and looked on him and passed by on the other side.

33. But a certain Samaritan, as he journeyed, came where he was: and when he saw him, he had compassion on him,

34. And went to him and bound up his wounds, pouring in oil and wine, and set him on his own beast, and brought him to an inn, and took care of him.

35. And on the morrow when he departed, he took out two pence, and gave them to the host, and said unto him, Take care of him; and whatsoever thou spendest more, when I come again I will repay thee.

36. Which now of these three, thinkest thou, was neighbor unto him that fell among the thieves?

37. And he said, He that shewed mercy on him. Then said Jesus unto him, Go, and do thou likewise.

As I walked round, I observed some men & women in the hatchway, in Irons; they were pleading for their deliverance, or that they rather than remain as they were, might receive instant death; what had been their offence I never learned. At sun down we were separated into small parties, and I was separated from my comrades, and bolts and bars for the first time in my life confined me to a small apartment, and language cannot describe more misery than I experienced that night. Solitude brought home to my tender, youthful mind, remembrance and reflection, two unwelcome messengers. But early next morning, all was bustle, noise and confusion; they weighed anchor, hoisted sail, and we sailed down the river; here to my sorrow I learned what the white men came to Morocco in,

which my father before had so imperfectly described to me, on his last return home. In a short time we came to anchor before a town called in my
language, Yellow Bonga, the English name of which place I could never
learn.

As before observed, the captain, super-cargo, and many of the English
gentlemen had been residents in this town for many months. During their
stay here they had ingratiated themselves with the natives, whose
credulity taught them to believe that they were as honest and innocent as
the natives were themselves. The ship lay before this place for some days
during which time there was much passing and repassing. One day a man
came on board, whom they paid particular reference to, who afterwards,
I learned, was the commander himself. He was about five feet two inches
in height, duck legged, high shoulders and hollow backed, his hair being
red as scarlet, cued down his back, to his hips, which were broad and
prominent, his nose aquiline, high cheek bones, with a face about the
color of what we call crimson grapes, but what is more familiar to our ideas
his complexion was that of a red beet. His nose eclipsed it. His eyes resembled a bowl of cream in a smoky house sprinkled with white ashes and
hemlock tan with a chin that defied them to examine his laced vest which
encompassed a huge paunch that would astonish a Bishop or host of a
London porter house. His mouth had destroyed about one third of his
face, and each wing was about attacking his ears, with ammunition within,
called teeth, that represented gourd seeds. His lips were about the thick-
ness of the blade of a case knife & appeared as if they had been at variance
for many years, for the barrier between them bid defiance to an union. His
hat resembled a triangle being cocked in the ancient mode, with three
sharp corners, brim laced with gold, and gold laced loops. Time had made
some impression upon its former beauty; but the ostentation of the wearer
made up all deficiencies; but the description is tedious, all things corresponded; yes, his mind agreed with his appearance, and his dress was emblematical of his feelings, which were bedaubed with iniquity and grown
very stale.

We had not remained many days in this situation before we learned by
the interpreter that the officers were courting some of the women and
were almost idolized by the natives, who were making public feasts for
their amusement and entertainment. At length it was announced that a
grand feast was to be held on board of the ship; apparent preparations
were made accordingly, and all the principal inhabitants of the Town were

to attend. This was considered as a civility due from that deluded people to the officers of the vessel, while the blackest perfidy rankled in the hearts of those traitorous villains, who conceived and executed the plot. A general invitation was accordingly given to all classes, without distinction. The day arrived, the boats of the ship were busily employed in bringing on board the visitors. The principal inhabitants of the Town came on board; in short, but few staid behind only the sick, lame, aged and children; they brought with them many valuable articles of plate, &c. When all were on board, the festivity commenced, but mark, the slaves were cautiously concealed in the cockpit, that vigilance might be kept asleep and suspicion lulled into security. When they had regaled themselves with food, brandy, spirits and wine were introduced and prepared in many ways to make it the more delicious. When they had drank freely, laudanum was secretly conveyed into their liquor. A general intoxication and sound sleep soon prevailed, and insensibility was the consequence. These dexterous dealers in iniquity seized upon the moment, fastened with implements already prepared each individual down upon their backs, with poles across their breasts and legs, with hands and feet drawn up by cords to certain loop holes therein. In this situation they were obliged to lie during a six months voyage, fed like hogs in the stye by their drivers. Their excrement however was taken out by women and sickly negroes, who were liberated from the situation before described, if they appeared to be that kind of valetudinarians who were incapable of relieving their fellow sufferers. But to return to the sufferers when the delirium was banished by the resumption of the operations of nature. A scene ensued that seemed to deny that there was a perfect supreme ruler and unerring governor of the universe. Behold three hundred men, women and children, who, twelve hours before, enjoyed the purest freedom that nature herself could bequeath to her natural offspring, who were untainted by vice, save only that corruption which those people had introduced among them.

During the foregoing scene, the ship's crew weighed anchor, leaving this hospitable village without regret almost desolated. In a few days we came to a city called in my language Guingana, where there was an English gentleman who had resided there many months trading with the natives, during which residence he had courted and married the princess, only daughter and heir. He understanding that an European vessel was going out, attempted to prevail upon his wife's father to consent that she might accompany him to his native country, but all entreaties were vain, until he interceded with the Judges whom he made believe that he would positively return with her in two years, and in the meantime give her an English education. The Judges interceded for him, and ultimately caused the prince to consent. On a solemn treaty being formed that he would take many ladies of honor to accompany her; with some young lads that were near allied to the throne; that he would give them all an European education, instruct them in all the arts of civilization in his power, and return in two years. For the true performance of this he pledged himself to the King and Judges in the most solemn manner.

Accordingly they all came on board the ship, accompanied with many of the nobility. The most solemn scene ensued that I ever beheld: offering up sacrifices, burning incense, washing and anointing their feet, and the consecrating their heir apparent of the throne to the God of the Ocean and to the protection of their great Father. The solemn dirge and the farewell sound of the trumpet added sublimity as well as solemnity to the scene.

At the close of this ceremony were introduced abundance of rich presents for the outset and expense of the voyage, such as gold-dust, ivory, corn, rice with many other very valuable articles, which loaded the ship as deep as she would swim. The bride was decorated in the style of an eastern princess, with gold bracelets, rings, beads, and in fact was completely decorated in gold from head to foot.

As soon as we had fairly got under way, and about bidding adieu to the African coast forever, the captain and many of the officers made choice of such of the young women as they chose to sleep with them in their Hammocks, whom they liberated from chains and introduced into their several apartments. After the officers had provided themselves with mistresses of color, they made arrangements for the keeping and feeding the slaves. We were fastened in rows, as before observed, so that we could set upon our rumps or lie upon our backs, as was most convenient, and as our exercises were not much, we, it was concluded, could do with little food; our allowance was put at two scanty meals per day, which consisted of about six ounces of boiled rice and Indian corn each meal, with the addition of about one gill of fresh water; while in this situation, the ship's crew had been butchering a goat, and threw some meat, which fell near me, but a boy caught too quick for me and swallowed it as soon as a hound would have done. I thought it was my right as it fell before me, and therefore clenched him, but one of my comrades interfered and admonishing us, said, it was extremely wrong for us to contend, as we had no parents or friends to take our parts, and could only bring disgrace upon ourselves. We desisted and mutually exchanged forgiveness.

Soon after this we were almost famished for want of water. We often begged salt water of the invalid who attended us. I would get it in my cap and cautiously drink it, which would run through us like salts. We were in such a situation that the officers liberated us, and Guy, the boy before mentioned, was so indecent as to drop some, from necessity upon the white man's deck. It was laid to another boy, who would not expose his friend, therefore he was saluted with only forty lashes, but poor Guy died a few days afterwards, and was thrown into the sea, which made food for sharks, as they continually followed us being well baited by the frequent deaths on board.

About this time the princess was delivered of a child, but the great disposer of all events was pleased to waft its infant soul to realms unknown to us. There was great mourning among the maids of honor; they cried aloud.

A boy, one of my comrade slaves by the name of Leo, forgetting his sufferings for a moment, was disposed to mirth; he observed, *"Cordier agong, cadwema arroho:"*—which in English is, Hark! there is a trumpeter among us.

In this situation upon the boisterous deep, where each gale wafted us to a returnless distance from our families and friends, almost famished with hunger and thirst, to add horror to the scene, the sailors who were not provided with mistresses, would force the women before the eyes of their husbands. A sailor one day forced the wife of a slave by the name of Blay, before his face. Blay, whose blood boiled with wrath and indignation, said to his comrades in chains, "Let us rise and take them and force them to conduct us back to our native country again; there is more of us than of them, and who is there among us, who had not rather die honorably, than live ignominious slaves?" The interpreter happened to overhear him, and gave information against him. Poor Blay was taken to the gunwale and received 80 lashes and was then put in chains with a double weight of iron. At this treatment well may we cry out with Ezekiel—"Behold their abomination in the sight of the Lord."

After a voyage of about five months, the vessel arrived at Barbadoes, in the West Indies, in the year of our Lord, one thousand seven hundred and fifty nine, or one thousand seven hundred and sixty, with the slaves who had not either died with disease, mourned themselves to death or starved. Many of the children actually died with hunger, pent up in the same ship where midnight and beastly intoxication bloated the miserable owner. The cries of the innocent African boy, destitute of the protection of a parent, if they reached the ears, could not penetrate the heart of a christian, so as to cause him to bestow a morsel of bread upon his infant captive, even enough to save his life.

The slaves, consisting of about three hundred in number, including women and children, were carefully taken out of the ship and put into a large prison, or rather house of subjection. In this house we were all, above twelve years of age, chained together, and sat in large circles round the room, and put to picking oakum.[2] A slave by the name of Syneyo, from the town of Yellow-Bonga, taken in the manner formerly described, and who was one of the Judges in that place, refused to work. He rose up and in his native language made the following speech to the captain, which was repeated to him by the interpreter:

Sir, we will sooner suffer death than submit to such abominable degradation. The brow of our great father, the sun, frowns with indignation on beholding the majesty of human nature abused, as we are, and rendered more brutal than the ravenous wild beasts, as ye are. Feel like mortal man, and what I say may prevent your spirit from being blotted out forever. You came to our country; you and your friends were treated with hospitality; we washed and anointed your feet; we gave you the best of our wines to drink, our most delicious food to eat; we entertained you with every amusement our country could afford. We prayed for you, burnt incense and offered up sacrifices for you; we gave you presents of gold, ivory, corn and rice, with many other valuable things; and what return did you make us? You invited us to see your ship, we were credulous, even vigilance was asleep; you traitorously gave us opiates, which caused us to sleep, you bound us captives and bore us away to this place; you and your myrmidons[3] ravished our wives and daughters, whipped us with many stripes, starved our children to death, and suffered others to die unnoticed. And now you hold us in bondage and oblige us to work unceasingly. Is this the reward of friendship, hospitality and protection? Are you a christian people? Then do unto us as we have done unto you; strip us of these chains, and conduct us back to our own shores. If christianity will not

2. Oakum is "loosely twisted hemp or jute fiber impregnated with tar or a tar derivative and used in caulking seams (as of wooden ships) and packing joints (as of pipes)" (Webster's *Ninth New Collegiate Dictionary*). Oakum could be obtained by untwisting and picking old rope.

3. Myrmidon: "a loyal follower, *esp:* a subordinate who executes orders unquestioningly or unscrupulously" (*Webster's Ninth New Collegiate Dictionary*).

move you to perform so just an act, look at those little fatherless children, whom you kidnapped from their parents;—hear their cries, behold their sufferings, think of the bewailing of their bereft parents, look across the great waters to that village where you were almost idolized—view the distresses your conduct has brought upon it, & if you have one spark of human sensibility, or even the least shade of humanity, if you are what you profess to be, a christian; repent and let us, whom you call heathens, return to our once happy shores, thereby, if you cannot obliterate, heal as much as possible the wounds you have made.

On the close of this speech, all was silent for a few minutes; but the captain in his turn made a speech more to the purpose. With a countenance that would terrify a crocodile and a voice like the braying of a jackass, he said:

Oh you impudent, rebellious, treasonable, cowardly, saucy, low, black slave, I will teach you discipline, obedience, and submission, and what is more, I will learn you your duty. You seem to speak as though you thought yourself equal to white people, you Ethiopian black brute, you shall have but twelve kernels of corn per day—your breakfast shall be fifty stripes—and if your work is not done, I leave you to the care of this my overseer, who will deal with you as you deserve.

This order was strictly complied with. From Monday until Wednesday following, no one received any other allowance, except water, which we were driven to, in drove, and obliged to lie down and drink.

From Wednesday until Saturday, we had each one ounce of biscuit in addition. All began to be subdued and to work according to their strength and abilities.

Chapter 5

A continuation of the narrative, with an account of Gow, a gentleman's daughter sent to this country for education, her being stripped and whipped to death in presence of her little brother Thry, who tried to wake her corpse—Progress of sales—Account of Mahoo and her brother—Scripture—Reflections—Account of the princess, daughter of the king of Guingana, her sufferings and death—Our subjugation—I am sold and sent away to one Welch—reflections in his stoop on death—My being whipped by him—Poem.

On Saturday morning, I sat next to a girl by the name of Gow, who was a gentleman's daughter sent from Guingana to this country for education. She was also accompanied by a little brother, about six years of age, who was under her protection. They both had been decorated in a style equal to their rank in their native country. Thry, her little brother, happened to be asleep, and we sat pensively working as fast as our enfeebled bodies and want of knowledge would permit.—All of us had been stripped of our ornaments; in fact, everything of value was taken from us, and instead of gold rings, bracelets of gold beads, chains and jewels, we had an old piece of sail cloth tied round our waists. She had been crying and sobbing all night. She said to me: "What do you think your father would say if he could see you in your present situation, stripped of his cap and all the ornaments he gave you to wear when you went a swimming in the Neboah; and now chained and obliged to work both day and night unceasingly, and be whipped by those awful creatures, if you do not do what is almost impossible to do."—On which nature gave way (perhaps moved by sympathy) I burst into a flood of tears. I being almost starved for want of necessary sustenance, even carrion[1] would have been delicious. My change of fortune stared me full in the face. I thought of home; I thought of a father's tenderness and a mother's love, a crowd of horrors burst upon me. We both cried aloud, until a feast of grief eased our swollen hearts; thus satiated we ceased to weep. Thry, her little brother, in the time awoke, and beginning to cry, he said to his sister, "Come Gow, do get me a piece of bread and some water, for I am almost starved and am so thirsty that I cannot live—Come Gow, why won't you get it for me; you used to get me everything I wanted." "O Thry," said she, "I hope you will not cry, come sit down as it is impossible for me to assist you; I could die with pleasure if you were with our parents again. I have nothing that I can give you to eat or drink, being almost starved myself, and here I am chained you see, and if I do not do more work than I am able to do, I must be whipped and I fear they will kill me."—They both burst into a flood of tears, which continued for some time. After their lamentation ceased, she spoke to me, saying, "I should not feel so bad if the white people had not taken from me the bracelet of gold, which was on my right arm, as my grandfather, when my grandmother died, took it from her arm and gave it to me (on account of my bearing her name) as a token of remembrance and affection, which was always expressed; and now I have nothing in this foreign land to remember her by. It makes me feel as if it would break my heart; but what is worse than all, I fear, if they don't kill me, they will take away my little brother; and if they don't starve him, he will mourn himself to death." At this instant the driver came in with a long whip under his arm and placed himself in the centre of the circle in which we were chained. He stood about four minutes, cast his eyes upon the slaves, a dead silence prevailed through the whole house except the re-echoing of sobs and sighs. He fixed his eye upon us, stepped up to the bunch of oakum which Gow had been picking, took it up in his hand with some vehemence, threw it down instantly, struck her upon the side of her head with the butt end of his whip, which laid her quivering upon the ground for one or two minutes. When she began to recover and to get upon her hands and feet, during which time he continued whipping her. Her little brother began to scream and cry, begging in his artless manner and unintelligible dialect for her relief. She at length regained her former situation, when he again turned the

1. Carrion: putrefying flesh from dead animals.

butt of his whip and struck her on the other temple, which leveled her with the ground; she seemed frantic and instantly rose upon her feet. The driver with a terrible grin and countenance that bespoke his brutality struck her with a drawing blow over the left shoulder, which came round under her right arm, near the pit of her stomach, and cut a hole through, out of which the blood gushed every breath. The wretch continued whipping until he had satiated his unprovoked vengeance, then he sat her up and handed her a rope to pick. He composedly walked round to see some of the rest of the slaves. She sat reeling backwards and forwards for about two or three minutes, the blood gushing from her wounds every breath, then fell down and expired. Thry, her little brother, went and laid his head upon her neck and said, "Come Gow, don't cry any more, come get up, don't go to sleep and leave me awake, because I am so lonesome I cannot bear it, do wake up; O! I wish my father and mother would come and give us some water, for I must choke to death with thirst, if I cannot get some." He cried over her corpse some time and then went to sleep upon the dead body of his sister and protector, who was thus whipped to death innocent as our mother Eve in her primitive state when first she was placed in the garden of Eden.

During this time the *humane christian* walked composedly up to me, and with a large tarred rope gave me about fifty stripes, which cut wails in every part of my body. At length I fainted, and when I recovered, this clement [2] christian white man had left this house of misery and its inhabitants to ruminate upon their situation and the prospect before them.

We remained in this mansion dedicated to the subjugation of our spirits for a few days, during which time many of my bosom friends were sold and sent away and I unable to learn their destiny. At length a most affecting scene ensued. Mahoo, a nobleman's daughter, who was also sent from Yellow Bonga to this country for education, accompanied by her brother two years younger by the name of Bangoo; they had pledged themselves never to part but by death, let whatsoever fate await them, they were to lose their lives for each other, rather than be separated. But alas! Bangoo was sold and called for by the *humane* christian purchaser, who had doubtless been devoted to the covenants of our Lord and Saviour, perhaps had crossed himself before the image of Christ, suspended upon

2. Clement: "Mild and humane in the exercise of power or authority; merciful, lenient, kindly, towards subjects of those in one's power" (Oxford English Dictionary).

the cross. These poor creatures clung together, and by signs the most impressive that the pure aborigines of Africa could make, entreated the owner to suffer them to remain with each other. But they forced him away, tied him to a cart and drove it off, dragging him after it. She clung to him until a ruffian ran up, and with the butt end of his whip, struck her such a blow that she fell motionless upon the ground. She lay senseless for sometime. As soon as she recovered, she was taken back to prison and here whipped forty lashes for her offence, or for the terror of others in like case offending. The poor creature was so maimed, that her life hung in doubt for three weeks. Thus were separated for ever these two African children, neither purchased or stolen from their native land, but entrusted with many rich presents of bars of solid gold and ivory, to an enlightened, scientific, christian people, who enjoy the light of divine revelation, and sent to this country, for the sole purpose of receiving a refined education.

Courteous reader, if you live in civilized society and enjoy the privileges of an enlightened people; under the immediate light of gospel inspiration; or if you are only a moralist, and believe that man can be virtuous without the restrictive influence of supernatural operation, ponder well upon these things. Proverbs, chap. 14, ver. 84.—Righteousness exalteth a nation; but sin is a reproach to any people.—We read again in sacred writ—Gen. chap. 9, ver. 6.—Who so sheddeth man's blood, by man shall his blood be shed, for in the image of God, made he man.—But what does the conduct of our advocates for slavery say to this doctrine, or divine decree.—"Not so, my Lord, you did not mean that the African negroes should be included in this, thy Law, because they bear a different complexion from us thy chosen people. You only meant your law should extend to us to whom the regions of the north have given a light complexion, and who have the knowledge of thy laws. The poor negroes although they may have descended from the patriarch Jethro, the priest of Midian, who was one of the elders of thy chosen people, shall be cast off from the benefits of thy law and promises of the gospel. Therefore we think the blood of this people will not be required at our hands. We can whip, scourge, torture and put them to death with impunity."

During our confinement in this prison the common sailors were allowed to come into the house and ravish the women in presence of all the assembly. Fathers and mothers were eye witnesses to their daughter's being despoiled. Husbands beheld their wives in the hands of the beastly destroyers. Children bore testimony of the brutality practised upon their mothers.—"Behold their abomination in the sight of the Lord." 2nd Ezekiel.

We formerly mentioned the princess, daughter of the King of Guingana, who had been married to an Englishman. He was a very rich planter and slave owner on this island. The reader will recollect her husband's engagements to her Father, the Judges' solicitations, their treaty, the whiteman's vows, the king's hospitality, his presents in gold, ivory, corn, wine and oil; the young nobility and maids of honor that came out with her— Then mark the sequel. She was taken to her husband's dwelling, stripped of her ornaments, which consisted of immense sums of gold, as also of her clothing. Her maids of honor were served in the same way, and all sent to the prison among the common slaves. She, on entering the house of subjection and beholding her doom before her, fell into a fit of delirium, which continued with little or no intermission for two days. When the vehemence of grief and despair subsided, she became by degrees more calm and sensible; she, not being chained, went out of the house, laid herself down upon the sand, and sang mournfully, in her native language, the following song.

1. Ye happy maids beyond the ocean's wave,
Who live secure from all these dread alarms,
Take heed from me, now dire affliction's slave,
Despise the beauties of the white man's charms.

2. Among my friends I play'd with every grace,
My hopes my prospects and my heart was free,
Amid this scene I view'd the white man's face,
He lur'd me trembling o'er the foaming sea.

3. With voice of Siren cloath'd with subtle guile,
He told the beauties of his native shore;
All these he said should court my placid smile,
All that my taste could wish or heart implore.

4. For him I left my home my mother's side,
For him I cross'd this boundless raging wave;
And now secur'd he spurns with haughty pride,
I'm lash'd and tortur'd, wretched, I'm a slave.

5. No friend endearing, wipes the falling tear,
No tender mother bends her pitying eye;
Far, far from home, no hopes my heart to cheer,
And none but monsters hear my dying sigh.

The driver whipped her back, tied her up and gave her eighty lashes, and set her picking oakum. Her tender fingers gave way and she could not sever the tarred cable. Her whipping had cut the flesh from her shoulder blades, so that the bone lay bare—her whole body was covered with wounds and wails of clotted blood. While in this situation her husband came in. As soon as her eye caught the image of her former adoration, and now author of her misery, she summoned all her strength and flew to his arms. But he, with a heart harder than the adamantine rock and colder than the mountains of ice in Greenland, calmly spurned her from him with brutal insensibility. She stood motionless for some minutes, with a countenance expressive of the keenness of her afflictions. One moment ten thousand lightenings darted from her eyes, the next instant the mildness of the morning sun portrayed the tender emotions of her heaving bosom. At length she said:—

Is it possible that the fair white man of the north, whose countenance is emblematical of the perfection of our great father the Sun, can thus spurn from his bosom an innocent princess of the kingdom of Guingana, who forsook the splendor of her Father's Castle for his sake, and who but a few months ago enjoyed all the blessings of paternal affections in the sunshine of native innocence and prosperity? But lo! You came to our dominions, your beautiful appearance caused my Father to invite you to our castle and suffer you to make it your home; the native splendor of our court was exhausted upon you; every attention that was productive of your happiness was paid to you by each member of the Court. I was ushered into your presence with all the splendor of African dignity! When you were weary, I strove to procure you rest, when thirsty, I gave you the best of our wines to drink; I washed and anointed your feet. When you were a-hungered I gave you the best of our fruits. When sick, I gave you medicine and consolation. I watched by day and night. You with every pretension of dignified love, with asseverations of the strongest, most pure and holy affection, solicited a union of our hands. At length you won my heart, and I consented to join our hands in the holy band of matrimony. Our Nuptials were celebrated, and we were both dedicated to the sun, according to the holy order of our religion.

Thus our matrimonial rites were consummated. I went into your arms with virgin purity and the most unparalleled love. When you wished to leave our dominions—my father refused to let me leave his Court, as I was his only child and heir to his Throne. But you interceded with the Judges and Councillors, who prevailed upon my father to make a treaty, the conditions of which you well knew. You swore before the alter of incense burning, to give my suit an English education, to instruct us in all the arts of civilization, and return with us in two years. O thou polluter of our holy institution! what have you done? Hear me and tremble. You have traitorously stolen me from my country and friends; you, with the subtlety of the demon of seduction, with perjury and deception in your mouth, have destroyed me. You have made a father and mother miserable. You have robbed me of all my precious jewels, and stripped me of my clothing, deprived me of liberty and even life itself, for I must soon die. See these wounds inflicted by your petty tyrants, see this tender flesh torn from my bones. Did you hate me? Why all that assiduity? Why not leave me with my father? Have you feelings? Look at this princely, tender, mangled frame, which you have so often embraced; see these wails inflicted by your order; upon whom? upon your wife, and mother of your deceased offspring, whose soul looks down from Heaven, and sees your perfidy and my sufferings, and beholds me fast approaching him.—O Christian, wretch, traitor; I have done, I must die.

She swooned away, came to, raved and tore her hair in frantic ejaculations, and then expired.[3] Luke, chap. 23, ver. 34—For if they do these things in a green tree, what shall be done in a dry.——James, iv—17—Therefore to him that knoweth to do good, and doeth it not, to him it is sin.—First Epistle of Peter, iv—18—And if the righteous scarcely be saved where shall the ungodly and sinner appear.

During all the foregoing scene, the planter stood apparently unmoved, but soon withdrew from the house, and I never saw him more. Thus we passed our time about two months, each day driven to water like beasts of the field, only we were chained together, and obliged to lie down in filthy brooks to drink, and the multitude would so roil the same that the excrements from their necessary houses would be sucked in as we drank. In the meantime my ankles got sore in consequence of the chains; in short they were so galled that the driver thought it prudent to take off my irons, as maggots were making considerable inroads upon the sinews. Many of

3. This story of betrayed love is reminiscent of Richard Ligon's 1657 tale of Inkle and Yarico, in which an American Indian woman named Yarico on the South American coast near Barbados rescues a young English man during a conflict between her people and the English in the mid-seventeenth century. She "upon first sight fell in love with him, and hid him close from her Country-men (the Indians) in a Cave, and there fed him, till they could safely go down to the shoar, where the ship lay at anchor" (Ligon 78). The English youth rewards his rescuer by selling her into slavery when they reach Barbados. Ligon asserts that Yarico was a slave in his house, although an earlier version of the story had been narrated in 1616 in Jean Mocquet's *Voyages* (Gallagher 190). In 1711 Richard Steele made Ligon's story famous by publishing an essay on it in *The Spectator*, No. 11 (March 13, 1711). Dozens of variations of the "Inkle and Yarico" story appeared in multiple languages and genres in the eighteenth century. In the later versions, Yarico was represented as a black slave.

my companions were set at liberty on the same account. We stole out to
beg for sustenance. The owners happened to be absent, and none but children were present. While a little girl was examining our appearance and
listening to our unintelligible dialect, one of the boys who was taken with
me went round into a back room, and got his cap full of stewed beans. He
called us and informed us that he had got something that would make us
feel better; we instantly left the house, went out and sat down in a circle
under some shades, upon the bank of a muddy brook and soon licked
them down to our great delight and benefit.

We had suffered for food in a manner and to a degree of which even a
faint description would be considered as fabulous, therefore I forbear to
disclose it. Thus I remained for about three months from the time I was
taken from the ship, starved, whipped and tortured in the most shameful
manner, obliged to work unceasingly, in order I suppose that the clement,
benevolent and charitable whiteman should be satisfied that the heathen
spirit of an African boy of noble birth should be sufficiently subdued, rendered tame, docile and submissive; and all for my good that I should
thereby become a tame, profitable and honest slave. The natural man
must be obliterated and degraded, that even the thought of liberty must
never be suffered to contaminate itself in a negro's mind; and the odious
thing, equality, should be taught by European discipline never to raise its
head.

At length I was sold to Capt. Isaac Mills,[4] who commanded a 44 gun
frigate, and was led without much ceremony from the house of subjection
to meet the man who thus owned me by right of purchase; which brings
to my mind the following song.

The Negro's Complaint
By W. COWPER, Esq.[5]

Forc'd from home and all its pleasures,
Afric's coast I left forlorn,
To increase a stranger's treasures,
O'er the raging billows borne.
Men, call'd Christians, bought & sold me,

---

4. Captain Isaac Mills (1728–1780) of Milford, Connecticut was active in the New
England–West Indies trade from at least 1755 to 1764. See Introduction.

5. William Cowper (1731–1800) was a popular English poet known for his gentle wit
and generous humanitarianism. First published in 1788 in the London newspapers *The*

Paid my price in paltry gold;
But though their's they have enroll'd me,
Minds are never to be sold.

Still in thought as free as ever,
What are Christian's rights, I ask,
Me from my delights to sever,
Me to torture, me to task?
Fleecy locks, and black complexion,
Cannot forfeit nature's claim;
Skins may differ, but affection
Dwells in black and white the same.

Why did all-creating nature
Make the plant for which we toil?
Sighs must fan it, tears must water,
Sweat of our's must dress the soil.
Think ye, masters, iron-hearted!
Lolling at your jovial boards,
Think, how many backs have smarted
For the sweets your cane affords!

Is there, as ye sometimes tell us,
Is there one who reigns on high?
Has he bid you buy and sell us,
Speaking from his throne, the sky?
Ask him, if your knotted scourges,
Fetters, blood-extorting screws,
Are the means which duty urges,
Agents of his will to use?

Hark! he answers—wild tornadoes
Strewing yonder sea with streaks,
Wasting towns, plantations, meadows,
Are the voice with which he speaks:
He, foreseeing what vexations
Afric's sons should undergo,

Public Advertiser and Stuart's Star, "The Negro's Complaint" was frequently reprinted.
Prentiss's copy varies slightly from the British version, in which lines 5, 7, 10, and 30 read:
"Men from England bought and sold me"; "But, though slave they have enroll'd me;"
"Where are England's rights, I ask;" and "Matches, blood extorting screws."

Fix'd their tyrant's habitations,
Where his whirlwinds answer—No.

By our blood in Afric wasted.
Ere our necks received the chain,
By the mis'ries which we tasted
Crossing, in your barks the main;
By our sufferings since ye bro't us
To the man-degrading mart,
All sustain'd with patience, taught us
Only by a broken heart.

Deem our nation brutes no longer,
Till some reason ye shall find
Worthier of regard, and stronger
Than the color of your kind.
Slaves of gold whose sordid dealings
Tarnish all your boasted powers,
Prove that you have human feelings
Ere you proudly question ours.

Here I would ask the reader and all mankind, whether a person or any other property, which is sold by any person, who has no other right save that he gains by stealth or theft can be valid, or by any parity of reasoning, rendered binding by the laws of this or any other civilized nation.— But pardon me for this digression; I wish not to attempt to legalize or moralize any transaction that has happened to me since my captivity, as I consider all to be illegal and immoral.

At any rate, I was conducted by two sailors, who led me as a beast to slaughter. I was so weak that I could not walk but a short distance before I was obliged to rest, for I was so exhausted for want of food that I was almost emaciated. And being forced from all of my comrades and placed in a situation that I could not converse with any person, it forced upon me a fullness of grief that caused me to cry aloud, and then I expected my doom was certain death. The sand was hot and the journey fatiguing, yet it is now impossible for me to measure the distance in my own mind. At length we came to an orange tree, where the oranges covered the ground; I would not ask for any, and dare not stoop down to pick any up, for fear of being whipped, although hunger that is indescribable, called aloud, urged, yes, almost forced me to partake of the forbidden fruit. We passed, and I was in an agony of despair; however, I was forced along to a house, which was inhabited by a man by the name of Welch.[6] He had a black wife and white maid. The wife was as brutish and ostentatious as was Welch himself. She was a large fat greasy Guinea[7] woman; flat nose, thick lips, with teeth as white as snow.—I was left in a stoop before the door. The captain who had bought me and Welch went into a room together, where they sat drinking and talking—perhaps this was his boarding house. While they sat regaling themselves with the inebriating drop, I remained in the stoop where I was first seated, imagining that they were planning my death.

While in this melancholy situation, as I sat musing upon my approaching fate, I discovered some Negroes and Mulattoes boiling something in a large kettle. They seemed to be jabbering to each other. I fancied they were talking about me, and concluded that I was to be boiled in the same kettle. The thoughts of this horrid death destroyed my hunger; every feeling except the thoughts of death, my native country and friends, sunk before the horror that pressed upon me. While I was thus situated, the white woman asked me into the house, or rather by signs she induced me to go in. She let me set down and put into my hands one spoonful of pork and onions, which appeared had been stewed together. Also, a small piece of biscuit, which I ate without much indignation. It being about dusk, Welch came in and conducted me to a small back room, where the floor was sanded, and locked me in; there was neither bed nor chair in the room, therefore, I laid me down upon the floor and went to sleep, but I soon awoke and found I was extremely sick. I tried to get out, but found my efforts were vain. Accordingly I was obliged to puke upon the floor, after which I felt extremely weak and thirsty, but laid me down again upon the floor and slept until sunrise. When I awoke, I heard some person at the door unlocking it. It was Welch himself. He opened the door, looked in and saw what I had done, returned, got a large whip, and the first salutation, after jabbering a few words, and frothing at the mouth, which was unintelligible to me, only I saw he was angry, he turned the butt of his whip, and knocked me down flat upon the floor. I, half stunned, attempted to get

6. Dozens of Welches lived in Bridgetown in the mid-eighteenth century. Most were white, but some were of mixed European and African ancestry. See Introduction.

7. The English began importing slaves from Guinea (a region of Africa now called the Gold Coast) in 1660.

up, but he caught hold of my shirt, drew it over my head, and while he continued whipping; almost suffocated me. At length he tore off my shirt, which left me entirely naked as I was born; he again knocked me down, and continued whipping me. At this time the white woman came to the door, they had some words; I believe she undertook to expostulate with him, for he shook his whip at her, and she retired, then he resumed his whipping, until I fainted. After I was brought to, by the white woman, I found I was much bruised and had bled much; and I could never to this day discover but the blood had every appearance and quality of white man's blood. It was after 12 o'clock at noon that I had any knowledge of any thing which transpired after I fainted. Thus I was sold, and thus was I whipped, without being able to expostulate or enquire of my tyrant the reason for treating me in the foregoing manner; which forces upon me the following description of

THE NEGRO BOY[8]

The African Prince who lately arrived in England, being asked what he had given for his watch, replied, "What I'll never give again.—I gave a fine boy for it."

When avarice enslaves the mind,
And selfish views alone bear sway:
Man turns a savage to his kind,
And blood and rapine mark his way.
Alas, for this poor simple toy,
I sold a blooming Negro Boy.

His father's hope his mother's pride,
Tho' black, yet comely to their view:
I tore him helpless from their side,
And gave him to a ruffian crew;
To fiends that Afric's coast annoy,
I sold the blooming Negro Boy.

From country, friends and parents torn,
His tender limbs in chains confin'd,
I saw him o'er the billows borne,

8. A popular abolitionist song, "The Negro Boy" was published in Washington, D.C., in 1802 in *Select and Fugitive Poetry*, ed. Richard Dinmore. It may have been written by Robert Wedderburn (1762–1834?), the son of a Jamaican slave and a Scottish planter. See Basker 565–66; Wood 310–12.

And mark'd his agony of mind:
But still to gain this simple toy,
I gave away the Negro Boy.

In isles that deck the western wave,
I doom'd the hopeless youth to dwell:
A poor forlorn insulted slave,
A beast that Christians buy and sell:
And in their cruel task employ,
The much enduring Negro boy.

His wretched parents long shall mourn;
Shall long explore the distant main,
In hopes to see the youth return;
But all their hopes and sighs are vain:
They never shall the sight enjoy,
Of their lamented Negro Boy.

Beneath a tyrants harsh command,
He wears away his youthful prime
Far distant from his native land
A stranger in a foreign clime:
No pleasing thoughts his mind employ,
A poor dejected Negro Boy.

But he who walks upon the wind,
Whose voice in thunder's heard on high,
Who doth the raging tempest bind,
Or wing the light'ning thro' the sky,
In his own time will soon destroy
Th' oppressors of the Negro Boy.

Chapter 6

*Meet with one of my countrywomen—conversation with her—Her narrative—
Extreme thirst—Charitable slave—Sickness—Carried on board Capt. Mills's
ship—Sail for New-Spain—lose sight of the fleet—action with a Spanish ship.*

When I was fairly awakened, or rather brought back to my natural senses,
I made shift to crawl out upon the stoop, where I sat down upon the bench
and wept. While I was thus weeping there came along a black woman
who discovered my tears. She asked me in the Bow-woo language what I
was weeping for. Although cheered, I was confounded. I felt as though it
was a delusion. I said nothing; caution taught me there was deception. She
then asked me what I wanted, when I ventured to speak, and tremulously
told her that I wanted nothing, for I dare not give any other answer. She
then asked me where I came from. I told her ingenuously that I came from
the kingdom of Bow-woo. "What part of Bow-woo?" said she. I answered,
The city of Deauyah and county of Hughlough. "Hughlough," she exclaimed, "What was your father's name?" Whryn Brinch, says I. "And your
mother's name was Whryn Dooden Wrogan—I knew her well—and
can you remember your grand-father and mother?" O yes, said I. "What
was your grand-mother's name?" Zoah. "How many children had she?"
Three. "Do you remember Vossea?" O yes, I know them all. "Who
preached in your church when you left home?" Caushee was our minister.
"Caushee," she exclaimed, "is my mother's brother; if you know Gow
Friendall's wife, you know my sister." That I do, and I well know Beaureau
her son, for he was taken with me when we went to swim in the Niger. "O
great father the sun," she exclaimed, "has friend Whryn Dooden Wrogan
a son in bondage, whom she will never more behold? And alas, has my

143

dear sister Friendall lost forever her only son, to linger out a miserable existence in this foreign land. He, poor boy, was a playful child, about four years of age, when I was taken. Do tell me where he is?" I told her he was sold some days before, and gone, I could not tell where. She wept for a few minutes, and then asked me to go into the house, and said she was sure I was hungry; I said no, I was not hungry, and that I did not wish to go in, as I was afraid of the white man. She told me the white woman was my friend and would take care of me; and that she had two little girls, and I might have one of them to make me a wife to take care of me.[1] I told her I did not want a wife, as I expected the white people would whip me to death, and I wished to die so that I could go back to my father and tell him what kind of beings there is in this country.[2]

They then took me up and carried me to the house, told me I must eat something or I should starve. They gave me an earthen pitcher that had something in it like chocolate, and I drank it.[3] They also gave me some bread and butter, but I could not eat it, as it looked so much like the pork that made me sick the night before. Then they gave me some crackers and I ate them. After I had eaten, she asked me a few questions and requested me to lie down, which I did. She told me she would stay by me and watch to see that no one offered to hurt me, but I must observe when her husband came, who was a whiteman, not to speak to her in my native tongue; neither would she speak to me, as it would displease him. I was anxious to learn her story, and, at my request, she retold it to me as follows:—

When I was about seventeen years of age, I went down from Bow-woo to Bearblea, the next province towards the sea. I remained there about three weeks on a visit, at my uncle's, Vroo Friendall. I being decorated in a style different from their nation, I received much attention from the young gentry of the town, the name of which was Ghana. This town is situated on a small river, called Zoo, and falls into the Niger about nine miles below the town. A party of us one day went down to

1. The "she" in this sentence likely refers not to the "white woman" but to Brace's countrywoman.

2. In 1694 Captain Phillips of the Royal Africa slave ship *Hannibal* described a similar view held by slaves from Whidaw in Africa. Philips wrote in his journal: "We had about 12 negroes did wilfully drown themselves, and others starved themselves to death; for 'tis belief that when they die they return home to their country and friends again" (qtd. in Beckles, *Natural Rebels* 154).

3. Two sweet beverages were sometimes allocated to slaves in Barbados. One, called "weak diversion," consisted of "rum and water sweetened with molasses." The other was simply water and molasses (Higman 205).

see the Niger and amuse ourselves with such delights as might be met with. We stood upon an high bank of the river, when we discovered a boat containing white people. We anticipated their object as many people had been taken before. We flew, we separated, but a young man, whom I had become attached to, said he would not leave me, let the consequence be what it would. We hid ourselves in a thicket until night, then cautiously leaving our retreat, traveled towards the town. We had got within about two miles of home, thinking ourselves out of danger, began to talk, when in an instant we found ourselves surrounded. To contend was in vain; to fly was impossible. We were without opposition bound and gagged, conducted to their boat which lay in the Zoo, not more than thirty rods from where we were taken. They had many there, and continued upon the search until morning, when they dropped down into the Niger, went down to the ship, which was anchored about thirty miles below the town; this was a French vessel. In short, we came to Martinico, where we were landed and were sold at auction. Vrocea, for that was my friend's name, was taken from me. I was sold to a French merchant and put into his kitchen. Vrocea found means to meet me afterwards, as he lived about two miles from town and came there often. Our affections increased, we contrived our escape. An English vessel lay at anchor in the harbor, the captain was frequently dining with my master. I found an opportunity to let him know my wishes, he promised me liberty and protection if I would go with him. Accordingly Vrocea and myself were conveyed on board the night before he was to sail. We met with nothing until we had been out about three days, when we were attacked by a Spanish vessel. They were beaten off altho' of far superior force; but alas! My beloved Vrocea bravely fell in the contest. Thus all my hopes of happiness were obliterated for ever.

We made a long voyage, and at length arrived at this island. I lived in the captain's house for about two years. He dressed me elegantly, treated me tenderly, seated me at the head of his table at all times; and as I then spoke French, I soon learned English. At length he offered me his hand. It was bettering my situation, therefore I accepted his offer. We were married about seven years ago, and have two little girls and a boy. My husband's name is Lecois, he has left the seas, & owns a small plantation; he is a man of pleasure and considerably dissipated; he is a natural tyrant, but has much feeling and uses me well, only[4] sometimes when intoxicated.

I listened to the foregoing account with delight, and notwithstanding my situation, I was overjoyed to see a distant relative, and one that came from my native place; but even that joy gave me pain. I lay musing for some time, burst into tears and cried myself to sleep. When I awoke, it was

4. I.e., except.

almost sun-down. The black woman was gone. I felt worse than ever, as I had no one to speak to, and thirst suffocated me almost to death, and I was so sore, I could not rise up alone. The white woman helped me up and led me to the stoop. While I sat there crying, a little Mulatto girl came and said something to me, and gave me a piece of ginger bread. This girl, I suppose, was daughter to my friendly country-woman; but I could not understand what she said, neither could I eat one atom of the bread, in consequence of my being so overcome with thirst. At this time an old black man came along and said to me, "Are you here today boy." I said, "Yes." "How do you do today?" says he. "O I am almost dead, for I want to see some friends, and I am whipped almost to death." Then I asked him if he had been to the slave prison today? He said he had, and that they were all well. "Ah!" said I, "I wish I was along with the boys again." He tried to cheer me up, told me they would use me better by and by. I saw he had a barrel on a dray.[5] I asked him what he had in his barrel? He said, "Nothing, but water, and that is old sea water, which is all rotten with maggots." I begged most earnestly, as I was almost dying with thirst. He got an old dish and brought me some. The slime and maggots almost thickened it, yet I drank, straining it as much as possible through my teeth. The most delicious wine, slaking the thirst of the most refined Prince on earth, was never more grateful to the taste than this water was to me. Neither was the good Samaritan better employed than was my humane African friend. When I reflect upon the wants, miseries, and dependencies of mankind, I cannot conceive of a more humane act than was thus performed by a slave.

After I had thus been relieved from the torments of thirst, I ate the gingerbread, but could not eat the biscuit and butter, before mentioned. It being dusk, Welch came, took me by the shoulder and put me into the back hole, and again locked me in. In this solitude I met the most horrid nightly visions that the human mind can experience. Whether I slept or was awake, I am unable to say. At any rate, I thought maggots were devouring my inwards and whips were scourging my back; the furies of unprovoked vengeance were preying upon me to that degree that I was almost tempted to wish for annihilation. In the morning, I was unable to rise. I found myself in a violent fever and lay three weeks in a most hopeless and abandoned situation. Nothing but the arm of Almighty Jehovah saved my life.

But to give Justice where Justice is due, the white woman paid every

5. A dray is a low cart used to haul things.

attention in her power, when Welch was gone; and my country woman paid every attention in her power,—but Welch's wife never entered the room during my sickness.

As soon as I was able to walk, Capt. Mills called for me to go on board his frigate. He brought me a sailor's jacket and kilts, and a new white shirt.

While I was putting them on in his cabin, he rubbed his hand across my back, then clapped them together, signified to me that I had been whipped, and made signs that he wished to learn the author. He called me upon deck, I pointed to the place, which was in sight, and by signs, as intelligible as possible for me, informed him, who had thus whipped me.

He expressed to me by signs the strongest indignation, and I believe would have revenged himself upon Welch, if he could have met him, but he was under sailing orders, and immediately put to sea, as I afterwards learned that he belonged to Admiral Hawk's fleet, which was then under sailing orders, upon a private expedition, against St. Croix.[6] I also learned that he had seen me in the house of subjection and purchased me for his cabin boy, or private waiter. But I being unable to understand the language did not answer his wishes; therefore I was put among the mariners and taught the military discipline by one William Burks, who taught me altogether by signs.[7] When we arrived at St. Croix, we received orders to sail for St. Augustine, where we tarried only two days, then sailed for the Havannah, or, as it was called new Spain, on the grand expedition to reduce that place.

On our passage we lost sight of the guide ship, just before day, in consequence of a thick fog. We got wind bound and could not find the fleet. While thus stranded, a Spanish 64 came up to us and ordered us to strike.[8] Capt. Mills told him that he would never strike to any Spanish or French force until he had given his English tars an opportunity to try their bravery, and demanded in turn their surrender. Our ship was prepared, and every man upon his post.

Here it is my duty to acknowledge that I saw heroism clothed in submission; bravery docile; the spirit of man commanded still independently

6. Sir Edward Hawke (1705–1781) served as Admiral of His Majesty's Fleet from February 1757 to October 1762. During the expedition against Havana, Hawke primarily worked to distract the Spanish off the coasts of Spain and Portugal while Admiral George Pocock commanded the squadron that attacked Spain in the West Indies (Clowes 565, 239).

7. William Burke (1697–1788) was a mariner in Bridgetown. See introduction.

8. I.e., to lower their flag in surrender.

brave, one gave a pledge of his fair mistress to his friend, with solemn in-
junctions; another a commission to his wife and children, and another to
his parents. Their only fear seemed to be that their friends could not learn
that they died bravely fighting for their king and country. In short, the
memory of their actions seemed to be their glory. The Spanish ship bore
down upon us; the captain had given orders to take the first broad side and
tack, so as to get the wind, and be prepared for the second fire, also that
our smoke might assist us and injure them. Strict orders were given that
there should not be a gun fired. I not understanding their language, when
we first received their broadside, thought it my duty to answer it, therefore took up my gun and fired upon them. When they came opposite to us
on the second tack, we immediately gave them a broadside.

The battle lasted about fourteen minutes, at the expiration of which
time they immediately struck and yielded themselves up to us as a lawful
prize.

Chapter 7

Ideas of futurity—Court death as a blessing—Am wounded—nicknamed—Sail to Havannah—Ingenuity of Capt. John Staley—Capture of Havannah—Arrive at Boston, where I am allowed to visit the town—Sold to Burrell—his cruelty and my sufferings—A friend appears—A vision.

But during this battle, I can observe that I felt no other sensation than that if they killed me, I should go to my great father the sun; therefore I courted death.

I stood upon the upper deck, exposed to all the enemy's shot for about seven minutes, contemplating a meeting with my grandfather, who had gone before me. I was disappointed, for I received five wounds and was conveyed to the surgeon's apartment; on examination of which three were upon my head very slight, one on my ankle, where a musket ball passed through; the fifth was caused by a musket ball entering by the side of my back bone and lodging in my right hip. The surgeon tried to extricate the ball, but I not understanding the object shouted like a loon and would not permit him to probe the wound.

In consequence of my firing without orders, instead of punishment with death, as would have been the fate of one doing the same understandingly, the captain gave me the honorable nick-name of Jeffrey. I say honorable, as I was named after Sir Jeffrey Amherst,[1] General and commander in chief of the expedition for the reduction of Canada, the year before. The reader will recollect the taking of Quebec, in consequence of the

---

1. Jeffrey Amherst (1717–1797), a British baron, was appointed Supreme Commander of British forces in America in 1758, in the midst of the Seven Years War.

memorable battle upon the plains of Abraham, before the city, fought by young General Wolfe, commander of the British army, and General Montcalm, who commanded the French, in which the former was victorious and caused the place to surrender to the arms of the English.[2]— Many have the mistaken idea that Wolfe was commander in chief; but the fact is, Amherst bore the chief command.[3] And his character was that he was one of the bravest men in the realm of Great Britain; but he possessed rather more courage than prudence. As my act of firing bore some resemblance of courage and want of prudence, and Jeffery being a suitable name for a negro boy, I was dubbed with it at that time and have ever borne it since, only they have lately added nick-name upon nick-name, for people call me old Jeff now. But to return—I was confined with my wounds for about two months, in which time we sailed to Savannah, in the state of Georgia, with the prize. We stayed in this place but few days, in order to make some repairs and take in fresh water; then we sailed to join the fleet. After we joined it, we were informed that the French and Spanish fleet had joined, and that they were about to attack Gibraltar.

Admiral Hawk gave orders for the fleet to stand for that place, but when we arrived we found we had been misinformed, therefore we sailed for the Havannah. While on the passage, Capt. John Staley, a brave commander of an English frigate, got becalmed and lost sight of the fleet.[4] While in this situation he was attacked by a Spanish ship of superior force. They fought about two hours and forty minutes. Staley having expended all his ammunition except one round, hoisted a flag of truce and informed the commander of the Spanish ship that he had two hours to determine whether he would surrender himself and force honorable prisoners of war, or be sunk; for if he had to spend any more lives, he would neither give nor take quarters. After a short consultation the Spaniards surrendered on certain honorable conditions. He conducted his prize to the fleet, and there was great rejoicing when he joined us. But when the Spanish captain learned the situation of the frigate when he surrendered, he was extremely mortified, and discovered some signs of insanity.

2. Although his forces decisively defeated the French forces, the British general James Wolfe (1727–1759) was killed at the Battle of Quebec in 1759, as was his defeated opponent, the Marquis Louis Joseph de Montcalm (1712–1759), the French Marshall in Canada.

3. Amherst was the supreme commander, but he arrived in Quebec too late to assist General Wolfe.

4. Possibly John Stanton, captain of the St. Florentine ("List of Commissioned Officers of the Royal Navy," National Maritime Museum).

We at length arrived before the fortress at the Havannah, where we remained about two months. When all the English forces were collected, we commenced the attack[5] in the following manner:—

We landed between four and five thousand troops, to make an attack by land. The Spanish made a sally from the fort, placed their cavalry in front, who commenced the attack on their part. They were met by a regiment of Scotch Highlanders, who fought with broad swords, and with great dexterity cut one rein of their horseman's bridles, which turned them round upon their foot and created great confusion and prodigious slaughter, which decided the battle.[6] In the meantime the fleet kept up a continual firing upon the town and fort.[7] I saw the steeple of their principal church shot down, and many public buildings. The form of the attack by the shipping was singular, and one of the most sublime sights ever seen by man. Figure to yourself thirty two seventy four gun ships of the line, and six frigates, passing in a circle as near to each other as possible, and when they came opposite the fort, they gave a broadside, which kept up a continual thundering of cannon for eighteen hours, which made a breach in the walls.[8] The Spanish sent a flag of truce and surrendered unconditionally to our forces, after which the whole island fell into the hands of the English.[9]

5. The siege began on June 8, 1762.

6. The Royal Highlanders formed the 42nd Regiment, including ten companies of men under in the First Battalion under the command of Lieutenant-General Lord John Murray (Syrett 126). On June 7, 1762 the British landed troops six miles east of Havana. "By the next evening they had scattered a screen of Spanish defenders and secured a position on high ground" (Anderson 499). The Highlanders won, but were decimated by disease. Albemarle wrote to Sir George Pocock: "The poor Highlanders die in numbers. I wish you could spare a frigate to send them to North America; it would perhaps be the only means of saving the remains of these poor people." He begged for some medicines, "as these poor wretches have none and their situation is most melancholy" (*Albemarle to Pocock*, 8 August 1762; Syrett 281).

7. Havana was surrounded by a bastioned wall, and "two stout forts, the Punta on the west and Morro Castle on the east, guarded its seaward approaches" (Anderson 498). The Royal Navy attacked from the harbor, as Brace describes. Morro Castle was partially blown up by a mine and then stormed by British troops on July 20, 1762. Afterwards the British fleet focused its fire on the Punta and the walls of the city proper.

8. Clowes lists 53 gun ships in the British fleet at Havana in 1762, including six with 74 guns, one with 90, one with 80, two with 70, six with 64, and so on (246).

9. No historians cite Brace as a source, yet Brace's description is strikingly similar to a modern historian's summary: "At dawn on 11 August the British batteries opened fire on Havana and the forts at La Punta and La Fuerza. Within several hours the superiority of British fire was apparent, for the guns of La Punta were quickly silenced and the Spanish were forced to abandon the fort. It was only a question of time before the walls of Havana

After this victory we sailed to Dublin, the capital of Ireland. This was the first time I ever saw a capital European city. We remained here about three weeks, then we sailed for Savannah, in Georgia, leaving the fleet behind. Here I was, by the kindness of Captain Mills, allowed many privileges; and to do Justice to his name, I must here observe that he was a brave and humane man. He was never rifled with passion, and in battle as unmoved as Mount Atlas. The whole ship's crew loved, respected, and revered him. He took great pains to learn me English, in which by this time I had made some progression. We spent about four weeks at Savannah, then we sailed for New York, where we staid about ten days, from thence we sailed to Newport, R. Island, here we made but a short stay and then sailed for Halifax; on our passage we caught many codfish, and I was sat to cleaning them, in doing which I cut my hand, and while it was bleeding one Pattle, who was bantering with my master for me, came and took hold of my nose and chin, opened my mouth as a jockey would a horse's, in order to see my age or to insult me. While my mouth was open, he spit a cud of tobacco into it which made me sick. I sat down and wept all day, and since then I could never chew that weed.

From Halifax we sailed to Boston, where we tarried about two months, where I was again indulged by my master, who allowed me to go about the town. I became acquainted with many free African descendants, who appeared to be well contented in their situation. They asked me many questions about my native country. I gave them the best account in my power, which appeared to gratify them and procure me much attention. I was extremely anxious to remain in this place, but was at length obliged by the authority that held me to sail to New Haven, Connecticut, where we arrived about the first of October. There were frost, snow and ice upon the ground which were the first I had ever seen. The reader may well judge, it was a miracle to me.

Here I bid adieu to the British fleet forever, as I was sold to a man belonging to Old Milford, west side of Oyster river. His name was John Burrell, a professed puritan.[10] The snow was about two inches deep, and I had

---

were breached and the British stormed the city. . . . White flags were hung out on the walls of the city" (Syrett xxxiii). By nightfall on August 11 the Spanish commandant "requested a truce to work out terms of capitulation" (Anderson 501). He formally surrendered the city on August 14, 1762.

10. See introduction for information on John Burwell and Samuel Eells.

on a thin linen jacket and one pair of trousers or sailor's kilts and no shoes. I was the first night put upon the naked hearth to sleep, but could not enjoy the sweets of repose, for a British man of war was a palace in comparison to my present situation, in which I had been upwards of two years. The next night I met the same fare, which was continued for about two weeks. My wounds, which I received from the Spaniards, broke out newly and I almost perished with cold and hunger, as this puritan christian could not condescend to give me any thing to eat but old crusts and bones, such as people generally throw to their dogs, and nothing to sleep upon but a cold stove. Not even a blanket or old quilt could be allowed. He would read the bible and pray both night and morning, for all mankind, recommend all to the sovereign mercy of the father of the universe; sit down to a good breakfast and when he had glutted himself he would throw down a bone upon the hearth before the block where I was allowed to sit, and sometimes it would be accompanied by a crust of bread, which would all perhaps make six ounces of coarse food. If it was Sunday morning he would dress himself, put on his best coat and wig, go to meeting, there sit and appear to suck in every word the minister should say. He would also suffer me to stand behind the door of his sanctuary.

One night I dreamed of being in my native country and conversing with one of my aunts, by the name of Zoah. In this vision a region of imaginary happiness appeared before me. I was in a complete transport of earthly felicity; but alas! a slave upon a cold stone in a foreign land; when I awoke I found it was a dream. I was also in extreme agitation and almost chilled to death, which frighted me so that I cried aloud. I rose up and put together some brands, attempting to make some fire to warm me. Something was said by my master. He spoke so quick that I did not understand him, then immediately jumped up, and the first salutation knocked me down with his fist. As I went to get up he took up a chair and struck me on the side of the head near where I had been wounded in the first battle I was engaged in, and pealed up a piece of my scalp about as big as my three fingers. I fell with the blow under a table, where he kicked and beat me until I became insensible. When I awoke in the morning I found myself in a most shocking situation. The blood had ran across the room and stood in a puddle. In short, I was covered with wounds and poorly fitted for the service of the day; but work I must, as there was no charity to be found in my master's breast. I was ordered to go up stairs to get some corn, and while I was going to the pen to give it to the swine, there being a hole in the bottom of the basket, some of the ears dropped upon the ground. My puritan master gave me two or three strokes with his whip. When they handed me my bones to pick I could not eat, and they thought I was sulky. Burrell handed me the bone, took his horse-whip, and lashed me until I gnawed it like a dog. When this was over, I was ordered to go about a quarter of a mile barefoot to get some turnips. As I could not move fast, it seemed as if it would freeze my feet. The keenness of the pain caused me to make use of every exertion to keep the frost from nipping my toes. In the meantime someone of the family had drawn some beer or cider, I went to drink some of it, my mistress saw me and knocked me down with the distaff and ordered me to go to chopping wood. I not being used to chopping cut my foot. It bled much and I bound it up with some husks, then laid down between two logs. While I lay in this situation, one Mr. Samuel Eals came and took me up, and very charitably led me into the house, told Burrell that such abuse was inhuman and unchristian; he also threatened to complain of him to the authority. They quarreled for some time then he gave me his great-coat and sat me down by the fire, and went to one James Parker,[11] got a pair of shoes and took me with him. Isaiah, 58 chap. 3, 4, 5, 6 and 7th verses—Amos, 5th verse 25th.—Often have I been caused to reflect upon the conduct of this man towards me, as he was one of the strongest professors in the church, and as strict in his family devotion as any man I was ever acquainted with; and he must have been a hypocrite, and never received that grace which worketh a change of heart and drives out that evil which was ingrafted into man by the fall. If he had charity, that crown of christian virtues, how could he pray for all mankind and then starve a poor negro boy, who could look to no other person for food. If he had a hope of grace and mercy from his Lord and Master, how could he freeze his slave, and then unmercifully beat him for attempting to make a fire to warm himself. Did he think me in possession of an immortal spirit? Then what could he make of the Lord's prayer—"Forgive us our trespass, as we forgive those that trespass against us." If I had done wrong how could he expect his sins to be forgiven him? In short, was there a single trait of a real and true christian in him? But the advocates of a distinction in human nature may say I have no right to examine into the acts

11. James Parker (1729–1807) was married to Mary Gillett and is listed as a head of family in Milford in the 1790 Census. A James Parker was the printer of *The Connecticut Gazette,* a New Haven newspaper established in 1755.

and feelings of white people. To such I answer, If I have the same propensities and feelings, and am endowed with the same intellectual reason, then where is the distinction? Is it the color or is it the power you have gained over me, which the once first angel in heaven, now the arch fiend of hell, attempted to gain over his creator? From what fountain does the Ethiopian, Turk, Indian, Chinese, Tartar or Englishman receive all their sensations. Is there more than one supernatural creating power; or is that power partial in the distribution of his spirit? No. The house of subjugation, the difference in education and situation, is all. Even in this country, where the African is degraded and disgraced; his heart broken, his hope destroyed, and almost generally deprived of education, do you not see some geniuses burst forth and rise above the tyranny and oppression they are under, and stand as monuments of admiration. Behold some of your ministers of the gospel! Go to the African churches, in the cities of New York and Philadelphia, see their devout attachment to the religion of their Savior. Hear the pathetic and persuasive eloquence of their preachers, and then answer my inquiries.—But to the narrative.

At night Mr. Eals made me a straw bed, which was the first bed I had slept upon after I was taken into bondage, until this time. This humanity and christian-like act opened my wounded feelings and brought my sorrows up afresh to my view. My mother's tenderness came to my recollection. Being so much subject to abuse, the least kindness brought upon me that kind of melancholy, which a real christian feels to see his brother devout in christian faith, depart this life. At night I dreamed that the good spirit came to me, took me by the hand, asked me to accompany him, which I did without the least hesitation. He ascended with me high above the earth, and wafted me through vast space—at length we arrived at the African coast and came in sight of the Niger, following its course up the river, about one hundred yards above the earth. He showed me the desolated town of Yellow Bonga. The shades of night seemed to break away, and all at once he gave me a fair view of Deauyah, my native town. The people were all asleep, and we hovered about the town until it was light. We then descended and sat upon the grass before the church.

Chapter 8

Continuation of my vision—Am sold to Pridon—Sold three times, the last to Widow Mary Stiles, who, like a real christian, taught me to read—Enter into the American army—Several skirmishes—A frolic—Kill a British light horseman—Narrow escape.

I then thought I had died of my wounds, and that our great father, the Sun, was the good spirit, who conducted me back to my town. The spirit left me, and seemed to ascend into the air with dazzling light, which overpowered the strength of my eyes to behold. I started at the sight and awoke. The fire from the kitchen hearth had blazed up and shone bright in my face—So I came from Africa without the help of any other spirit save only necessity, much quicker than I went, and found myself still a forlorn slave as I went to sleep. Mr. Samuel Eals used me very well while I remained with him; but as soon as I was able to work, I was sold to one Peter Pridon, son of the old priest Pridon, of Old Milford.[1] I lived with him about two months and got five severe whippings for crying nights. From Pridon I was bartered away for some old horses to one Gibbs, who was a man of very inferior talents, possessing great pride and ostentation, always at work and in a hurry.[2] He had the longest nose and chin I ever saw at-

---

1. Peter Prudden was the son of Job Prudden (1715–1774), who pastored the Second Church of Milford (formed by Presbyterian dissenters) for twenty-seven years (1742–1774). Job was the great-grandson of the original Peter Prudden, the founder and first pastor of Milford's Congregational Church (Barber 233). The Peter Prudden House is still standing in Milford.

2. John Gibbs (1730–1809) was the son of Thomas Gibbs (1692–?), who was one of Captain Isaac Mills's partners in the shipping business. Like his father, John Gibbs was a

tached to a man's face, thin lips, and a voice that was less pleasing than the ravens. With this man I stayed about three months, and to describe the particular management of his family would only mortify those who live in the same way at the present time. I have thought he took a peculiar delight in whipping me, as I uniformly received about four whippings per day. If I was awkward, cried too much, or was lazy, it was sure to purchase me a good drubbing. Sometimes I got a flogging for freezing my feet while I was foddering and cutting the ice out of the watering place. And one day, while I was getting corn up stairs, I designedly pushed his boy down stairs, for while I had the basket upon my shoulder he began whipping me & chirping to me, as would a driver to his horse. For this I was knocked down stairs, basket, corn and all shared the same fate; and to complete my punishment, the next morning I received fifty lashes with a horse-whip. Next I was sold to Phineas Baldwin of the town of Old Milford. I continued with him until summer, or rather spring, when I went to live with his son Phineas, who had two small children to tend.[3] In his nursery I was engaged until the last of May, when I was sold to Jones Green, of the same place.[4] Green did not whip me but about twice in a week, except now and then a kicking. From Green I was transferred to one Murrier, a tanner,[5] where I remained until September, at which time the widow Mary Stiles, of Woodbury, Connecticut, bought me. This was a glorious era in my life, as widow Stiles was one of the finest women in the world; she possessed

---

Milford merchant engaged in the maritime trade (*History of Milford* 40; Scott 456). A newspaper ad in 1762 indicates that the younger Gibbs and Mills co-owned horses, which Mills may have exported to the West Indies (Scott 128).

3. The elder Phineas Baldwin of Milford (1700–1789) was Captain Isaac Mills's father-in-law. His son Phineas (1733–ca. 1777), the brother of Mills's wife Katherine, had four children with his wife Mehitable Peck (1735–1805): Phineas (b. 1751), Thadeus (b. 1760), Mehitable (b. 1763), and Catherine (b. 1767). Since Brace was enslaved in their household around 1765, Thadeus and Mehitable would have been the two small children he tended. All three generations of Phineas Baldwins lived in Milford.

4. Jonas Green (1731–1789) was born in Middletown, Connecticut, and moved to Milford by 1755. He was John Burwell's brother-in-law, having married Ann Smith (1734–1805), the sister of Burwell's first wife, Sarah Smith. In 1762 Green launched the *Sarah Ann*, a 35-ton schooner of which he was the Captain and owner. "In 1776 he was surveyor of highways and in 1781 collector of taxes. He owned the home across the street from St. Peter's Church" (*Families of Early Milford* 313).

5. Although no records survive of a family named "Murrier" in Milford, tanneries had been in operation there since the 1640s. Edward Adams opened the first Milford tannery in 1646, and Miles Merwin set up the second in 1654. Local tanneries continued to operate through the nineteenth century (*History of Milford* 19, 74).

every christian virtue. This same woman was the mother of Benjamin Stiles, Esq. whose illustrious character is rewarded in the heart of every person living who knew him.

Here the prospects of the negro boy began to wear a more pleasing appearance. To mention all the incidents of my life during my residence in this family, for sixteen years, would make a volume; therefore I will only mention a few. This good lady learned me to read. One day I was sent to school, where I was taught to read by the master. I could not speak plain, therefore when I came to W I could not pronounce it and when I attempted so to do, I was understood to say "devil you." He thought I said so in order to insult him, and therefore was angry, and with his ferule[6] struck me. The second time he struck me his ferule broke, and he ordered me to sit down; but I concluded I would not stay there to be whipped by a schoolmaster, therefore I walked out instead of sitting down. He called me back; but I had not the least idea of stopping, therefore composedly walked off. I expected he would follow me and had determined in my own mind to give him a whipping, as I verily believed the task would be easy. Anger prompted me to this determination; but he did not follow me. Prudence kept him back, and vengeance melted me into pity, for I pitied his want of discernment and just judgment. Thus I became a child again; I went into the nursery and shed tears, where I sat about an hour. At length I went in and Mrs. Stiles asked me what they had done to me, and how I liked going to school. She was questioning me as her grand children had told her what happened. I felt some compunction, although not guilty of any intentional wrong. She questioned me for some time with all the humanity of a saint, then generously told me I should not be whipped at school, for she would learn me to read herself. Accordingly she with intentions as good and pure as virtue itself taught me to read and speak the English language. She was indefatigable until I could read in the bible and expound the scriptures. In the meantime she taught me the prayer usually communicated to children, and some general principles of the christian religion. Both day and night she most kindly taught me, by which I am enabled to enjoy the light of the gospel.

When this lady died I descended like real estate, in fee simple to her son Benjamin Stiles, Esq. About four years after her death, her two sons,

6. Ferule: a flat piece of wood used to punish schoolchildren.

Benjamin and David, were drafted to fight in the revolution.[7] I also entered the banners of freedom. Alas! Poor African Slave, to liberate freemen, my tyrants. I had contemplated going to Barbadoes to avenge myself and my country, in which I justified myself by Samson's prayer, when he prayed God to give him strength that he might avenge himself upon the Philistines, and God gave him the strength he prayed for.

I went into Capt. Granger's company,[8] from thence I was drafted into Capt. Barker's[9] company of light infantry, as they wanted six feet men. I then wanted but a quarter of an inch of being 6 feet 3 inches. We marched to Frog Plain, from there to second hill, between Reading and Ridgold. In the spring we came to Pauncludg there to Salem. General Worcester commanded the British under the command of General How, who attacked us.[10] We beat them back; the fight was continued all day, and the victory was sometime doubtful. From thence we marched to White Plains.[11] I devoted myself to study, making some philosophical observations on vegetation & c.

From White Plains, we marched to Fort Montgomery, at which place we remained until June.[12] From thence we proceeded to Mud-Fort, where we encamped until August.

In the latter part of the month of August the Fort was attacked, and

7. Benjamin Stiles's sons, David and Nathan, enlisted in Woodbury, Connecticut on June 18, 1777. See introduction.

8. Samuel Granger of Connecticut was Captain of the Second Connecticut from January 1, 1777 to December 24, 1777 (Heitman 196). The American army was organized in 1775 as follows: "Each regiment was to contain 728 men, divided among eight companies; and each company was to consist of a captain, two lieutenants, an ensign, four sergeants, four corporals, two fifers or drummers, and 76 privates" (*Compiled Service Records* 1). This structure was reorganized in 1776, 1778, and 1781.

9. Samuel Barker was captain of the 6th Connecticut from 1 January 1777 to 15 November 1778 (Heitman 75).

10. General William Howe (1729–1814) was commander-in-chief of His Majesty's forces in America from 1776 to 1778. He landed on Staten Island, New York on July 2, 1776, commanding a British army of 32,000.

11. A French officer at White Plains observed that New England's troops arrived poorly dressed but in good spirits. He stated that "a quarter of them were negroes, merry, confident, and sturdy." He added: "Three-quarters of the Rhode Island regiment consists of negroes, and that regiment is the most neatly dressed, the best under arms, and the most precise in its maneuver" (qtd. in White 35).

12. Fort Montgomery was a large unfinished garrison located on a high point above the range of fire from warships and bomb-ketches on the west bank of the Hudson River, north of New York City. The British took the fort in the fall of 1777.

after every exertion we could possibly make, we were obliged to surrender to superior force; and we retreated to Kingsbridge.[13] Soon after our
arrival at Kingsbridge, New York was evacuated, and we entered the city
under the command of Col. Owin, from Rhode Island.[14]

However, previous to the evacuation of New York, I was one of a hundred selected for the purpose of plundering a certain British store, which
was completed without the loss of a single man—but with the gain of
seven loads of excellent Provisions.

We were overtaken by the British, after we had marched about a mile
towards North Castle.[15] The party that pursued us were 60 light dragoons,
whom we saluted so warmly with a well aimed fire that they were obliged
to return for additional force. They again overtook us about 3 miles from
New York, but as we had also some new forces, they thought most proper
to return without an engagement.

We then proceeded to North Castle, uninterrupted, where we continued about 2 months. From thence we marched to New Windsor, where
we spent the remainder of the season. From thence we marched to West
Point, and took up winter quarters.[16] While we remained here the soldiers
played many boyish pranks. One Samuel Shaw,[17] a brave soldier but as
complete a petty thief as ever graced a camp; not that I would represent
him a thievish character, as honesty was never more predominant in any
human being than it was in him, when he pledged himself to any fellow
soldier. However, he with myself and some others from our camp, the day
before we were to be reviewed by his Excellency, Gen. George Washington,[18] concluded we would have a soldier-like frolic. Accordingly we se-

13. King's Bridge was a strategic site in New York.
14. Brace is probably referring to Colonel Jeremiah Olney (1749–1812) of Rhode Island, who commanded a regiment that included many black soldiers. Connecticut's Second
and Fourth Regiments (headed by Heman Swift and Zebulon Butler, respectively) aligned
with Olney's Rhode Island Regiment in battle formations in 1781 and 1782, and African
American soldiers from both Rhode Island and Connecticut served under Olney's command. They had winter quarters in New York State.
15. The Continental Army had a headquarters at North Castle (now called Armonk).
16. West Point was a few miles south of New Windsor, on the Hudson's west bank
17. Samuel Shaw (1748–1834) served on the New York Line. Born in North Carolina,
he got married in 1775 in North Stonington, Connecticut, but lived most of his life in New
York. He was awarded a disability pension in 1808 (*Genealogical Abstracts* 3090).
18. A slaveholder who would become the first President of the United States, George
Washington (1732–1799) was commander-in-chief of the Continental army from 1775 to
1783.

cretly stole from the lines, went to a Farm not many miles distant, which was occupied by a Tory. From him we stole a shoat.[19] Shaw was the principle manager in this affair, and we got into camp just before day. We laid the shoat in the middle of the camp and sat down, and in the language of gratitude began conversing upon our success; but short was our confab. As we soon saw the frothing Tory coming for his hog, we immediately covered ourselves with our blankets and effected to be asleep. He recognized his property; he went to the Col. to whose regiment we then belonged and reported that we had stolen one of his shoats. Col. Meigs[20] came immediately to our company, and with a countenance that plainly bespoke a determination of punishing us if guilty, he asked how we came by that shoat. I answered immediately that the owner had brought it for sale, but that from his manner of conversation (knowing him to have been a Tory) we unanimously suspected him to have come as a spy, and were determined to keep the shoat until the officers might have an opportunity of being acquainted with his designs. My fellow soldiers were glad of the opportunity of confirming the truth of my assertion—which so completely satisfied the Col. of our innocence, together with the circumstance of its lying in fair view, in the middle of the Camp—that he severely reprimanded the man for his insult on him and his soldiers. The man, a little frightened at so unexpected a charge of guilt that he really had the appearance of a condemned culprit, was glad to escape with his dead pig upon his back.

A few days after this circumstance took place—Shaw with two others of which I was one, had been out on an expedition in which we became extremely hungry. Shaw proposed to furnish meat if we would procure bread; all accordingly offered to do it. Shaw went to a Dutchman's house not far distant and with artful affection of great fatigue and an ingenious

---

19. Shoat: a young hog.

20. Col. Return Jonathan Meigs of Connecticut was an officer in the Continental army from May 1, 1775 to January 1, 1781. An Act of Congress on July 25, 1777 commended "Lieutenant-Colonel Meigs, and the officers and men under his command, who distinguished their prudence, activity, enterprise and valor in the late expedition to Long Island" (Heitman 291). Promoted to Colonel of the 6th Connecticut on September 10, 1777, Col. Meigs wrote a letter to Governor Trumbull of Connecticut in December 1778 itemizing the many promises made and broken to his soldiers. He described how the army was suffering from lack of provisions, "the trifling value of wages," and lack of adequate clothing, and he warned, "'If the next Assembly should rise without positively doing something for them, it is my opinion that mutiny or desertion will reduce our battalions to nothing before Spring'" (qtd. in Buel 181).

representation of his sufferings excited the old lady's compassion to a great degree—and she offered him a bottle of rum. He took a good draught of rum and pretended to be greatly strangled. The woman pitying his situation went to the well for water. Shaw improved that opportunity to put a large gammon[21] that hung in the chimney-corner into his knapsack. The woman returned with some water, which soon relieved Shaw—he then asked for some bread and milk—while he was eating, he was also busy in putting spoons into the legs of his stockings. After we had got some distance from the house, we asked Shaw what could tempt him to take so much from the seemingly good old woman. He said that he had long known the old Dutchman to aid and assist the British, or he could not have had a heart to do it, which account of the Dutchman we afterwards learned was correct.

Nothing of consequence took place that related to me till spring, when we moved to Hackensack in the Jerseys. Soon after our arrival there, the enemy stole some cattle from our lines. Capt. Granger with twenty chosen men was sent in pursuit of them, with orders to go about two miles to a place called Hackensack-four-corners. I was one of the number, but when we arrived at the destined place, we discovered that they had passed with the cattle; one Ahiel Bradley,[22] a sergeant in the company said if myself and one Adam Waggonor would accompany him, he would go and find them, as he believed that they were driven to a certain meadow back from the road, which meadow he was acquainted with. The captain consented and we pursued our course upon the track, to a pasture fronting the meadow, into which we discovered they had been driven. We came to a small hill or rise of land over which they must have passed. This rise being covered with bushes, it was thought prudent that I should wait upon the hither side of the hill while they went over and examined into the fact, whether the cattle were actually in the meadow or not, and at the same time, to keep a look out for the enemy. While I stood there anxiously waiting for their return, I suddenly discovered a man riding up to me not more than eight rods distant on full speed with a pistol in his hand, and ordered me to lay down my arms. But not being so instructed by my officers you may well suppose that I did not. At first I thought he was a Jerseyman and

21. Gammon: a ham or a side of bacon.
22. Possibly Alling Bradley or Elihu Bradley, both of whom were soldiers from Connecticut.

was attempting to fool me, as they had played some such pranks before upon some of the soldiers belonging to our line—therefore in return I demanded to whom I was to surrender and by what authority he demanded it.—He said I must surrender to him who demanded me in the name of the King his majesty of Great Britain. I then plainly told him that neither him nor his King's majesty would get my arms unless he took them by force. He immediately cocked his pistol and fired; I fell flat upon the ground in order to dodge his ball, and did so effectually do it that he missed me. I rose, he drew his sword and rode up to me so quick that I had no time to take aim before he struck my gun barrel with his cutlass, and cut it almost one third off—also cut off the bone of my middle finger on my hand. As he struck the horse jumped before he could wheel upon me again. Altho' my gun barrel was cut, I fired and killed him. As he fell I caught his horse and sword. He was a British light horseman in disguise.— I mounted immediately, and that instant discovered four men on horse back approaching me from different directions. I fled, passed one man, just before I came to a stone wall. Both of our horses were upon the full run. He fired and missed me. My horse leaped the wall like a deer; they all pursued me. When we got into the road, they were joined by many more; and all with swords in hand pursued me in full career. I drove my horse as fast as possible, stabbed him with my sword and gun, kicked my heels in his side, but having no spurs, and not being so good a horseman they gained upon me. I looked forward and saw my Capt. in full view, almost a mile distant. This encouraged me, and the long-shanked negro soldier with a leather cap, mounted on an elegant English gelding light horse, made all whistle again. When I came in about twenty or thirty rods, I heard the Captain say, "There come one of our leather caps, and it is Jeffrey. Reserve your fire so as not to kill him." However the men fired, and three balls cut my garments, one struck my coat sleeve, the next hit my bayonet belt, and the third went through the back side of my leather-cap. They were so close upon me that the same fire killed four of the British and five horses—and wounded some more. I did not stop for this salute, but pulled on for head quarters. When our men fired the enemy were within two or three jumps of me; but being so handsomely saluted upon surprise, as our men were concealed from their view, they made the best retreat possible.

Chapter 9

Return to the Camp—Suffered much from my wounds—Defrauded of my horse and equipments—Several skirmishes—Return home—Emancipation—Travel to Vermont, and commence work for myself—Vicissitudes at Poultney and Manchester—Marriage.

I made no halt until I arrived within our Camp. When I dismounted, tied my horse and went to set up my gun, I found I could not open my hand which was the first time that I discovered that I was wounded. Slight fear and precipitation had turned me almost as white as my fellow soldiers. In consequence of my wounds, I was unfit for duty again for almost three months. But after all the poor simple Negro was cheated out of his horse; as I sold horse, saddle and bridle, holsters, pistols and sword, to Col. Roger Sherman for his contract of two hundred and fifty dollars, who thought proper never to pay the same.[1] Yet I felt more gratitude towards the horse than regret for the loss of him, as he with the assistance of divine providence saved my life.

1. A Connecticut lawyer and politician, Roger Sherman (1721–1793) was one of five men appointed by the Continental Congress in June 1776 to develop an explanation for colonial discontent and a rationale for independence. The other men were Thomas Jefferson, Benjamin Franklin, John Adams, and Robert Livingston. Their Declaration of Independence (drafted by Jefferson) opened with the statement: "We hold these truths to be self-evident, that all men are created equal." Despite his purported belief in equality and disapproval of the slave trade, Sherman brokered a deal with South Carolina delegate John Rutledge at the Constitutional Convention whereby he supported allowing slavery to continue in exchange for the southern delegates' support on issues that he regarded crucial to the Connecticut economy. Sherman's failure to pay his debt to Brace may have sprung from

And here I will observe that I can give no other reason why the enemy did not fire upon me, only I presume they chose to take me alive, which they had full faith in, as they when our men fired upon them were fast approaching me—and what caused me to form this opinion, I had been one of the standing sentry upon the outposts for some time, therefore I presume they concluded that I would acquaint them with the state of our army. Perhaps the soldiers thought I might be sold by them and enrich their coffers; as these mercenary beings seem rather more inclined to deal in human flesh and blood than in fighting.

I belonged to one Capt. Baker's company when the attack was made upon us at Hackensack.[2] I was on the flank and the charge was made there; we gave them a warmer salute, and lost many brave Yankee-boys. Our battalion was charged by their light horse, and we beat them off with our bayonets.

After this battle, we heard that the enemy were making their way to Stanford. We marched there immediately, and arrived before them. A party marched down into some meadows to watch their motion; on discovering their superior force, we fired upon them and ran off fully believing,

> That he who fights and runs away,
> May live to fight another day—

We concealed ourselves behind a stone wall for some minutes, they lost sight of us, but continued firing for some time. As we were passing over a small rise of ground several balls whistled by us, and what was peculiarly diverting to us; one Caleb Nicholas dodged a bullet after it had passed us for about 5 seconds. We ran to the fort at Stanford but the enemy had gotten possession; we then took again to our heels. We then retreated to Salem; from thence we marched to West Point, where we remained until September. From thence we went to Horseneck—where

---

greed; men as prominent as Benjamin Rush sometimes charged Sherman with supporting legislation out of personal financial interest (Collier 292). Sherman had been in dire financial straits since 1777, despite having formerly been one of the wealthiest men and largest landholders in Litchfield County. Brace also may have been the victim of bad blood between Sherman and Benjamin Stiles, who had known each other for decades.

2. Two Captain Bakers, both with the first name John and both from Massachusetts, served in the Continental Army, one as Captain of the 12th Continental Infantry (Jan. 1 to Dec. 31, 1777) and the other as Captain of the 27th Continental Infantry (Jan. 1 to Dec. 31, 1777) (Heitman 71). Brace may have been referring to Capt. Barker, mentioned above.

we remained until winter; frequently searching about the adjacent country.[3] Finally I was in the battles at Cambridge, White Plains, Monmouth, Princeton, Newark, Frog's Point, Horseneck where I had a ball pass through my knapsack.[4] All which battles the reader can obtain a more perfect account of in history, than I can give. At last we returned to West Point and were discharged; as the war was over.[5]—Thus was I, a slave, for five years fighting for liberty.

After we were disbanded, I returned to my old master at Woodbury, with whom I lived one year; my services in the American war having emancipated me from further slavery and from being bartered or sold.— My master consented that I might go where I pleased and seek my fortune. Hearing flattering accounts of the new state of Vermont, I left Woodbury and traveled as far as the town of Lenox, in Massachusetts, where for the first time I made a bargain as a freeman for labor; I let myself to a Mr. Elisha Orsborn[6] for one month, at the price of five dollars.[7] When I had fulfilled this contract, I traveled to the town of Poultney[8] in Vermont, there again I let myself to a Mr. Abiel Parker,[9] for the sum of thirteen pounds ten shillings, for six months. Here I enjoyed the pleasures

3. Regiments were stationed at Horseneck, New York to protect the southwestern frontier.

4. A battle took place at White Plains, New York, in 1777. The Battle of Monmouth, New Jersey, was fought in June 1778. Sir Henry Clinton, who replaced General Howe as the British commander, narrowly escaped defeat at the hands of General George Washington. Brace may have been in either Horseneck, New York (see note above) or in Horseneck, Connecticut (now called Greenwich), which was in 1779 "a no-man's-land . . . filled with Tories. Plundering bands robbed and looted almost at will. It was also filled with ample supplies of food, ammunition, and salt" (Stember 361). A skirmish took place there on February 26, 1779.

5. Brace was honorably discharged with a badge of merit in 1783.

6. Lenox is located in western Massachusetts about halfway between Connecticut and Vermont. One of the first white settlers was Josiah Osborne, likely a relation of Elisha "Orsborn." He arrived in 1773, "bringing his goods in an ox-cart, and settled in what was unbroken forest" (Palmer 1). Jeremiah Osborn from Lenox fought in the Revolutionary War, as did two Osborns (Joel and Thomas) from Richmond, an adjacent town (Palmer 22). Brace may have become acquainted with the Osborn family during the war.

7. Daniel Osborn, a schoolteacher in Lenox, was paid $6.42 for teaching 71½ days in 1801, which suggests that Brace's $5 for one month's work in 1784 was not a bad rate of pay (Wood 51).

8. The town of Poultney in southwestern Vermont was chartered on September 21, 1761. It had 1121 inhabitants in 1790, a few years after Brace arrived (Joslin 49).

9. Abel Parker was a large landowner who built a saw mill near the East Poultney waterfall some time before 1800 (Joslin 49, 317).

of a freeman; my food was sweet, my labor pleasure: and one bright gleam of life seemed to shine upon me. However he not fulfilling his agreement, I let myself to Wm. Hooker, a Constable, with whom I worked only a few days.[10] I directly contracted with Mr. Belias Hill,[11] a shop joiner; but my stay with him was also of short duration; indeed it still seemed to me as it ever had done that I was fortune's football and must depend upon her gentle kicks. When I left Mr. Hill, I made an agreement with a Mr. Craw who was by trade a Tanner.[12] I determined to obtain some property, that I might in some measure enjoy the independence of the freedom I possessed. I purchased by agreement twenty five acres of land of Mr. Craw, which lay in the East Part of the town; for this land I was to work six months; he promising before witnesses to pay me $250, in failure of his procuring me a good indisputable title.

When I had paid for my land by faithfully laboring for the term agreed on, I made a tour to the pool at new Lebanon—from thence I returned to Dorset.—I bargained with John Manly a tavern-keeper, to work for him for some considerable time; in fact our agreement was that while each party was contented, I should serve him.[13]

During my servile situation with Mr. Manly I became acquainted with Widow Susannah Dublin. In the spring I settled with Mr. Manly and returned to Poultney. On my arrival in Poultney Mr. Craw solicited me to work again for him, I preferring to work in a family with whom I had once been acquainted. I bargained and continued with him until fall— well may the reader imagine that during the sun's diurnal course this summer I most fondly gazed on his last glittering beams at eve; and impatiently sighed to behold him peep from his eastern chambers, in the morn. Yes even at this late and advanced period of my life, the delightful idea of enjoying the bliss of hymen kindled warm and pleasing sensation in a heart

10. William Hooker was also a Trustee of Schools in 1784 (Joslin 42, 44).

11. Belias Hill is named in the Poultney Town Clerk's Grand List in 1785, 1786, 1787, and 1790.

12. During the 1780s and 1790s Joseph Craw appears on multiple documents regarding land, taxes, and petitions in the Poultney Town Clerk's office.

13. John Manley (1738–1816) was one of the original settlers of the "wilderness" town of Dorset, Vermont, moving there with five other men in 1768. Manley's Tavern on the West Road served food and alcohol. Manley was married to Benedict Arnold's half-sister, and their 1770s house was the first ever built using Dorset marble. He was elected first deacon of the Dorset Congregational Church in 1785, at which time it had about forty members. Manley died in 1816 and is buried in Dorset.

that ever glowed in the participation of true and mutual friendship. So long had I been acquainted with and so long had I been enervated to the keen smarts of disappointment that it seemed impossible that I should ever realize the supreme joy of being united in the holy band of matrimony, to a native African female, who possessed a reciprocal abhorrence to slavery and whose sufferings had been equal to any that can be delineated by the pen or endured by the bravest of the human race, whose history I must omit as it will swell these memoirs beyond the bounds of my limits. But in justice to her memory, I think it my duty to observe that she proved to me a virtuous, patient, loving, and prudent wife, and industry was as habitual with her as was tenderness and affection for her children. By her I was blessed with children, who prove a comfort to me in my declining years. To raise and educate my children, and instruct them in those moral virtues and religious principles which should render them useful and honest citizens in this life, was my anxious care. And if possible to lay a foundation of religious virtue on which, with the blessings of a Saviour, they might build a fabric which would insure them a blissful eternity. And it is my delight to say, I see none of them prone to the ways of evil doings.

I was married in the month of November, and moved my wife to Poultney soon after. I built me a snug log house, near one Mr. Solomon Norton,[14] where I resided one year. At the expiration of which time, I was solicited to move into the middle of the town, which I did, and went to live with the Rev. Ithamer Hibbard, Pastor of the Presbyterian Church in that town, with whom I resided about one year and six months.[15] Nothing material transpired in that time. But at the close of this period, there came one of the most distressing famines I ever knew. Many people were in danger of starving, and others were obliged to live weeks without bread.[16]

14. A prominent citizen of Poultney, Solomon Norton "built the first grist and saw mills at the Hampton Bridge Place" (Joslin 315). He was a member of the Baptist Church.

15. Ithamer Hibbard, the first settled minister in Poultney, arrived in 1780. He was a Congregationalist, and although the settlers were divided in nearly equal numbers between Congregationalists and Baptists, they united in "settling" him (Joslin 40–41). Other Hibbards (Jedadiah, John, and Asa) were active as Baptist elders throughout the state of Vermont from the 1780s through the early nineteenth century (Vermont Baptist Historical Society Papers).

16. Nathan Perkins's diary confirms Brace's description of famine in the late 1780s. Perkins notes that following two years of bad seasons, "the year 1789 will be remembered by Vermont as a day of calamity and famine – *dearness of truck & want of bread in all their dwellings.* It is supposed by the most judicious & knowing that more than 1/4 part of the people will have neither bread nor meat for 8 weeks – and that some will starve" (22).

In the time of this famine among the people, I went to chopping cole-wood for Mr. Samuel Joslin, to get iron to carry to Manchester, a distance of about 30 miles.[17] When I got one hundred weight of iron, it was my practice to take it upon my shoulder and carry it over the mountains to Manchester, and get two bushes of grain upon my back, and return to my family.[18] Thus I supported them through this distressing time.

While performing these duties, I became acquainted with my wife's old Mistress in Manchester. She owned part of a gristmill,[19] and requested me to move to Manchester, and remain until a better opportunity offered me, to clear my land.[20] Accordingly I complied with her request, and we moved down soon after, by the assistance of one Mr. Daniel Beckwith.[21] During my residence here, I raised good crops of corn and other grain, and life glided along greatly to my satisfaction.

And here it is a pleasure to observe, during all this time after my good Mrs. Stiles died, who taught me to read and expound the Bible, I continued strictly to read the same and endeavor to learn its divinity.

While in this prosperous way, Mrs. Powell[22] entered a complaint to the selectmen against me. She was instigated by a Mr. Dixon, one of the

17. Samuel Joslin and Abel Darling built a forge in Poultney. "This was actively run for some years, and furnished the blacksmiths and others with wrought iron" (Joslin 51).

18. Brace's feat became legendary in Poultney history. In 1875 the town historians wrote: "we have one instance in which a man took a hundred pounds of iron upon his shoulders, carried the same to Manchester, and exchanged for its equivalent in meal, and brought that to his home in Poultney on his shoulders. The man's name is forgotten, but there is no doubt of the fact" (Joslin 28).

19. A mill for grinding grain. Susannah Dublin's unnamed mistress may have been a partner of Timothy Mead (below) who built one of the first gristmills in Manchester.

20. Chartered in the 1760s, Manchester, Vermont, was a booming town with a reputation for religious diversity, drinking, gambling, and "immorality." Between 1776 and 1791 the population of Manchester more than doubled, from less than 600 to 1,276 (Bigelow 28, 25).

21. The Beckwiths were an established family in Manchester (Bigelow 293).

22. Elizabeth (Harris) Powell (b. 1748) was the second wife of Martin Powell (1731–1800), an extensive landholder who was one of the most powerful men in early Manchester. A former lieutenant in the Continental Army, Powell (also spelled Powel) worked in Manchester as an innkeeper, selectman, town clerk, treasurer, jail keeper, justice of the peace, and judge of probate. He was elected to the Vermont Legislature and served on several powerful state committees. After marrying Martin Powell in 1778, Elizabeth Powell bore three children, and the 1790 U.S. Census lists one free person of color (most likely Bersheba) in the Powell household along with three white children (two girls and a boy). The nine children that Martin Powell had with his first wife, Rhoda Thompson, were already grown (Bigelow 270–72).

selectmen.[23]—The complaint amounted to this, that I was a black man. The corruption and superstition, mingled with the old Connecticut bigotry and puritanism, made certain people think a Negro had no right to raise their own children. Therefore I was complained of, that the selectmen might be enabled to bind out the children which my wife had by her first husband. Dixon wanted the boy; that was the moving spring to the complaint.

As he was about twelve years of age, and began to be useful, and could earn more than his living, it was sufficient to induce almost any honest selectman to procure a complaint to be entered, that he might have the profits of his labors.

Dixon and one Timothy Mead[24] came to my house one day to take him away, but I expostulated with them and told them that it was unchristian in human religion and unnatural for them to attempt it. As Moses had made his special canon in which he was inspired by the father of the Universe, which was that we must not afflict a fatherless child or oppress a stranger. I quoted many passages of scripture to prove the impropriety of a christian people holding in chains of bondage their fellow beings, who are commanded to unite as one and must partake of the blood of Christ our Saviour, and while thus partaking the Sacrament hold the cup in one hand and the scourge or whip in the other; for cannot an African slave become a christian and member of the same church, with a miserable owner; certainly, and no man dare object to it. No! not even an Indian, Mahomitan, Turk or Ethiopian heathen would perform such a deed.— But all my entreaties were in vain. They scorned at my expostulation. They took away the boy and bound him out. One further reason I gave them, which was that I came to Manchester to stay for a season, and that I had land in Poultney which was paid for, and that I intended to move there immediately, and very much wanted the boy's assistance in clearing the same. But Dixon told me it would be in vain for me to attempt to clear my land, as I had no oxen, without which I could do nothing. I asked him how many

23. Archibald Dixon is listed in the 1790 U.S. Census as a head of family in Poultney, and his household contained one free person of color (most likely Brace's stepson).

24. One of Manchester's original proprietors, Timothy Mead (1724–1802) owned 200 acres on which he built a gristmill, sawmill, fulling mill, distillery, and store. Although "no professor of faith," he eventually donated land for building the Baptist church. All his children but one were said to be heavy drinkers, and his entire estate passed out of the family on his death (Bigelow 27, 274).

young Americans left their fathers' dwellings, in the old towns, and traveled far into the wilds of Vermont and commenced clearing farms for their future residence, with no other tool of husbandry, save only the ax upon his shoulder; and when he had walked over the lands of his anticipated residence, pitched upon some favorite spot for his and his offspring's future dwellings, and when he struck his ax into a fair towering maple of the forest, whether his heart did not swell and vibrate with a glow of anticipated delight indescribable. And if he would return me my poor little negro boy, my prospects would be as good as theirs. But I might as well laid pearl before swine, as all this had no effect.

And to close the scene of oppression, my wife had a little girl by the name of Bersheba. She also must be bound out by the authority, or by my consent, and to alleviate her situation, I consented to have her bound out to a Mrs. Powell, on her indenture or agreement to learn the girl to read, and to give her a good feather bed, when she should arrive at the age of eighteen, at which time she had fulfilled her indentures and was free.

But that good christian woman never attempted to learn her to read, neither did she ever give her the bed. I could get no redress—for what lawyer would undertake the cause of an old African Negro against a respectable widow in Manchester, who had many respectable acquaintances. None, for if there had been one willing to take up in my defense, he would have been flung out of business for taking up so dirty a cause against so respectable a personage as the Widow Powell, on no other evidence only the Negro's family, who might swear to the contract.[25] Therefore as no gentleman of the Bar would disgrace himself so much as to engage in the cause, Mrs. Powell went free and escaped in her iniquity with impunity.

25. Elizabeth Powell was widowed in 1800, and Bersheba most likely turned eighteen shortly thereafter.

Chapter 10

Return to Poultney—Vicissitudes there, the persecutions of Jery Goram—attempts to bind out my children—obliged to sell my land—removal to Shelden—Vicissitudes there—removal to Georgia on the shoals of Lake Champlain—residence there—loss of my beloved companion—reflections thereon.

Soon after these Christian salutes, I returned to Poultney, settled upon my land and went to clearing it up as fast as was in my power. The first season I cleared about seven acres, and sowed it with wheat, enclosed the same with an excellent pole and log fence. But one Jery Goram,[1] who wanted my land, & to whom I refused to sell it, pulled down my fence and let in cattle. The same year I had a crop of good corn, which land I had cleared off early in the spring, he also turned his cattle into that and destroyed it, so that I did not get five bushels from 8 Acres, which otherwise would have produced me more than one hundred bushels.

The next year Goram came to me, and wished to join with me in making sugar, and offered to find kettles, as I had none, also to help me make troughs if I would find trees, and do a share of the work, which was agreed to, by me. At the close of the season, I had 8 lb. When we came to divide, he and his family had found means to get away the remainder; as we had

---

1. Jared ("Jery") Goram and two of his brothers, James and Seth, settled in Poultney after the Revolution. (Their name is spelled "Goram" in the Poultney Town Clerk's Grand List of 1785, but "Gorham" in later lists.) Jared Goram and Jeffery Brace settled south of an area known as Ames Hollow on rocky, wooded land surrounded by mountains. Jared owned significantly less land than his two brothers and apparently achieved little in life. Poultney town historians stated in 1875 that Jared "married Asenath Morgan, and had several children. He died many years ago, and his children are all dead" (Joslin 269).

two hundred trees tapped, I thought the complement was small, and expostulated but to no effect.

The next Spring, while I went to town to buy a kettle, Susan went to tapping trees, as she said she had frequently made sugar while with her old master. Goram saw her at work and came down to drive her off, as he said he had the possession there, and would not suffer her to work upon the land. She then asked him whether Jeffery had not bought that land of Mr. Craw. Goram said if he had, it was his land, and he would occupy it, and she should not tap the trees, and then attempted to take the pail, which contained the spouts, from her. They both pulled and broke the pail; he got it away from her and dashed it into the brook, which broke it into pieces. He also flung away her tapping iron: at which she got away his ax, and flung that into the brook after her things. Then he clinched and attempted to fling her in after them all; but she proving too stout for him, like to have wrestled him into the brook; at any rate she got him down, and rubbed him well in the face and neck, with good white March snow. She then threatened to complain to the authority; he tried to dissuade her but to no effect, as she was determined to have redress, and went to Capt. Josiah Grant,[2] and entered a complaint.

It was late when I returned; or before I slept I should have avenged the injury. The majesty of Guina rose indignant in my breast, and I was determined to give him a drubbing. But the next morning, Capt. Grant and Joseph Adams,[3] came up and we left the matter to them, as neighbors; who said we ought under all circumstances keep peace in the neighborhood. As Goram claimed a share in the troughs, he must ask Susan's pardon, and occupy one share of the sugar place for that season. Thus this affair was settled.

After spring opened, I went to the Town of Wells, which was situated south of Poultney, on the line of the state of New York, where I purchased me a very handsome yoke of young oxen. After I had been in possession of my oxen a few days, I purchased me twenty five apple trees, and while setting them out, I directed my boys to drive the oxen down into my meadow, in order to bate them before I went to plowing. While thus bating, the division fence between Goram and myself, not being made, as it belonged

2. Josiah Grant, one of Poultney's early settlers, served on town committees in the 1780s (Joslin 269).

3. Joseph Adams appears in the Poultney Town Clerk's Grand List of October 4, 1781.

to him to make that part—my cattle got across the line into his meadow;
he ran after them, flung a large stone, and broke the leg of one of them,
which matter we left to men, Judge Ward[4] and Stephen Clark,[5] who decided that he must give me fifteen dollars and take the ox. Mortified at this
decision, Goram entered a complaint to the selectmen, in order to get my
children bound out by the town. The authority came to me about the business; but I plainly told them that as I had suffered so much by bondage
myself, my children should never be under the direction of any other
person whilst I lived. That if they would keep Goram from destroying my
property, I could support my family, as well as Goram could his, and they
never wanted for wholesome food or clean linen, neither were they back-
ward in education.

Some short time after, my pigs got out of the pasture and went into
Goram's corn; as soon as it was discovered by my family, my wife went
after them. Mrs. Goram had caught one; Susan expostulated with her,
but she would not let her have the pig; therefore, Susan took the Pig by
the hind legs, and forced it from her. For this affair, Goram and his wife
brought an action of assault and battery against me and my wife, for the
assault and battery committed by Susan, wife of Jeffery Brace, upon the
body of Goram's wife. But on the trial it appearing that there was no assault, the court acquitted us and immersed him with costs, which judgment so vexed Goram, that he again complained to the authority, in order
to get my children bound out. The selectmen came, and when we were arguing upon the subject, I asked, if they were strangers in Africa, whether
they would be willing to have their children bound out to Negroes; they
said that was a different case, for white men were more capable than
Africans of taking care themselves. I turned with indignation from them
and their arguments, by telling them that while I lived no authority should
bind out my children. After this Goram went to Middletown, and got one
Clark to come to Poultney to try me, which he did, and judged me to pay
twelve dollars; thus I was hunted down at last.

4. Judge William Ward (1743–1819), an original settler, served as a moderator of town
meetings in the 1770s and was elected to be Poultney's first representative in the Vermont
General Assembly in 1778 (Joslin 24, 33, 39). A member of the Poultney Baptist Church,
he became the town's Probate Judge and built Poultney's first court house in the second
story of his late-eighteenth-century house, which is still standing in an area known as Fenel
Hollow. Brace's farm was located about a half mile down the road.
5. Stephen Clark is listed on two petitions filed in Poultney in 1806 and 1825.

The next spring, I said to one of my neighbors, if Goram pulled down my fence and destroyed my crops that year, I should be tempted to burn his barn. For this I was arrested and tried by two justices, who, on a fair and full examination of the matter, honorably acquitted me.

At length Goram swore he would whip me, and when I went up to him, in order to take it, he would run away from me, and thereby save me from a good drubbing; and to wind up this scene of difficulty, we had each of us, an excellent ram, they met, and as I suppose mine so maimed his that he died of the wounds. It was secretly reported around the neighborhood that Old Jef. had killed Goram's ram, and his wife had made the meat into mince pies for Thanksgiving; and one David Varnum[6] was sent as a spy in order to enquire of my wife where she got the meat to make her mince pies. She very ingeniously told him that Jeffery had wrought for Major Dewey,[7] who paid him in Beef, which proving to be the truth, put an end to their slander.

As it was against the law in Vermont to let rams go at large in a certain season of the year, mine was fastened to a stake in my meadow near the house. One night the stake was pulled up and the ram went off. While my boys were looking for him in the morning, Goram gave them the halter with which he was held, but said he had not seen the ram; in consequence of which my ram got among his sheep and was forfeited.

These insults were more patiently borne by me than they were by my children, whose feelings were alive to every opprobrium that was cast upon their father. They would often threaten to avenge my wrongs, but this I always discouraged. Frequently would I expostulate with them and instruct them in the lessons of divine patience. I told them the best way for us, as we were of a sable race, to get redress was to return good for evil, and thereby shame and mortify the ostentatious destroyer of our rights. This to them seemed like false doctrine. However they generally paid due attention to my instruction.

6. David Varnum was probably the "mulatto" son of Joseph Varnum, a white man whose household contained four free people of color (and no other whites) in the town of Sunderland, which was adjacent to Manchester (1800 U.S. Census). As another family of color, the Varnums most likely socialized with the Braces. Members of both families later moved to St. Albans. A notice in northern Vermont's first newspaper, the *St. Albans Adviser,* reveals that the Varnum children were as vulnerable as the Brace children to being forced into indentured servitude: "Ran away from the subscriber, on the 7th of March . . . an indented boy, named JOHN VARNUM" 2 June 1808).

7. Zebadiah Dewey, one of the original settlers of Poultney.

But to end this disagreeable relation, after living about seven years in this unhappy situation by the side of Goram, who was determined to be a thorn in my side, I sold my land to the best advantage possible, and was determined to move to some distant part of the country where I might enjoy the evening of life in a more tranquil and peaceable manner than I possibly could do in this place. I got about half of the value of my land; as Goram pretended to have an adverse claim, therefore no man would give me the value of it and have to quiet Goram.

When I had sold, I talked some of going to Kentucky with Colonel Mathew Lyon.[8] But I did not know that being so near slavery again, they might haul me in; or that I should say something which would cause me to be prosecuted and punished as a seditious person. Therefore, after all matters were settled in Poultney, I removed to Sheldon in Vermont, a new town, about 114 miles north of Poultney.[9] As I never received half of the value of my land, and after arriving with my family in Sheldon, a new town, almost destitute of provisions, I underwent many difficulties for the want of the remainder, being among strangers who felt but little kindness for people of my color. However fortune placed me in a happy spot.

I went to live on some land belonging to Major Jedediah Clark, who had been a neighbor to me.[10] I also lived near Josiah Tuttle, Esq. who was to me a benefactor, as I was greatly indebted to him for many acts of kindness.[11]

On this land I resided almost two years, when I purchased fifty acres of land of Major Samuel Shelden.[12] I paid him down in cash twenty five dollars, and he was to wait six years for the remainder, the price being five

8. Brace had met Matthew Lyon when he was a young indentured servant in the household of Jabez Bacon in Woodbury, Connecticut. See introduction.

9. A village near the Canadian border (eleven miles north of St. Albans), Sheldon was chartered in 1792 and was named in honor of Elisha Sheldon, a lawyer and judge from Litchfield County, Connecticut who had served for eighteen years in the Upper House of Connecticut's General Assembly and thus was acquainted with Benjamin Stiles, Sr. His son, Col. Elisha Sheldon, Jr. commanded the Second Regiment of Light Dragoons in the Continental army (*History of Litchfield County* 122; Aldrich 617).

10. Jedediah Clark had been Brace's neighbor in Woodbury, Connecticut, where he married Susannah Smith in May 1756. They had a son also named Jedediah, born in Woodbury in 1766. A Benjamin Clark opened the first store in Sheldon around 1803.

11. Josiah Tuttle, Esq. was born in New Haven, Connecticut in 1774. After marrying Sarah Ann Weeks in Rutland, Vermont, in 1795, he became a clergyman and landholder in Sheldon, where he died in 1816.

12. This land transaction took place in May 1804 (see introduction and appendix C).

dollars per Acre. I cleared about ten acres fit for corn; but there came a man, and wanted the whole lot; his name was Crocker, and Shelden sold him the whole lot, and told me he would pay me for the betterments, and let me have a lot near the middle of the town, which was never performed: yet I have that charity for the memory of Major Shelden, that if he had lived, he would have amply satisfied me.[13]

Finding I could not get the land contemplated I removed in the spring of 1804,[14] to Georgia, a pleasant situated town on the banks of Lake Champlain, where I purchased with my son-in-law sixty acres of land of Esq. Evtets,[15] and where I contemplated spending my days.

Here I settled down in the peaceful sunshine of anticipated delight. Industry caused prosperity to hover round my cot. But alas! when gliding along in the peace and sunshine of earthly felicity—veiled were the Heavens in black. The partner of my life was called from me, and her soul wafted into a boundless eternity. Short was the warning, but heavy the blow. She was taken sick on the 8th of March, 1807, and died 19th of the same month. The throbbing and tender emotion of my bosom during her illness are indescribable, but death sealed the fate as indelible; and it was my duty to be content, but I was left without an earthly companion, to linger out the remainder of my days.

13. See introduction and deed dated 24 June 1805 in appendix C. Samuel B. Sheldon died suddenly in 1807.

14. The date more likely was June 1805.

15. Either James Evarts (1754–1825) or Reuben Evarts (1763–1839), brothers who were Revolutionary War veterans and founding members of the town of Georgia, Vermont. They each owned a great deal of land and engaged in dozens of land transactions during the period. Brace's name does not appear in the Georgia town records of land transactions, so it is likely that he purchased the land in his son-in-law's name, which he does not give us.

Chapter 11

Manner of conversion—conversion—ideas of baptism—baptised at Georgia— conclusion.

Here I think it my duty to take a review of my life, so far as to give an account of my religious experiences. As before observed, during my residence with the Widow Stiles, she taught me to read the Bible, as that contained those religious truths which were necessary for the salvation of my soul. She also had me baptised according to the religious tenets of the church to which she belonged. During my services in the American war, I paid but little attention to her instructions. But after my emancipation and arrival at Poultney and during my residence with the good old Mr. Joseph Craw, I not speaking very good English for my own amusement and instruction employed all my leisure hours in reading the Bible. This opened my eyes in some degree, and I began seriously to reflect on my situation, as it related to man, and what I was to my Creator. The first aid I received from scripture was Moses' declaration "the Lord our God, has no respect of persons." Then I read in the tenth chapter of the Acts of the apostles the following truth:

Ver 34. Then Peter opened his mouth, and said, Of a truth I perceive that God is no respecter of persons:

35 But in every nation he that feareth him, and worketh righteousness, is accepted with him.

36 The word which God sent unto the children of Israel, preaching peace by Jesus Christ; (he is Lord of all;)

37 That word, I say, ye know, which was published throughout all Judea, and began from Galilee, after the baptism which John preached;

38 How God anointed Jesus of Nazareth with the Holy Ghost, and with power; who went about doing good, and healing all that were oppressed of the devil: for God was with him.

39 And we are witnesses of all things which he did, both in the land of the Jews and in Jerusalem; whom they slew, and hanged on a tree:

40 Him God raised up the third day, and shewed him openly;

41 Not to all the people, but unto witnesses chosen before of God, even to us who did eat and drink with him after he rose from the dead.

42 And he commanded us to preach unto the people, and to testify that it is he which was ordained of God to be the Judge of quick and dead.

43 To him give all the prophets witness, that through his name, whosoever believeth in him shall receive remission of sins.

44 While Peter yet spake these words, the Holy Ghost fell on all them which heard the word.

45 And they of the circumcision which believed were astonished, as many as came with Peter, because that on the Gentiles also was poured out the gifts of Holy ghost.

46 For they heard them speak with tongues, and magnify God. Then answered Peter,

47 Can any man forbid water, that these should not be baptized, which have received the Holy Ghost as well as we?

48 And he commanded them to be baptized in the name of the Lord. Then prayed they him to tarry certain days.

When I seriously reflected upon the assurances contained in the foregoing scripture, my eyes were opened, and I was encouraged and verily believed that I was equally acceptable with all mankind.

Revelations, Chap. 4, Ver. 2.

Thou art worthy, O Lord, to receive glory, and honor, and power; for thou hast created all things; and for thy pleasure they are and were created.

Also, I read that God made man after his own image and breathed the breath of life into him, and man became a living soul. Here I reflected there was nothing intimated what color either God or man was. And in Psalms, it is said—"Look unto me all ye ends of the earth, and believe and ye shall be saved, for I am God, and none else besides me."

Thus I was strengthened. I reflected upon my lonesome situation among the sons of men, I could discover no hope of consolation only in a redeemer, I ventured to address the throne of grace. I began to behold the beauty, power, majesty, and glory of an all wise and just God, who is able to save me, even in the remotest ends of the earth; who had supported and protected me through all trials and suffering while in the hands of my tyrants. Groaning under the lash of unnatural masters, I fancied my life had been preserved by his Almighty shield for some good ends. I hoped I was to be made an instrument for the redemption of my African brethren, from the galling chains of bondage; or for conveying the light of christianity to my native land. This taste of divine goodness gave me courage. "Ask and ye shall receive, seek and ye shall find, knock and it shall be opened unto you."

St. John, 3d Chap. 16th verse. For God so loved the world, that he gave his only begotten son, that whosoever believeth in him should not perish, but have everlasting life.

17th For God sent not his son into the world to condemn the world, but that the world through him might be saved.

Here I thought it my duty to pray to God, in and through the Savior Jesus Christ. Accordingly I went down into a distant meadow, chose a silent spot by the side of a large birch log; the sun was just setting, and the heavens seemed to be perfectly serene, all nature were retiring to rest. I kneeled me down and attempted in humble adoration to offer up my fervent ejaculations, to the throne of grace. I prayed for all mankind, for all my African brethren, whether at home, or in foreign lands, groaning out a miserable existence in slavery; in short for all heathen and christian nations, that those in darkness might receive the knowledge of the Mediator and savior Jesus Christ.

This was on Friday evening, I felt some relief, but I was in great darkness, and heavily pressed with the weight of my sins.

On Saturday morning Mr. Craw told me he wanted me to go to the north of his farm and get some lime stones. We went and wrought all day. On Saturday evening I met some of my associates, who invited me to go and amuse ourselves on the Sabbath as we were wont to do. I felt such a weight of guilt pressing upon me, I could not admonish them. I therefore turned from them and gave an evasive or no answer.

On Sunday morning, Mr. Craw, that good old christian, addressed the throne of grace. I secretly prayed in my heart that my load of guilt might be removed that I could join with him in christian faith. But such was my situation, all my iniquities stared me full in the face. I sunk before it and acknowledged my guilt. On Monday morning, I went into the woods to cut some timber, to use about the lime pit. The wind blew upon the tops of the trees, and I thought they cursed me; in short it seemed as though all nature held me in abhorrence. I dare not begin to chop, and walked backwards and forwards for some time. I dare not attempt to pray, it appeared my prayers would be the height of iniquity; I thought Mr. Craw would blame me if I did not work. At length I ventured to say the Lord's prayer, this gave me considerable relief. I then began to chop, Mr. Craw's son came down, and we wrought until noon; we went up to dinner, but I could not eat one morsel. Mrs. Craw took notice of it and enquired the cause. I could not say one word. In the afternoon, I took the oxen and went to drawing the timber we had chopped. All nature seemed to frown upon me. I was so weak I could not load the logs upon the sled. Young Craw came to my assistance; we continued our labor until night. I went to the barn to turn out the cattle and fodder. After I had flung down the hay and while still on the mow, I ventured to pray. I prayed for some time. All at once, I felt light as air. I prayed more fervently, a region of happiness seemed to be opened before me. My load of guilt was removed, and I thought I heard a voice say, God can be just and justify the chief of sinners. That night I enjoyed all the sweets and felt all the consolation which appertains to man this side of the Grave. I prayed and felt the immediate assistance of the redeeming spirit of all perfection. I was strengthened by faith, and hope seemed to soothe all my anxieties. I remained in this situation for some weeks; my knowledge of Christ seemed to increase daily.

Then I began to think of baptism. As before observed, I had once been baptized, but for what reason I then did not understand; I viewed it as a favor of my good mistress Stiles. And if I had been told that it was a covenant necessary to be performed, I did not understand it; therefore I thought at this time, it was my duty to search for myself; I read in Matthew:—Go ye therefore, and teach all nations, and he that believeth, and is baptized shall be saved. I also read in the four Evangelists, the same doctrine.

Then I began to reflect what belief was, and what we must believe; and it seemed to me that I must believe in the Lord Jesus Christ as the son of God, as the only Mediator and Savior of mankind. Then what is baptism. I read in the 3d Chap. Matthew, the following Scripture—Ver. 13 Then cometh Jesus from Galilee to Jordan unto John, to be baptized of him:

14 But John forbade him saying, I have need to be baptized of thee, and comest thou to me.

15. And Jesus answering, said unto him, suffer it to be so now: for thus it becometh us to fulfill all righteousness. Then he suffered him.

16 And Jesus, when he was baptized, went up strait way out of the water: and Lo! the Heavens were opened unto him, and he saw the spirit of God descending like a dove, and lighting upon him.

17 And Lo! a voice from Heaven, saying, this is my beloved Son, in whom I am well pleased.

Believing it my duty as much as possible to follow the examples of the savior, I was convinced by the foregoing scripture that plunging or being immersed in water was the true baptism contemplated in the gospel. Therefore I concluded to follow the example (in this respect) of the redeemer. Also the Apostle Paul said, "Be ye buried with Christ in baptism."

I continued in this belief searching for a church with whom I could commune, until my settling in Georgia before mentioned. There I believed it my duty to enter into full communion. Accordingly on the 6th of June 1805, I was baptized in Georgia, by the Rev. Elder David Hulebert, Pastor of the Baptist Church in Swanton, by which I became a member of the Baptist Church in Georgia, with which I have walked to this time endeavoring as much as possible not to fall out by the way.[1]

And now after having passed through so many varying scenes of life, and having lost my beloved companion, as before mentioned, and being left as it were, alone in this world, I have concluded it my duty to myself, to all Africans who can read, to the Church, in short to all mankind, to thus publish these my memoirs, that all may see how poor Africans have been and perhaps now are abused by a christian and enlightened people. Being old and blind, almost destitute of property, it may bring me something to make me comfortable in my declining days, but above all, it is my anxious wish that this simple narrative may be the means of opening the hearts of those who hold slaves and move them to consent to give them that freedom which they themselves enjoy, and which all mankind have an equal right to possess.

Jeremiah, 9th Chap. Ver. 1st. Oh that my head were waters, and mine eyes a fountain of tears, that I might weep day and night for the slain of the daughter of my people.

1. The Baptist Church in Georgia, Vermont, was organized without a pastor in 1793. David Hurlburt was ordained pastor of the Swanton Baptist Church in 1802 (Vermont Baptist Historical Society Papers). The 1800 U.S. Census counted 858 people (excluding Indians) in Swanton, including 13 free people of color, all of whom lived singly in white households. Many of Brace's descendants have remained in the St. Albans–Swanton region, which is just south of Quebec and is one of the most vital centers of Abenaki Indian life in Vermont.

Apology

The writer of the foregoing memoirs deems it his duty to apologize to those who read them for many apparent repetitions in the narrative which were unavoidable, as the narrator not speaking plain English, it was extremely difficult to get a regular chain of his ideas; also in relating, he would frequently recollect circumstances, which he had omitted in their proper places.

But the writer has taken unwearied pains to render it as amusing and correct as possible, carefully avoiding every circumstance which might tend to wound the feelings of any individual or society of men.

The scripture is inserted by the request of the narrator, and under his immediate direction and every fact recorded according to his relation, and much in his own language.

The Author.

Appendix A

Deeds of Manumission Drawn by William Welch

Copied from copies in the Barbados Department of Archives

Edward Bridges—Clerk to James Sutherland of Birchin lane, London, maketh oath and saith that he this Deponent was present and did see William Welch of London Mariner Master and Commander of the Ship Berwick trading from the Port of London to the Island of Barbados and now at the Port of London sign seal and as and for his act and deed in due form of Law deliver the Deed of Manumission hereunto annexed and marked A bearing date the Eighteenth Day of October now last past, and being a Deed of Manumission from the said William Welch to his Negroe man slave named Michael, that James Alexander Sutherland of Birchin lane aforesaid was also the present, and that he this Deponent and the said James Alexander Sutherland did severally subscribe their Names as witnesses to the due Execution of the said annexed Deed of Manumission

Edwd Bridges

Sworn at London this 22nd November one thousand Eight Hundred and Six—Before me.—

Wm. Leighton—

To all to whom these presents shall come, William Welch of London Mariner Master and Commander of the Ship Berwick trading from the Port of London to the Island of Barbadoes and now at the Port of London sendeth Greeting. Whereas by a certain Deed of Conveyance bearing date the twenty fourth day of July in the year of our Lord one thousand eight hundred and six Sarah Hartle of the Parish of Saint Michael in the Island of Barbadoes free Negroe for the considerations therein mentioned did grant bargain and sell alien remise release enseosse and confirm unto the said William Welch his heirs and assigns a certain negroe man slave named Michael to hold unto the said William Welch his heirs and assigns to the sole and only proper use benefit and behoof of the said William Welch his heirs and assigns forever as by the said Deed of Conveyance herein before in part recited reference being thereunto had may more fully and at large appear, and whereas the said William Welch for the considerations herein after mentioned is desirous of manumising his said Negroe man slave named Michael now in the Island of Barbadoes of and from all Bondage and future servitude and slavery whatsoever Now therefore know ye and these presents witness that the said William Welch for and in consideration of the sum of ten shillings of good and lawful money of the United Kingdom of Great Britain and Ireland current in Great Britain at or before the sealing and delivery of these presents to him the said William Welch in hand well and truly paid by or on behalf of the said negroe man slave named Michael (the Receipt whereof he the said William Welch doth hereby confess and acknowledge) and for other good causes and valuable considerations him the said William Welch thereunto moving He the said William Welch hath manumitted enfranchised released and forever set free and by these presents doth manumise enfranchise release and forever set free the said negroe man slave named Michael of and from all and all manner of bondage future servitude and slavery whatsoever as well in the said Island of Barbadoes as in any other Island Part Port or Place whatsoever and wheresoever whereat or wherein Providence may order his Lot to be at all times forever hereafter and the said William Welch for the considerations aforesaid the freedom of the said Negroe man slave named Michael against him the said William Welch his heirs executors and administrators and all and every other person and persons whomsoever lawfully claiming or to claim by from under or in trust for him them or any of them shall and will warrant and forever defend by these presents.—In witness whereof the said William Welch in presence of James Sutherland of the City of London Notary Public and the witnesses hereunto subscribing hath hereunto set his hand seal at London this eighteenth day of October in the forty sixth year of the Reign of our Sovereign Lord George the third by the Grace of God of the United Kingdom of Great Britain and Ireland King Defender of the Faith of and in the year of our Lord one thousand eight hundred and six—And in further confirmation thereof the said James Sutherland hath hereunto set his Hand and Notarial Seal.

    Wm Welch SEAL

Signed Sealed and Delivered being first duly stamped in the presence of Edwd Bridges—J.A. Sutherland—Received the Day and year last above written of and from the above mentioned negroe man slave named Michael the sum of ten shillings of good and lawful money of the United Kingdom of Great Britain and Ireland current in Great Britain being the consideration money above mentioned to be paid by him or on his behalf to me./

Wm Welch

Witness   Edwd. Bridges   J.A. Sutherland.
                Jas. Sutherland—Not. Pub./ seal

Source: Barbados Department of Archives, RB1/235/27-29

To all to whom these presents shall come William Welch of the Island of Barbados Mariner now in London sendeth greeting. Whereas Florella Clark of the Parish of Saint Michael and Island of Barbados a Free Negro, by a certain Bill of Sale or Deed of Conveyance bearing date the thirteenth day of April one thousand eight hundred and seven did for the considerations therein mentioned grant bargain sell alien remise release enseosse and confirm unto the said William Welch his heirs and assigns forever, a certain Negro man slave named John Clarke and also a certain Negro Boy slave named James George Clarke and the reversion and reversions remainder and remainders, rents, issues, services, and proffits of the said slaves thereby granted bargained sold released and confirmed or meant mentioned or intended so to be and all the estate right title interest use trust possession property benefit claim and demand whatsoever both at law or equity of her the said Florella Clarke of into and out of or from the said slaves, to hold the said slaves hereby granted and confirmed or meant mentioned or intended so to be unto the said William Welch his heirs and assigns forever as by the said Bill of Sale or Deed of Conveyance reference being thereunto had may more fully and at large appear which said Negro man slave named John Clarke, he the said William Welch for the considerations herein after mentioned is desirious of manumitting. Now therefore know ye and these presents witness that the said William Welch for and in consideration of the faithful services of the said Negro man slave named John Clarke rendered to him the said William Welch since he became his slave and also for and in consideration of the sum of ten shillings of good and lawful money of the United Kingdom of Great Britian and Ireland current in Great Britian and as money is valued in England by or on behalf of the said Negro man slave named John Clarke to him the said William Welch at or before the ensealing and delivery of these presents in hand well and truly paid (the receipt whereof he the said William Welch doth hereby confess and acknowledge) and for other good and valuable causes and considerations him the said William Welch thereunto moveing, he the said William Welch hath manumitted enfranchised released and forever set free and by these presents doth manumit enfranchise release and forever set free the said Negro man slave named John Clarke of and from all and all manner of bondage, future servitude and slavery whatsoever as well in the said Island of Barbados as in any other Island part or place whatsoever and wheresoever where at or wherein

Providence may order his lot to be at all times and time forever hereafter
and the said William Welch in consideration of the promises the freedom
of the said Negro man slave named John Clarke against him the said
William Welch his heirs executors and administrators and all and every
other person and persons whomsoever lawfully claiming or to claim by
from under or in trust for him them or any of them shall and will warrant
and forever defend by these presents. In witness whereof the said William
Welch in the presence of James Sutherland of the City of London Notary
Public and the witnesses hereunto subscribing hath hereunto set his hand
and seal at London this seventeenth day of June in the forty seventh year
of the Reign of our Sovereign Lord George the third by the Grace of God
of the United Kingdom of Great Britian and Ireland King Defender of the
Faith to and in the year of our Lord one thousand eight hundred & seven
and in further confirmation thereof the said James Sutherland hath hereunto set his hand & seal:/

William Welch SEAL

Signed sealed and delivered being first duly stampt, in the presence of:/
the words shall and will warrant and forever defend by these presents being first interlined

Edward Bridges

Received on the day of the date of the foregoing Deed of Manumission of
and from the above named Negro man slave named John Clarke, the sum
of ten shillings of good and lawful money of the United Kingdom of Great
Britian and Ireland current in Great Britian and as money is valued in England being the consideration money abovementioned to be paid by or on
his behalf to me.

0—10.0.

Wm Welch

Witness Edwd. Bridges
    Quad. Attestor—   Jas. Sutherland
NOTARIAL SEAL   Notary Public

Source: Barbados Department of Archives, RB3/41/130-132

Barbados:/ To all to whom these presents shall come William Welch late of the Parish of Saint Michael & Island of Barbados, Mariner now in London sendeth greeting. Whereas by a certain Bill of Sale or Deed of Conveyance bearing date the fifteenth day of April one thousand eight hundred and seven, Christman Small of the said Parish and Island aforesaid a free Man of Colour for divers good causes and considerations him thereunto moveing & also for & in consideration of the sum of ten shillings of good and lawful money of the said Island of Barbados to him in hand well and truly paid by the said William Welch, he the said Christman Small did grant bargain and sell alien remise release enseosse and confirm unto the said William Welch his heirs and assigns, those two several slaves to wit:/ Henrietta a woman and Molly Sue a girl with the issue and increase of the said slaves thereafter to be born, and the reversion and reversions, remainder and remainders rents issues services and proffits thereof and all the estate right, title, interest, use, trust, inheritance, possession properly claim benefit and demand whatsoever either at law or in equity of him the said Christman Small of into and out of the said slaves and premises. To hold the said slaves with their issue and increase thereby granted & conveyed or intended so to be unto the said William Welch his heirs and assigns to the sole and only proper use benefit and behoof of the said William Welch his heirs and assigns forever, as by the said Bill of Sale or Deed of Conveyance. Reference being thereunto had may more fully and at Large appear which said several slaves the said William Welch for divers good causes & considerations him thereunto moveing is desirious of manumitting. Now therefore know ye, and these presents witness that the said William Welch for and in consideration of the faithful services of the said woman slave named Henrietta rendered to him the said William Welch since she became his slave & for and in consideration of the sum of ten shillings of good and lawful money of the United Kingdom of Great Britian & Ireland, current in Great Britian and as money is valued in England to him the said William Welch in hand at or before the ensealing and delivery of these presents by or on behalf of the said woman slave named Henrietta well and truly paid (the Receipt whereof he doth hereby confess and acknowledge) and for other good & valuable causes and considerations him the said William Welch hereunto moveing he the said William Welch hath manumitted enfranchised, released, and forever set free and by these presents, doth manumise, enfranchise, release, and forever set free the said woman slave named Henrietta with her future issue offspring and increase hereafter to be born of & from all and all manner of bondage, future servitude and slavery whatsoever as well in the said Island of Barbados as in any other Island Port or Parcel whatsoever and wheresoever whereas or wherein Providence may order her and their respective lots to be at all time and times forever hereafter, and the said William Welch for the considerations aforesaid the freedom of the said woman slave named Henrietta and her future issue offspring and increase hereafter to be born against him the said William Welch his heirs executors and administrators and all and every other person and persons whomsoever lawfully claiming or to claim by from or under or in trust for him, them, or any of them, shall and will forever defend by these presents, In witness whereof the said William Welch in presence of James Sutherland of the City of London, Notary Public and the witnesses hereunto subscribing hath hereunto set his hand and seal at London the seventeenth day of June in the Forty Seventh year of the Reign of Our Sovereign George the third by the Grace of God of the United Kingdom of Great Britian and Ireland King Defender of the Faith to and in the year of Our Lord one thousand eight hundred and seven and in further confirmation thereof the said James Sutherland hath hereunto set his hand and notarial seal.

Wm Welch SEAL

Signed sealed & delivered being first duly stamped in the presence of:/
  Edward Bridges

Received the day of the date of the above written deed of manumission of and from the abovenamed woman slave Henrietta the sum of ten shillings of good and lawful money of Great Britian (being the consideration money mentioned) to be paid by or on her behalf to me

Wm Welch
Quod Attestor
Jas. Sutherland, Notary Public
NOTARIAL SEAL

Witness:/
  Edward Bridges

Source: Barbados Department of Archives, RB3/41/145-146

Appendix B

Legal Documents Related to Jeffrey Brace's Pension Application, 1818–1821

State of Vermont   On this fourth day of April 1818 before me the
Franklin County   subscriber one of the Judges of Franklin Count
                    Court personally appears Jeffery Brace, aged,
about seventy eight-years resident in Georgia in said County of Franklin
who being by me first duly sworn according to law doth on his oath make
the following declaration in order to obtain the provisions made by the late
act of Congress entitled "An Act to provide for certain persons engaged in
the land and naval service of the United States in the Revolutionary War":
That he the said Jeffery Brace enlisted in Woodbury in the State of Connecticutt in the fall of the year—but the year does not recollect but thinks
it was in the year 1777 in the Company commanded by Lt. Trawbridge afterwards commanded by Capt.Granger in Col. Meigs regiment in the
Connecticut line afterwards was transferred to Capt. Baker's Company.
He enlisted for three years or he thought but was returned for during the
War. That he continued in said Corps and in the service of the United
States until the summer 1783 when he was discharged from said service
in West Point by receiving an honorable discharge with a badge of merritt
which discharge is part—that he was in the battles of White Plains at
Stamford, West-chester at Mud-Fort in New Jersey and received a wound
in his leg at the Capture of Mud-Fort and retreated with the American
Army to Red Bank. He says, although he supposed he enlisted for three
years yet as he was returned for during the War he cheerfully served five
years and nine months—and that he is in reduced circumstances
and stands in need of the assistance of his Country for support—and
that he has no other [illegible] in his [illegible] of his said services than
transcribed.

	his
Witness to and declared before me	Jeffery X Brace
the day & year aforesaid	Mark
	Frederic Bliss asst Judge
	of Franklin County Court

I Frederic Bliss Judge of Franklin County Court in & for the County of Franklin & State of Vermont do certify that it appears to my satisfaction that the said Jeffery Brace did serve in the Revolutionary War as stated in his said declaration against the Common enemy for the full term of nine months and more & that the said service was continued nine months & more in the Continental establishment—and also am personally acquainted with the said Jeffery Brace & am knowing to his being blind having lost the sight of both of his eyes, and destitute of property and dependant on the public for a support. That he is in reduced Circumstances & stands in need of the assistance of his Country for support—that the said Jeffery Brace reputation for truth & veracity stands unimpeached & will gain Credit where ever he is known.—I further certify the Court over which I preside is a Court of Record and I now transmit the proceedings & testimony taken & had before me to the Secretary of the department of War pursuant to the Act of Congress described in the written declaration. In testimony whereof I have herein set my hand this 20th day of June, AD 1818.

at St. Albans—

> Frederic Bliss Asst. Judge of
> Franklin County Court

State of Vermont   I Horace Janes Clerk of the County
Franklin County   Court in & for said County do hereby
Certify that Frederic Bliss Esqr before whom
the annexed declaration of Jeffery Brace and
affidavit of Samuel C. Booge was made was at
the [illegible] dates thereof and now is Judge of
Franklin County Court in the State of Vermont
and duly qualified for that purpose acting under
the authority of this State and his name therewith
subscribed is his own proper signature and also
the Court over which he presides is a Court of
Record—In testimony whereof I have herewith
set my hand & seal of said County Court this
18th day of July 1818
     Horace Janes Clerk

S.C. Booges' Deposition in
Case of Jeffery Brace
Jeffery Brace
'77 to 83—war—
Meigs Connecticut Regt.
          4 Apr. 1818

Rejected [crossed out] ([illegible] letter to Hon.
Sam. C. Crafts, House of Rep. U.S. 11 Feby 1820)

St. Albans, Vt. [illegible] 30, 1820
additional evidence annexed as per Letter to Sam. C. Crafts, Esq.
          Seth Wetmore
Submitted

I, Samuel C. Booge, of Fairfax in the County of Franklin & State of Vermont aged sixty three years being duly sworn depose & say—that Jeffery
Brace now of Georgia in sd. County was in the American Service in the
years 1777 & 1778, was knowing him to belong to Cap. Bakers Company
& Col. Meigs Regiment—also was knowing that he was attached to Cap
Grangers Company. This deponent saith that he was in the American Service in the Capacity of Lt. in Col. Chandlers, Col. Durgees & Col. Webb's
Regiment. That this deponent was knowing that the said Jeffery Brace was
a faithful Soldier and can say there was no better Soldier in the Army—
This deponent has resided in the same Town of the said Brace for several
years and now resides in an adjoining Town and can say that he is a man of
Truth, that he is poor & blind and has depended on the Town of Georgia
& his friends for support for about two years Past part—and without the
assistance of the Public & friends he must suffer—.
          Samuel C. Booge

Sworn & subscribed before me this 4th of April 1818 & I further certify
that the sd. Sam. C. Booge is a credible witness.
          Frederic Bliss Asst. Judge
          of Franklin County Court

St. Albans. Dec. 28, 1819

Hon. Sam. C. Crafts

Dear Sir,

A Colored man, residing in Georgia made his declaration, before the Hon. Frederic Bliss to obtain a pension as a revolutionary soldier—the substance of which as I am informed by Judge Bliss is that he by the name of Jeffery Brace, in 1776 enlisted in Col. Meigs' regiment in the Connecticutt line, that he served till the close of the War making five years & nine months service—which declaration was by Judge Bliss forwarded to the Secretary of War—

In May last Judge Bliss received a Letter dated "War Dept. Pension Office May 5, 1819" signed by J. L. Edwards, in which among other subjects observes: "The papers of Jeffrey Brace are retained there being strong belief that they are not founded on truth"—since which some further information has been received—and as Judge Bliss health is poor, he has handed me over the Letter with request that I would examine into the business & write or send to the Secretary for the benefit of Jeffery—I would here observe that I have been personally acquainted with Jeffrey about 12 years. He has always sustained a good character. No one can suspect that he has wilfully made any false statement—He is a member of a respectable Baptist Church in Georgia—He is aged and infirm, totally blind—and on conversing with him on the subject I find that he is forgetful relative to dates—but has a strong impression on his mind that he enlisted for three years—but tarried 5 years & nine months till peace—He says he always went by the name of Jeffery Stiles till he enlisted when he took on himself the name of Jeffery Brace & by that name he answered in the Army—but his memory is poor, owing to his advanced age—Since Judge Bliss has handed me over the Letter above refered to—I have seen & conversed with a Capt. Brooks of Swanton, a reputable man—who informs me that he knew Jeffery when a boy,—he was a slave to one Stiles of Woodbury in Connecticutt about the commencement of the revolution he Brooks removed from Woodbury to Williamstown in Massachusetts that during the war he was frequently in Woodbury that he thinks that Jeffery is mistaken in many respects. —As he Brooks understood that in 1775 there was a draft for an eight month tour—that a son of Mr. Stiles (the master of Jeffery) was drafted—that Jeffery went & performed the eight months tour in the militia—that soon after he enlisted he thinks for eighteen months but whether it was in the militia or Continental service does not know that he heard—that after Jeffrey's return, from his 18 month tour—he challenged his freedom, a considerable difficulty arose. Many of the inhabitants were in favor of Jeffery—whilst his master contended that he was still his slave—In order to obtain his freedom he then enlisted for during [the duration of] the War. Capt. Brooks says that he has no knowledge of the foregoing but such was the information which he observed at the time—He Brooks thinks that Jeffery did not take the name of Brace till he obtained his freedom. He says whilst Jeffery was in the 8 months service he was nicknamed Pomp London—

Now Sir at the request of sundry respected inhabitants of Georgia I write this & their request is that you would call at the Secretary Office & see Mr. Edwards. & if possible to discern the Error. —Jeffery is poor: dependant on his children for support. & his children are also poor— Your attention will oblige the cause of humanity—

Yours respectfully
Seth Wetmore

[Envelope addressed to] Hon. Samuel C. Crafts, Member of Congress, City of Washington

[Crafts wrote in corner:] Seth Wetmore's letter for Jeffery Brace— obtained the papers & sent them back to Wetmore Feb. 6th

War Department
Pension Office
February 4, 1820

Sir,

Your letter of the 26th Dec. has been received. It was not meant by the observation "the papers of Jeffery Brace are retained there being a strong belief that they are not founded on truth" to insinuate in the slightest manner that the Judge before whom the declaration of this applicant was made would knowingly sanction any act of fraud, but as the roll of the regiment in which the party stated to have served is considered correct and his name "Jeffrey Brace" not having been found thereon, there is as strong reason to believe that the statement of this man was erroneous. —His papers with the letter from Seth Wetmore, Esq. in relation to the case, are herewith enclosed to your care. It is stated that this man had another name at, or previous to, the date of his enlistment; if he will make an affidavit stating in it all the circumstances relating to his change of name and the time of it having been done & procure the witness of two persons to whose credibility the Judge can certify, to prove that he served as stated in his declaration, and have the same transmitted to this Department, an examination of his papers will be made.—

I am, respectfully,
Your obedient servant,
J. L. Edwards

Hon. Frederic Bliss retiring from Office, Jeffery Brace requested me to take such measures as I should consider advancable relating to his pension. According I wrote to the Hon. Samuel C. Craft, member of the House of Representatives on the subject. On Febr. 4, I received the papers of Jeffery, together with your letter adding to Mr. Craft—In consequence of Jeffery being blind & destitute of property, he has been unable to make that search for evidence which he otherwise might have done— He has made his affidavit [illegible] which he has found after a considerable lapse of time.

If consistent with the duties of your Office, it would be desirable that re-examination of his papers be made as soon as possible—Should he be entitled to his pension he might have the benefit. More than two years has ensued since he made application, owing to his circumstance of being poor—

yours respectfully,

[Because the page has decayed, some words on the right side and the signature are missing.]

Letter from Seth Wetmore to Samuel Crafts, February 1820. *Crafts Family Papers, Special Collections, University of Vermont Library.*

St. Albans. Feb. 10, 1820

Hon. Sam. C. Crafts

Dear Sir,

I wrote you some time since in behalf
of the Hon. Fred. Bliss relative to the pension of Jeffery Brace—Brace's
children are frequently at my office making the enquiry—whether I had
heard from you—As they are poor & feel an anxiety to know the
prospects, I am induced to write you requesting that you would write me
relating to the business—whether you have seen the Sec. of War & have
learnt the views of the Hon. Secretary—

Yours respectfully,

Seth Wetmore

N.B. Please to mention whether you have purchased me the pamphlet I
wrote for——

[In a letter dated 1 Jan. 1820 Wetmore had requested Crafts to obtain a
pamphlet for him from Washington D.C.]

[Note written by Crafts on back of letter:]
Seth Wetmore's letter—have already written him on these subjects

State of Vermont   On this 9 day of May 1820
Franklin County   before me, Seth Wetmore, Judge of Probate
                       for the district of Georgia, in the State of Vermont,
personally appears Jeffery Brace of the town of Georgia, in said County—
aged between seventy and eighty years of age—a Man of Color, who being by me first duly sworn according to law & carefully examined and in-
terogated made the following declaration in addition to his declaration
made before the Hon. Frederic Bliss Esq, on the 4 day of April 1818, and
says that at the time he enlisted agreeably to his said declaration he was a
slave to Benjamin Stiles, Esq. of Southbury in Connecticutt that he went
by the name of Jeffery Stiles— Afterwards he altered his name to Jeffery
Brace. He had the impression that he altered his name at the time of his
enlistment, but when more mature to reflection he thinks that he must
have altered his name at the time of his discharge. The reason for altering
his name was that he was imported from Affrica when a lad. That his
fathers name was Brace. After he considered himself discharged from his
master, he concluded to take the name of his Father—Brace—was the
reason for his altering his name.

his

Jeffery X Brace

mark

sworn, signed, & declared before me the day & year above said. I further
certify that the Hon. Frederic Bliss, the Judge before whom, the applicant's declaration was made is not now in Office—Seth Wetmore Judge
of Probate

State of Vermont   On this 9 day of May 1820
Franklin County   before me the subscriber Judge of
                                        Probate, personally

appears Jonathan Brooks of Swanton in the County of Franklin & State of
Vermont, aged seventy four years—who being by me first duly sworn according to law, doth on his oath state that previous to the commencement
of the American Revolution he resided in Southbury in Connecticutt. He
knew a slave by the name of Jeffery—he is now present & known by the
name of Jeffery Brace—The deponent saith that a short period before the
commencement of the revolution, he removed from Southbury. In the
year 1776, he was at Southbury on a visit, & then understood from several
persons at Southbury that Jeffery was then in the service for his freedom—I have known Jeffery about ten years in this County—and was informed by Jeffery that he had altered his name to Jeffery Brace, and explained the reason by stating that after he obtained his freedom took the
name of his father—Brace—Jeffery at Connecticutt & since my knowledge of him in this Country sustained the Character of an honest man.
                        Jonathan Brooks
sworn & subscribed before me the
day & year above said. Seth Wetmore, Judge of Probate

I further certify that I am personally
acquainted with Jonathan Brooks and that
he is a credible witness.
                        Seth Wetmore, Judge of Probate

State of Vermont   On this 30 day of Dec. 1820
Franklin County   before me the subscriber, Judge
           of the Court of Probate, for the
           District of Georgia personally

appears Silas Strong aged sixty seven years resident in St. Armand, Province of Lower Canada, who being by me first sworn according to Law deposes & saith that he in the years 1778 & 1779 resided in Southbury in the State of Connecticutt, was well acquainted with Stiles, Esq, given name cannot recollect, that he was the owner of a Negro slave called Jeffery Stiles, was well acquainted with Jeffery—That he then well understood that Jeffery had enlisted in the army to obtain his freedom—but what Regiment Jeffery belonged to does not now recollect but remembers that he saw Jeffery a number of times after his enlistment in a soldiers uniform with a Leather Cap. He further recollects that, some time in the War, but the year does not recollect but thinks it might be in the year 1780 he was in the State of New York, near West Point—met a Sergeants Guard, all in Uniform. Among the Guard saw Jeffery & conversed with him.—I now am acquainted with a Colored man calling himself Jeffery Brace & know him to be the same person then known by Jeffery Stiles—Jeffery sometimes was nicked named Pomp London—

        Silas Strong

sworn & subscribed before me the day & year above said & I further certify that the deponent is a credible witness. I further certify this the Hon. Frederic Bliss before whom Jeffery made his declaration is not now in Office.

        Seth Wetmore, Judge of Probate

State of Vermont   Franklin County Clerks Office
Franklin County   December 30th, 1820   I Horace
                           Janes, of St. Albans Clerk of the County
                           Court in and for the County of Franklin
  [State   do hereby Certify that Seth Wetmore Esqr.
  Seal]   of St. Albans, is and was Judge of Probate within
                           and for the district of Georgia duly appointed
                           by the Legislature of this State to that
Office and that the foregoing Certificates are signed by him
in his own proper handwriting.   In testimony whereof
I have hereunto set my hand and affixed the Public
Seal of said Court—
                           Horace Janes Clerk

St. Albans (Vermont) 22 March 1821

Hon. the Secretary for the department of War

Enclosed is the deposition of Ansel Patterson
to be used as additional evidence in the declaration
of Jeffery Brace, alias Jeffery Stiles. It is requested that
the deposition may be annexed to said declaration.
Jeffery is aged & totally destitute of property & blind,
dependant on his Children for a support, and they are
all poor—Therefore as soon as the official duties
of the Hon. Secretary will permit it is requested
that the papers of Jeffery may be examined.

respectfully . . . for Jeffery

Seth Wetmore

State of Vermont   On this 3 day of March 1821
Franklin County   before me Seth Wetmore one of
                     the Executive Council & Justices
for the whole State of Vermont, personally appearing Ansel Patterson, last
of Barre in this State now residing in Georgia in the County of Franklin &
State of Vermont, aged fifty six years who being by me first duly sworn according to law do depose & say, that he was a Soldier in Col. Butlers regiment of Infantry & of the fourth Company in the Connecticut line for
three years, commencing about the year 1780 in the revolutionary army—
and that the deponent has this day seen & conversed with a Colored man
calling his name Jeffery Brace who says he was in Col. Meigs regiment afterwards Col. Butlers Regiment of Infantry. The deponent cannot at this
length of time identify this person. As Capt. Barkers Company in said
Regiment was composed of Colored persons & this deponent had but
little intercourse with said Company this deponent does not recollect the
name of the Captain who commanded the Colored men—The deponent
had the impression it was Capt. Potter. Of this the deponent may be mistaken. The deponent says that the Company of Negroes was generally pa-
raded on the right of the fourth Company—This deponent thinks he has
a clear recollection of the name of Jeffery as belonging to the Negro Company—This deponent in conversing with Jeffery is well persuaded that
he was a Soldier of Col. Butlers Regiment and belonged to the Negro
Company from his narrating so many transactions which took place in the
service which he could not have done had he not been in the service. He
narrates the transactions of a mutiny in the Regiment the plan when the
Regiment lay of the young leaders and especially of one Gaylor being
hung, as supposed to be one of the leaders—the plan of his execution—
He also narrates the circumstances of many tricks performed by a Negro
boy nicked named the Cat. He also states many circumstances of the Negro boxing, which the deponent recollects. Also the different movement
of the regiment that I have no doubt in my mind but what he was a Soldier
in said Regiment.—After conversing with him & a faint impression in my
mind as to the name of Stiles I think he may have gone by the name of
Jeffery Stiles—

                     Ansel Patterson

Duly noted & sworn before me that day & year above said—
and I further certify that the deponent is a credible witness
    Seth Wetmore Jus. Peace

The deponent further states in addition to the above that Jeffery is now
blind and aged, which may be the reason of the deponent not being able
to identify him at this great length of time. He also shows me a wound,
which he received which I have a clear recollection of some one Negro
having such a Wound—
    Ansel Patterson
Sworn & submitted the day & year above said before me Seth Wetmore
Jus. Peace

State of Vermont
Franklin County   Franklin County Clerks Office
                           March 22, 1821. I Horace Janes
                           Clerk of the County Court aforesaid
                           do hereby certify that Seth Wetmore
                           Esq. of St. Albans in said County is one
                           of the Executive Council and by virtue
of said office Ex officio Justice Peace for the whole State
and that the foregoing certificate is signed by him in
his own proper hand writing. In Testimony whereof
I have hereunto set my hand and affixed the Public
Seal of said Court.
    Horace Janes Clerk

Inform the claimant that if he will send a schedule to the Dept. that his case will have a final decision—the objections as to his service & the alteration of his name having been removed.

This case is referred to Mr. E. because he has rejected it under the name of "Brace," but there appears on the Connecticut roll Meigs' Regiment the name of Jeff Sill enlisted May 26, 1777 in Cap. Humphries' Company.

See letter // [?] 10121

[dated 11 April 1821]

Jeffrey Brace or Stiles
Declaration
Supreme Court July Special
Term 1821—
Copy of Record

St. Albans, Vt July 3, 1821

Hon. J. L. Edwards,

Your letter of 11th April 1821 duly received, in which you observe "the objections to the name of Jeffery Brace and the alterations of the name having been removed, a final decision in his case will be made when a schedule of his property shall be received"—The Supreme Court now in session is the first Court since the reception of your Letter—He has complied with the Act of Congress of May 1820 accompanying this— As it appears from his schedule which is the point that he has for years been dependant on the public & his Children for a support—that he is blind & unable to perform any Labor— It is requested if consistent with the various duties of your Office that a decision may be made in his case before the 4 Sept next—or as soon as conveniently can be made.

Respectfully
Your [illegible],
Seth Wetmore

Revolutionary Claim, under Act of Congress, May 1, 1820

STATE OF VERMONT   Franklin County Supreme Court July Special
                    Term 1821

    Franklin County   ON this third day of July
1821 personally appeared in open Court, being the Supreme Court for the
County of Franklin / State of Vermont and a Court of Record for said
County, and State, Jeffery Brace alias Jeffery Stiles as to my age I am not
certain being born in Africa but I believe I am aged about 85 years, resident late of Georgia and now in St. Albans in said County, who being duly
sworn, according to law, doth on his oath, declare that he served in the
revolutionary war, as follows—I cannot recollect that precise time that I
entered the revolutionary war but am sure it was about five years before
the close of the war. I enlisted in Capt. Barkers Company in Col. Meigs
Regiment, afterwards commanded by Capt. Butler in the Connecticut
line but I was frequently transferred and did duty in other regiments but
served principally in said Meigs and Butlers Regt. & I continued in the
Continental army untill the close of the war in 1783 and was discharged at
West Point but have lost my discharge.

    And I do solemnly swear, that I was a resident of the United States, on
the 18th day March, 1818; and that I have not, since that time, by gift, sale,
or in any manner, disposed of my property, or any part thereof, with intent
thereby to diminish it, as to bring myself within the provisions of an act
of Congress, entitled "An act to provide for certain persons engaged in the
land and naval service of the United States, in the Revolutionary war,"
passed on the 18th day of March, 1818; and that I have not, nor has any
person in trust for me any property or securities, contracts, or debts, due to
me: nor have I any income other than what is contained in the schedule
here-to annexed and by me subscribed. I have no property of any kind
and have been supported for a number of years by Public and private
Charity. I have no family. I am by occupation a farmer or labourer but have
been totally blind for about seven years and unable to do any thing for my
support

                                        his
                            Jeffery X Brace or Stiles
Witness I Janes   mark

Sworn to and declared on the 3rd
       day of July 1821
             Before the Court Attest   Horace Janes, Clerk

STATE OF VERMONT
       COUNTY, ss. I, Horace Janes, Clerk of the Supreme
             Court, do hereby certify that the foregoing oath and
             the schedule thereto annexed, are truly copied from
             the record of said court; and I do further certify, that it
             is the opinion of the said court that the total amount
             in value of the property exhibited in the afore-Said
             schedule, is Nothing dollars and—cents. In testimony
             whereof, I have hereunto set my hand and affixed the
             seal of the said court, on this 3rd day of July 1821
                       Horace Janes ———Clerk.

18.206   See letter to W. White late per Ag
                               Act of 1831.

Vermont

Jeffery Brace alias Jeff Stiles
of St. Albans in the State of Vermont
who was a private in the Regiment
commanded by Colonel Meigs of the
Connecticut line, for the term of
the war ————1777.

Inscribed on the Roll of Vermont
at the rate of 8 dollars per month, to commence on
the 4th of April 1818

Certificate of Pension issued on the 11th of July 1821
and sent to Seth Wetmore, Esq.
St. Albans, Vermont
Arrears to the 4th of March 1821 $280.23
Semi—anl.all'ce ending 4 Sept. 1821.   48.00
2 yrs. 10 mo.   27/50   4/31 $328.23
                          Revolutionary claim
                          Act 18th March, 1818
                          & 1st May 1820
      Franklin County

Appendix C

Documents Related to Jeffrey Brace's
Land Transactions and Estate

Town of Sheldon Land Records, Book 1, p. 197
Saml. B. Sheldon
Know all men by these presents that I, Saml. B. Sheldon of Sheldon in the County of Franklin and State of Vermont, for and in consideration of friendship received in full to my satisfaction of Jefre Brace of Sheldon aforesaid. The receipt whereof I do hereby acknowledge have given granted bargained and sold and by these presents do give, grant, bargain sell alien convey and confirm unto the said Jefre his heirs and assigns forever, the northwest fifty acres out of the third division of Lot No. 48 in the Town of Sheldon. The said Jefre paying all taxes now laying on said land to have and to hold the same granted and bargained premises with all the privileges and appurtenances thereof and thereto belonging to him the said Jefre his heirs and assigns to them and their own proper use benefit and behoof forever. And I the said Saml. B. do for myself any heirs executors and administrators covenant to and with the said Jefre his heirs executors administrators and assigns that at and with the ensealing of these presents I am well heired of the premises in fee simple, that I have good right and lawful authority to bargain and sell the same in manner and form as above written that they are free and clear of all incumbrances and that I will warrant and defend the same against all lawful claims and demand of any person or persons whatever. In witness whereof I have hereunto set my hand and seal this first day of May Ano Domini one thousand eight hundred and four.

                    Saml. B. Sheldon   SEAL

Signed sealed and delivered
      in presence of
Thos. Jowsey
Zalmon Ames
          State of Vermont May 1st Ano Domini
          Franklin County / One thousand eight hundred and four

Personally appeared Saml. B. Sheldon the signer and
sealer of the above written instrument and acknowledges the same to be his free voluntary act & Deed
before me

Elnathan Keyes Justice Peace

The above is a true copy of a deed left for record 19th May 1804
and recorded May 22, 1804   attest —

Saml B. Sheldon T Clerk

Town of Sheldon Land Records, Book 1, p. 269
Jefre Brace

Know all men by these presents that I, Jefre Brace, of Sheldon in the County of Franklin in the State of Vermont, for and in consideration of two hundred fifty dollars, and in full to my satisfaction of Saml. B. Sheldon aforesaid. The note whereof I do hereby acknowledge and have given, granted, bargained, sold and quitclaimed by this presents do forever quitclaim unto, the said Saml. B., his heirs, assigns forever in the northwesterly fifty out of the third division of Lot No. 48 in the Town of Sheldon, it being the same land which said Samuel B. Sheldon deeded to me on the 5th day of May, 1804 as will appear by the said deed to have sold the above granted and quitclaimed premises with all the privileges and appurtenances thereof and thereto belonging to him, the said Saml. B., to his heirs and assigns, to them and their own proper use and benefit. Furthermore, I, the said Jefre do for myself, my heirs, executor, administrators, assigns, now and with the said Samuel B., his heirs, executor, administrators, assigns, that at and until the unsealing of these presents, I have never conveyed away the above mentioned premises that I will warrant and defend the same against the lawful claims of any person or persons by, from or under me. In witness whereof I have hereunto set my hand and seal at Sheldon this 24th day of June A.D. 1805.
Signed, sealed and delivered
in the presence of
Thos. Jowsey
Elisha Sheldon

State of Vermont
Franklin Countyship}   Sheldon June 25th 1805
Personally appeared before me, Jefre Brace, signer and sealer of the above written instrument and acknowledges the same to be his free and voluntary act and Deed before me
[illegible], Justice of the Peace

St. Albans, Vermont. Probate Court Records Vol. O, p. 311b
Jeffrey Brace's Estate

STATE OF VERMONT, }   BE it remembered, that at a
}   Probate Court holden
}   at St. Albans, in and for the District
}   of Georgia, on
Georgia District, ss. }   the 8th day of September, A.D. 1831
Present   William Bridges *Judge*

IT is represented to this Court, that Jeffrey Brace late of St. Albans in the District of Georgia, deceased intestate, leaving goods, chattel, rights, credits, and estate, in said District. . . . . Therefore it is decreed by this Court that John L. Chandler be appointed to administer upon said estate. It is ordered by this Court, that before the said John L. Chandler enter upon the duties of his said trust, give bonds with sufficient surety, in the penal sum of one hundred dollars, conditioned for the faithful discharge of his trust, as the law directs.

It appearing to this Court that the said J. L. Chandler executed a bond agreeably to the order of this Court, whereupon the Court decree that the said John L. Chandler be, and he is, hereby appointed Administrator on all the goods, chattels, rights, credits, and estate, of which the deceased died seized and possessed in this state. It is further decreed by this Court, that the said Administrator make or cause to be made a true and correct inventory of all the estate, both real and personal, of which the said Jeffrey Brace died seized and possessed, that shall come to his knowledge or possession, and present the same to a committee of appraisal to be appointed by this Court, and cause the same to be appraised on or before the 2nd Monday of November A.D. 1831. And it is further decreed that the said Administrator make or cause to be made a just and fair account of his administration, and present the same to the Court for examination and allowance on or before the eighth day of September A.D. 1832.

Wm. Bridges, Judge

Appendix D

A Brace Chronology

ca. 1742	Boyrereau Brinch is born in West Africa.
ca. 1758	Captured and enslaved.
1759–60	Arrives in Barbados. Endures slave-breaking. Sold to Captain Isaac Mills.
1760–62	Fights as an enslaved sailor in Seven Years War and travels in British Empire.
1762	Participates in the British capture of Havana, Cuba. June–August.
1762–63	Sails with Mills to Dublin, Ireland; Savannah, Georgia; New York City; Newport, Rhode Island; Halifax, Nova Scotia; Boston, Massachusetts.
1763	Arrives in New Haven, Connecticut, in late fall. Mills sells him to John Burwell of Milford.
1764	Captain Isaac Mills buys a new ship, the sloop *Seaflower*, with his Milford business partners Edward Allen and Thomas Gibb in February and sails from New Haven to Barbados.
1764–68	Brace is enslaved by a series of cruel Connecticut masters.
ca. 1768	Brace is purchased by Widow Mary Stiles, who teaches him to read.
ca. 1773	Mary Stiles dies. Brace passes to her son, Benjamin Stiles, Esq.
ca. 1777	Brace enlists in the Revolutionary Army.
1783	Brace is honorably discharged with a badge of merit and manumitted.
1784	Brace heads for Vermont, stopping in Lenox, Massachusetts, for one month.
1784–89	Brace buys uncleared land in Poultney. Works in Poultney, Dorset, and Manchester. Marries Susannah (Susan) Dublin, an African-born widow. They clear and farm Brace's land in Poultney.
1789	Olaudah Equiano publishes *The Interesting Narrative of the Life of Olaudah Equiano, or Gustavus Vassa, the African* in London.
1789	A major famine in Vermont. Brace supports his family by carrying iron on his back over the mountains to Manchester and returning to Poultney with grain.

1790–91	Jeffrey Bran [*sic*] is listed in U.S. Census as head of household of five free people of color in Poultney, which suggests that he and Susan had three children. Martin Powell's household in Manchester contains one free person of color, probably Susan's daughter Bersheba, who was forced into indentured servitude. Archibald Dixon's household in Poultney contains one free person of color, probably Susan's son, who was forced into indentured servitude.
1791–1803	Slave revolt in St. Dominique, a French West Indian colony.
1802	The Braces move to Sheldon in northern Vermont.
1804	Brace acquires fifty acres of land from Samuel B. Sheldon (May).
1805	Brace returns the fifty acres to Samuel B. Sheldon for his pledge of $250 (June).
1805	Jeffrey Brace is baptized in Georgia, Vermont, on June 6 and joins the Baptist Church.
1807	Susannah (Susan) Dublin Brace dies on March 19. Great Britain abolishes the transatlantic slave trade, but it continues illicitly.
1808	The United States abolishes the transatlantic slave trade, but it continues illicitly.
1809	Ishmael Brace (a son?) is mentioned three times in January in the St. Albans Adviser (a letter is waiting for him at the post office).
1810	*The Blind African Slave* is published on October 18.
1811	Benjamin Prentiss is warned out of Milton, Vermont.
1812	Brace is warned out of Milton, Vermont.
1816	A grandson, Theodore, is born in St. Albans to Jeff Brace Jr. and Diana.
1818	Brace files a pension claim as a Revolutionary War veteran.
1821	Brace receives his pension ($8 per month), plus arrears ($328.23), from the federal government.
1827	Brace dies in Georgia, Vermont, on April 20.
1831	Nat Turner leads a slave revolt in Southampton County, Virginia (21 August).
	St. Albans Probate Court appoints an executor to administer Brace's estate (8 September).

Bibliography

Archival Sources

"Barbados/ An Account of What Numbers of New Negroes are Imported into this Island from the Ninth day of May 1757 to the Ninth of May One thousand Seven hundred and Fifty Eight." London. Public Records Office. PRO CO 28/31.

"Barbados/ An Account of What Numbers of New Negroes are Imported into this Island from the Ninth day of May 1758 to the Ninth of May One thousand Seven hundred and Fifty Ninth." London. Public Records Office. PRO CO 28/31.

"Barbados/An Account of What Numbers of New Negroes are Imported into this Island from the Ninth day of May 1759 to the Ninth of May 1760." London. Public Records Office. PRO CO 28/32.

Boston Weekly Magazine. Library of Congress. Microform 01104, reel 6.

Burial Records. Heald Funeral Home. St. Albans, Vermont.

Burial Register. Barbados Department of Archives.

Compiled Service Records of Soldiers Who Served in the American Army During the Revolutionary War. Washington D.C. National Archives Microfilm Publications.

Connecticut Courant. Connecticut State Library. Hartford.

Connecticut Journal and New-Haven Post-Boy. Connecticut State Library. Hartford.

Crafts Family Papers. Special Collections, Bailey-Howe Library, University of Vermont.

Franklin County Advertiser. Library of Congress.

Historical and Genealogical Material. Town Clerk's Office. Poultney, Vermont.

Inventories, Wills and Deeds. Barbados Department of Archives.

"List of Commissioned Officers of the Royal Navy." National Maritime Museum. Greenwich, England.

"A List of the Number of Inhabitants in each Town in the Colony of Connecticut

Taken in the Year 1762." Census ordered by Connecticut's General Assembly. Manuscript. Connecticut Historical Society. Hartford.

"A List of Ships and Vessels Which Have Enter'd Inwards in the Port of Bridge-town in the Island of Barbados Between the 1st day of January 1764 and the 1st of April follow: being the Quarter ended April 1st with the particular Quantity and Quality of the Loading of each Vessel." London. Public Records Office. PRO CO 33/17.

"A List of Such Ships & Vessels Which Have Cleared Outwards the Port of Bridgetown in the Island of Barbados Between the 1st day of January and the 1st day of April follow: being the Quarter ended April 1st." London. Public Records Office. PRO CO 33/17.

Marriage Register. Barbados Department of Archives.

Milton Town Meeting Records. Town Clerk's Office. Milton, Vermont.

Northern Spectator (Poultney, Vermont). Vermont Law Library. Montpelier, Vermont, and Library of Congress.

Probate Court Records. St. Albans, Vermont.

St. Albans Adviser (newspaper). St. Albans Historical Society and Museum. St. Albans, Vermont.

Town Clerk's Grand List. Town Clerk's Office. Poultney, Vermont.

Town of Georgia Land Records. Town Clerk's Office. Georgia, Vermont.

Town of Sheldon Land Records. Town Clerk's Office. Sheldon, Vermont.

Vermont Baptist Historical Society Papers. Special Collections, Bailey-Howe Library, University of Vermont.

Vital Records. Town Clerk's Office. Dorset, Vermont.

Vital Records. Town Clerk's Office. Manchester, Vermont.

Vital Records. Town Clerk's Office. Milton, Vermont.

Vital Records. Town Clerk's Office. St. Albans, Vermont.

Vital Records. Town Clerk's Office. Sheldon, Vermont.

Vital Records. Vermont State Archives. Waterbury, Vermont.

Published Sources

Adams, Alice Dana. *The Neglected Period of Anti-Slavery in American (1808–1831)*. Williamstown, MA: Corner House, 1973.

Aldrich, Lewis Cass, ed. *History of Franklin and Grand Isle Counties, Vermont*. Syracuse, NY: D. Mason, 1891.

Alleyne, Warren. *Historic Bridgetown*. Bridgetown: Barbados National Trust, 1978.

Allison, Robert J., ed. "Introduction" and historical annotations. Equiano, Olaudah. *The Interesting Narrative of the Life of Olaudah Equiano, Written by Himself.* 1789, 1791. Boston: Bedford, 1995.

Anderson, Fred. *Crucible of War: The Seven Years' War and the Fate of Empire in British North America, 1754–1766.* New York: Knopf, 2000.

Andrews, William L. "Dialogue in Antebellum Afro-American Autobiography." *Studies in Autobiography.* Ed. James Olney. New York: Oxford, 1988. 89–98.

———. *To Tell a Free Story: The First Century of Afro-American Autobiography, 1760–1865.* Urbana: U of Illinois P, 1986.

Appiah, Kwame Anthony and Henry Louis Gates, Jr., eds. *Africana: The Encyclopedia of the African and African American Experience.* New York: Basic Civitas Books, 1999.

Baldwin, Ebenezer. *Observations on the Physical, Intellectual, and Moral Qualities of Our Colored Population, With Remarks on the Subject of Emancipation and Colonization.* New Haven: L.H. Young, Press of Whitmore and Buckingham, 1834.

Barber, John Warner. *Historical Collections, Containing a General Collection of Interesting Facts, Traditions, Biographical Sketches, Anecdotes, Etc., Relating to the History and Antiquities of Every Town in Connecticut, With Geographical Descriptions.* New Haven: Durrie & Peck and J. W. Barber, 1838.

Barry, Boubacar. *Senegambia and the Atlantic Slave Trade.* Cambridge: Cambridge UP, 1988.

Basker, James G., ed. *Amazing Grace: An Anthology of Poems about Slavery, 1660–1810.* New Haven: Yale UP, 2002.

Baugh, Daniel A., ed. *Naval Administration, 1715–1750.* London: Naval Records Society, 1977.

Beckles, Hilary McD. *Centering Woman: Gender Discourses in Caribbean Slave Society.* Kingston: Ian Randle, 1999.

———. *A History of Barbados: From Amerindian Settlement to Nation-State.* Cambridge: Cambridge UP, 1990.

———. *Natural Rebels: A Social History of Enslaved Black Women in Barbados.* New Brunswick: Rutgers UP, 1989.

Behn, Aphra. *Oroonoka; or, The Royal Slave.* 1688. Boston: Bedford, 2000.

Behrendt, Stephen D., David Eltis, and David Richardson. "The Cost of Coercion: African Agency in the Pre-Modern Atlantic World." *Economic History Review* 54 (2001): 454–76.

Belinda. "Petition of an African slave, to the legislature of Massachusetts." Boston, 1782. *Unchained Voices: An Anthology of Black Authors in the English-Speaking World of the Eighteenth Century.* Ed. Vincent Carretta. Lexington: U of Kentucky P, 1996. 142–44.

Benezet, Anthony. *Some Historical Account of Guinea, Its Situation, Produce, and the General Disposition of Its Inhabitants. With an Inquiry into the Rise and Progress of the Slave Trade, Its Nature, and Lamentable Effects.* London: 1788.

Bigelow, Edwin L. and Nancy H. Otis. *Manchester, Vermont: A Pleasant Land Among the Mountains, 1761–1961.* Published by the Town of Manchester, 1961.

Billington, Ray A. *American History before 1877.* Totowa, NJ: Littlefield, 1965.

Blakeley, Phyllis R. "Boston King: A Black Loyalist." In *Eleven Exiles: Accounts of Loyalists of the American Revolution.* Toronto: Dunburn, 1982. 265–87.

Boardman, Roger Sherman. *Roger Sherman: Signer and Statesman.* 1938. New York: Da Capo, 1971.

Brown, William Wells. *The Black Man, His Antecedents, His Genius, and His Achievements.* 1865. Miami: Mnemosyne, 1969.

Bruce, Dickson D., Jr. *The Origins of African American Literature.* Charlottesville: UP of Virginia, 2001.

Buechler, John. "Brace, Bran, and St. Albans." *New-England Galaxy* 20.2 (1978): 35–41.

Buel, Richard Jr. *Dear Liberty: Connecticut's Mobilization for the Revolutionary War.* Middletown, CT: Wesleyan UP, 1980.

Bull, Lisa A. "The Negro." *The Ethnic Contribution to the American Revolution.* Eds. Frederick Hailing and Martin Kaufman. Westfield, MA: Westfield Bicentennial Committee, 1976. 67–74.

Calhoun, John C. "Report on the Subject of Civilizing the Indians, Communicated to the House of Representatives, January 17th, 1820." *Reports and Public Letters of John C. Calhoun.* Ed. Richard K. Cralle. New York: Russell, 1968. 68–70.

Capers, Gerald M. *John C. Calhoun—Opportunist: A Reappraisal.* Gainesville: U of Florida P, 1960.

Carretta, Vincent. "Defining a Gentleman: The Status of Olaudah Equiano or Gustavus Vassa." *Language Sciences* 22 (2000): 385–99.

Clowes, William Laird. *The Royal Navy: A History From the Earliest Times to the Present.* London: Sampson Low Marston, 1868. Reprinted. New York: AMS, 1966.

Connecticut Revolutionary Pensioners. Compiled by the Connecticut Daughters of the American Revolution. Baltimore: Clearfield, 1997.

Cothren, William. *History of Ancient Woodbury, Connecticut, from the First Indian Deed in 1659 to 1854, Including the Present Towns of Washington, Southbury, Bethlem, Roxbury, and a part of Oxford and Middlebury.* Vol. 1. Waterbury, CT: Bronson Brothers, 1854.

———. *History of Ancient Woodbury, Connecticut from the First Indian Deed in 1659 to 1854, Including the Present Towns of Washington, Southbury, Bethlem, Roxbury, and a part of Oxford and Middlebury, Containing the Genealogical Statistics of the Same, and of Ancient Stratford, from 1639 to 1728.* Vol. 3. Woodbury, CT: William Cothren, 1879.

Cowper, William. Poems. Vol. II. London: Chiswick, Whittingham, 1824.

Cromwell, Adelaide M. *The Other Brahmins: Boston's Black Upper Class, 1750–1950.* Fayetteville: U of Arkansas P, 1994.

Cugoano, Quobna Ottobah. *Thoughts and Sentiments on the Evil and Wicked Traffic of the Slavery and Commerce of the Human Species, Humbly Submitted to the Inhabitants of Great-Britain, by Ottobah Cugoano, A Native of Africa.* London, 1787. *Unchained Voices: An Anthology of Black Authors in the English-Speaking World of the Eighteenth Century.* Ed. Vincent Carretta. Lexington: U of Kentucky P, 1996. 145–84.

Curtin, Philip D. *The Atlantic Slave Trade: A Census.* Madison: U of Wisconsin P, 1969.

Davis, Charles T. and Henry Louis Gates Jr., eds. *The Slave's Narrative.* New York: Oxford UP, 1985.

Donnan, Elizabeth. *Documents Illustrative of the History of the Slave Trade to America.* Vol. 3. Washington, D.C.: Carnegie Institution, 1930–35.

Douglass, Frederick. *My Bondage and My Freedom.* 1855. Urbana: U of Illinois P, 1987.

Drake, Thomas E. *Quakers and Slavery in America.* New Haven: Yale UP, 1950.

Ellison, Ralph. *Invisible Man.* 1952. New York: Vintage, 1990.

Equiano, Olaudah. *The Interesting Narrative of the Life of Olaudah Equiano, Written by Himself.* 1789. Ed. Vincent Carretta. New York: Penguin, 1995.

Families of Early Milford, Connecticut. Comp. Susan Woodruff Abbot. Ed. Jacquelyn L. Ricker. Baltimore: Genealogical Publishing, 1979.

Fuller, James. *Men of Color, to Arms! Vermont African Americans in the Civil War.* San Jose: iUniverse, 2001.

Gallagher, Catherine, ed. *Oroonoko; or, The Royal Slave.* Boston: Bedford Cultural Edition, 2000.

Genealogical Abstracts of Revolutionary War Pension Files. Volume 3: N–Z. Abstracted by Virgil D. White. Waynesboro, TN: National Historical Publishing, 1992.

Genovese, Eugene D. *Roll, Jordan, Roll: The World the Slaves Made.* New York: Vintage, 1974.

Graf, Alfred Byrd. *Hortica: Color Cyclopedia of Garden Flora in All Climates Worldwide and Exotic Plants Indoors.* East Rutherford, NJ: Roehrs, 1992.

Greene, Lorenzo Johnston. *The Negro in Colonial New England.* 1942. New York: Atheneum, 1968.

Griaule, Marcel. *Conversations with Ogotemmeli: An Introduction to Dogon Religious Ideas.* London: International African Institute/Oxford UP, 1965.

Hahn, Michael T. *Alexander Twilight: Vermont's African-American Pioneer.* Shelburne, Vermont: New England UP, 1998.

Hall, David D. *Witch-Hunting in Seventeenth-Century New England: A Documentary History, 1638–1692.* Boston: Northeastern UP, 1991.

Handler, Jerome. *A Guide to Source Materials for the Study of Barbados History, 1627–1834.* Carbondale, Illinois: Southern Illinois UP, 1971.

———. "Survivors of the Middle Passage: Life Histories of Enslaved Africans in British America." *Slavery and Abolition* 23.1 (2002): 25–56.

Handler, Jerome, Ronald Hughes, and Ernest M. Wiltshire. *Freedmen of Barbados: Names and Notes for Genealogical and Family History Research.* Charlottesville, Virginia: Virginia Foundation for the Humanities and Public Policy, 1999.

Handler, Jerome S. and Frederick W. Lange. *Plantation Slavery in Barbados: An Archaeological and Historical Investigation.* Cambridge: Harvard UP, 1978.

Heads of Families at the First Census of the United States Taken in the Year 1790: Connecticut. Washington, D.C.: Government Printing Office, 1908.

Heads of Families at the Second Census of the United States Taken in the Year 1800: Vermont. Montpelier, VT: Vermont Historical Society, 1938.

Hemenway, Abby Maria. *Vermont Historical Gazetteer.* Vol. II. Burlington, VT: Published by Miss A. M. Hemenway, 1871.

Higman, B. W. *Slave Populations of the British Caribbean, 1807–1834.* Baltimore: Johns Hopkins UP, 1984.

History of Milford, Connecticut, 1639–1939. Compiled and written by the Federal Writers' Project of the Works Projects Administration for the State of Connecticut. Bridgeport, CT: Braunworth, 1939.

Horton, James Oliver and Lois E. Horton. *In Hope of Liberty: Culture, Community, and Protest Among Northern Free Blacks, 1700–1860.* New York: Oxford UP, 1997.

Ingersoll, Thomas N. "'Riches and Honour Were Rejected by Them as Loathsome Vomit': The Fear of Leveling in New England." *Inequality in Early America.* Eds. Carla Gardina Pestana and Sharon V. Salinger. Hanover: UP of New England, 1999. 46–66.

Joslin, J., B. Frisbie, and F. Ruggles. *A History of the Town of Poultney, Vermont, From Its Settlement to the Year 1875, with Family and Biographical Sketches and Incidents.* Poultney, Vermont: Journal Printing Office, 1875.

Kaplan, Sidney and Emma Nogrady Kaplan. *The Black Presence in the Era of the American Revolution.* Amherst: U of Massachusetts P, 1989.

Karlsen, Carol F. *The Devil in the Shape of a Woman: Witchcraft in Colonial New England.* New York: Norton, 1987.

King, Boston. "Memoirs of the Life of Boston King, a Black Preacher, Written by Himself, During his Residence at Kingswood-School." *Arminian* [or *Methodist*] *Magazine* 21 (March, April, May, June 1798): 105–11, 157–61, 209–13, 261–65.

Levy, Claude. *Emancipation, Sugar and Federalism: Barbados and the West Indies, 1833–1876.* Gainesville: U of Florida P, 1980.

Lewis, John W. *The Life, Labors, and Travels of Elder Charles Bowles of the Free Will Baptist Revival.* Watertown, MA: Ingal's and Stowell's, 1852.

Ligon, Richard. *The True and Exact History of Barbadoes.* 1657. Ed. J. Edward Hutton. St. Michael, Barbados: Cole's Printery, 2000.

Lipking, Joanna. "The New World Slavery—An Introduction." *Oroonoko.* New York: Norton, 1997. 75–89.

Ludlum, David M. *Social Ferment in Vermont, 1791–1850.* New York: Columbia UP, 1939.

MacLeod, Duncan J. *Slavery, Race, and the American Revolution.* London: Cambridge UP, 1974.

Main, Jackson Turner. *Society and Economy in Colonial Connecticut.* Princeton: Princeton UP, 1985.

Mars, James. *Life of James Mars, A Slave Born and Sold in Connecticut. Written by Himself.* Hartford: Case, Lockwood, 1864.

Marsters, Kate Ferguson. "Introduction." *Travels in the Interior Districts of Africa,* by Mungo Park. Durham: Duke UP, 2000. 1–28.

Merrill, Perry H. *Montpelier: The Capital City's History, 1780–1976.* Montpelier: Northlight Studio P, 1977.

Morgan, Philip D. "Rethinking Early American Slavery." *Inequality in Early America.* Eds. Carla Gardina Pestana and Sharon V. Salinger. Hanover: UP of New England, 1999. 239–66.

Morse, Jedidiah. *The American Geography; or, A View of the Present Situation of the United States of America: Containing Astronomical Geography.—Geographical Definitions, Discovery, and General Description . . . With a Particular Description of Kentucky, the Western Territory, and Vermont . . . To Which Is Added, An Abridgement of the Geography of the British, Spanish, French and Dutch Dominions in America and the West Indies.—of Europe, Asia, and Africa.* 2nd Ed. London: John Stockdale, Piccadilly, 1792.

Nash, Gary B. "Forging Freedom: The Emancipation Experience in the Northern Seaport Cities, 1775–1820." *Slavery and Freedom in the Age of the American Revolution.* Eds. Ira Berlin and Ronald Hoffman. Urbana: U of Illinois P, 1983. 3–48.

Nell, William C. *The Colored Patriots of the American Revolution, With Sketches of Several Distinguished Colored Persons.* 1855. Salem, New Hampshire: Ayer, 1986.

Newton, Earle. *The Vermont Story: A History of the People of the Green Mountain State.* Montpelier, VT: Vermont Historical Society, 1949.

Norton, Mary Beth. "'Either Married or to Bee Married': Women's Legal Inequality in Early America." *Inequality in Early America.* Eds. Carla Gardina Pestana and Sharon V. Salinger. Hanover: UP of New England, 1999. 25–45.

Orcutt, Samuel. *A History of the Old Town of Stratford and the City of Bridge-port, Connecticut, 1639–1886.* 2 Volumes. New Haven: Fairfield County Historical Society, 1886.

Park, Mungo. *Travels in the Interior Districts of Africa.* Ed. Kate Ferguson Marsters. Durham: Duke UP, 2000.

Patterson, Orlando. *Slavery and Social Death: A Comparative Study.* Cambridge: Harvard UP. 1982.

Perkins, Nathan. *A Narrative of a Tour Through the State of Vermont From April 27 to June 12, 1789.* Woodstock, Vermont: Elm Tree P, 1920.

Pierson, William D. *Black Yankees: The Development of an Afro-American Sub-culture in Eighteenth-Century New England.* Amherst: U of Massachusetts P, 1988.

Poyer, John. *The History of Barbados From the First Discovery of the Island in the Year 1605 till the Accession of Lord Seaforth 1801.* 1808. London: Frank Cass, 1971.

Public Records of the Colony of Connecticut, 1726–1735. Charles J. Hoadly, transcriber and ed. Hartford: Case, Lockwood, and Brainard, 1873.

Public Records of the Colony of Connecticut, 1757–1762. Charles J. Hoadly, transcriber and ed. Hartford: Case, Lockwood, and Brainard, 1880.

Public Records of the Colony of Connecticut, 1762–1767. Charles J. Hoadly, transcriber and ed. Hartford: Case, Lockwood, and Brainard, 1881.

Public Records of the Colony of Connecticut, 1772–75. Charles J. Hoadly, transcriber and ed. Hartford: Case, Lockwood, and Brainard, 1887.

Public Records of the Colony of Connecticut, 1775–76. Charles J. Hoadly, transcriber and ed. Hartford: Case, Lockwood, and Brainard, 1887.

Public Records of the Colony of Connecticut, 1776–1778. Charles J. Hoadly, transcriber and ed. Hartford: Case, Lockwood, and Brainard, 1890.

Public Records of the Colony of Connecticut, 1789–1792. Leonard Wood Labaree, compiler. Hartford: State of Connecticut, 1948.

Public Records of the Colony of Connecticut, 1793–1796. Leonard Wood Labaree and Catherine Fennelly, compilers. Hartford: Connecticut State Library, 1951.

Public Records of the Colony of Connecticut, 1797–1799. Albert E. Van Dusen, compiler. Hartford: Connecticut State Library, 1953.

Quarles, Benjamin. *Black Mosaic: Essays in Afro-American History and Histori-ography.* Amherst: U of Massachusetts P, 1988.

Rawley, James A. *The Transatlantic Slave Trade: A History.* New York: Norton, 1981.

Resch, Tyler. *Dorset: In the Shadow of the Marble Mountain.* Published for the Dorset Historical Society. West Kennebunk, ME: Phoenix, 1989.

Reynolds, Edward. "Human Cargoes: Enslavement and the Middle Passage."

Transatlantic Slavery: Against Human Dignity. Ed. Anthony Tibbles. London: HMSO, 1994. 29–34.

Richardson, David. "The British Empire and the Atlantic Slave Trade, 1660–1807." *The Oxford History of the British Empire. Vol. II: The Eighteenth Century.* Ed. P. J. Marshall. Oxford: Oxford UP, 1998. 440–64.

Roberts, James. *The Narrative of James Roberts, A Soldier Under Gen. Washington in the Revolutionary War, and Under Gen. Jackson at the Battle of New Orleans, in the War of 1812: "a Battle Which Cost Me a Limb, Some Blood, and Almost My Life.* Chicago: Printed for the Author, 1858. Electronic Version: http://docsouth.unc.edu

Roberts, Richard L. *Warriors, Merchants, and Slaves: The State and the Economy in the Middle Niger Valley, 1700–1914.* Stanford, CA: Stanford UP, 1987.

Rodger, N. A. M. "The Douglas Papers, 1760–1762." *The Naval Miscellany.* Vol. 4. Ed. N. A. M. Rodger. London: George Allen and Unwin for the Navy Records Society, 1984. 244–83.

Rolls and Lists of Connecticut Men in the Revolution, 1775–1783. Hartford: Connecticut Historical Society, 1901.

Rolls of Connecticut Men in the French and Indian War, 1755–1762. 2 Volumes. Hartford: Connecticut Historical Society, 1903–05.

Rollins, Alden M. *Vermont Warnings Out.* Vol. I: Northern Vermont. Camden, Maine: Picton P, 1995.

———. *Vermont Warnings Out.* Vol. II: Southern Vermont Plus Additions to Vol. I, Northern Vermont. Camden, Maine: Picton P, 1997.

Rolls and Lists of Connecticut Men in the Revolution, 1775–1783. Hartford: Connecticut Historical Society, 1901.

Roth, David M. *Connecticut: A Bicentennial History.* New York: Norton, 1979.

Roth, Randolph A. *The Democratic Dilemma: Religion, Reform, and the Social Order of the Connecticut River Valley of Vermont, 1791–1850.* Cambridge: Cambridge UP, 1987.

Sanders, Joanne McRee, compiler and ed. *Barbados Records: Baptisms 1643–1800.* Baltimore: Genealogical Publishing, 1984.

———. *Barbados Records: Marriages, 1643–1800.* 2 Volumes. Baltimore: Genealogical Publishing, 1984.

Scott, Kenneth and Rosanne Conway, compilers. *Genealogical Data from Colonial New Haven Newspapers.* Baltimore: Genealogical Publishing, 1979.

Sekora, John. "Black Message/White Envelope: Genre, Authenticity, and Authority in the Antebellum Slave Narrative." *Callaloo* 32 (1987): 482–515.

———. "Is the Slave Narrative a Species of Autobiography?" *Studies in Autobiography.* Ed. James Olney. New York: Oxford, 1988. 99–111.

Shillington, Kevin. *History of Africa.* New York: St. Martin's P, 1989.

Shy, John. "The American Colonies in War and Revolution, 1748–1783." *The Oxford History of the British Empire. Vol. II: The Eighteenth Century.* Ed. P. J. Marshall. Oxford: Oxford UP, 1998. 300–24.

Siebert, Wilbur H. *Vermont's Anti-Slavery Record.* New York: Negro UP, 1937.

Sloane, Hans. *A Voyage to the Islands . . . with the Natural History of Jamaica.* 1707. In *Oroonoko.* Ed. Joanna Lipking. New York: Norton, 1997. 112–13.

Smith, Venture. *A Narrative of the Life and Adventures of Venture, A Native of Africa: But resident above sixty years in the United States of America. Related by Himself.* New-London: C. Holt, 1798.

"Swanton, Vermont. 175th Anniversary, 1768–1938." Swanton Historical Committee, n.d.

Syrett, David, ed. *The Siege and Capture of Havana, 1762.* London: Naval Records Society, 1970.

Thornton, John K. "The African Background to American Colonization." *Cambridge Economic History of the United States.* Eds. S. L. Engerman and R.E. Gallman. New York: Cambridge UP, 1996.

Tindall, George Brown and David E. Shi. *America: A Narrative History.* New York: Norton, 1999.

Udo, Reuben K. *A Comprehensive Geography of West Africa.* Ibadan, Nigeria: Heinemann, 1978.

Ullery, Jacob G, compiler. *Men of Vermont: An Illustrated Biographical History of Vermont and Sons of Vermont.* Brattleboro, VT: Transcript Publishing, 1894.

Ulrich, Laurel. *Good Wives: Image and Reality in the Lives of Women in Northern New England, 1650–1750.* New York: Alfred A. Knopf, 1982.

Van Beek, Walter E. A. *Dogon: Africa's People of the Cliffs.* Photographs by Stephenie Hollyman. New York: Harry N. Abrams, 2001.

Vermont Imprints. 1778–1820 : A Check list of Books, Pamphlets, and Broadsides. Compiled by Marcus A. McCorison. Worcester [MA]: American Antiquarian Society, 1963.

Walker, David. "An Appeal to the Colored Citizens of the World." 1829. *Against Slavery: An Abolitionist Reader.* Ed. Mason Lowance. New York: Penguin, 2000. 133–43.

Waller, John A. *A Voyage in the West Indies.* London: Sir Richard Phillips, 1820.

Welch, Pedro L. V. and Richard A. Goodridge. *"Red" and Black Over White: Free Coloured Women in Pre-Emancipation Barbados.* Bridgetown: Carib Research, 2000.

White, David O. *Connecticut's Black Soldiers, 1775–1783.* Chester, CT: Pequot, 1973.

Wideman, John Edgar. "In Praise of Silence." *Callaloo* 22.3 (1999): 547–49.

Willis, Susan. "Crushed Geraniums: Juan Francisco Manzano and the Language of Slavery." In *The Slave's Narrative*. Eds. Charles T. Davis and Henry Louis Gates, Jr. New York: Oxford UP, 1985. 199–224.

Wilson, Harriet E. *Our Nig; or, Sketches from the Life of a Free Black*. 1859. New York: Vintage, 1983.

Winthrop, John. "A Modell of Christian Charity." *American Ideas: Source Readings in the Intellectual History of the United States*. Vol. 1. New York: Free, 1963. 37–38.

Wiseman, Frederick. "Abenaki." *The Vermont Encyclopedia*. Eds. John J. Duffy, Samuel B. Hand, and Ralph H. Orth. Hanover: UP of New England, 2003. 31.

Wood, Marcus, ed. *The Poetry of Slavery: An Anglo-American Anthology, 1764–1865*. New York: Oxford UP, 2003.

Yang, Guocon. *From Slavery to Emancipation: The African Americans of Connecticut, 1650s to 1820s*. Ph.D. dissertation. University of Connecticut, 1999.

Zirblis, Ray. "Lemuel Haynes," "John W. Lewis," and "Lucy Terry Prince and Abijiah Prince." *The Vermont Encyclopedia*. Eds. John J. Duffy, Samuel B. Hand, and Ralph H. Orth. Hanover: UP of New England, 2003. 154, 187, 240.

Index

Wisconsin Studies in Autobiography

WILLIAM L. ANDREWS
General Editor

ROBERT F. SAYRE
The Examined Self: Benjamin Franklin, Henry Adams, Henry James

DANIEL B. SHEA
Spiritual Autobiography in Early America

LOIS MARK STALVEY
The Education of a WASP

MARGARET SAMS
Forbidden Family: A Wartime Memoir of the Philippines, 1941–1945
Edited, with an introduction, by Lynn Z. Bloom

CHARLOTTE PERKINS GILMAN
The Living of Charlotte Perkins Gilman: An Autobiography
Introduction by Ann J. Lane

MARK TWAIN
*Mark Twain's Own Autobiography: The Chapters from
the* North American Review
Edited, with an introduction, by Michael Kiskik

Journeys in New Worlds: Early American Women's Narratives
Edited by William L. Andrews

American Autobiography: Retrospect and Prospect
Edited by Paul John Eakin

CAROLINE SEABURY
The Diary of Caroline Seabury, 1854–1863
Edited, with an introduction, by Suzanne L. Bunkers

MARIAN ANDERSON
My Lord, What a Morning
Introduction by Nellie Y. McKay